A Poetic Language of Ageing

Bloomsbury Studies in the Humanities, Ageing and Later Life

Series Editor
Kate de Medeiros

Bloomsbury Studies in the Humanities, Ageing and Later Life responds to the growing need for scholarship focused on age, identity and meaning in late life in a time of unprecedented longevity. For the first time in human history, there are more people in the world aged 60 years and over than under age five. In response, empirical gerontological research on how and why we age has seen exponential growth. An unintended consequence of this growth, however, has been an increasing chasm between the need to study age through generalizable data – the 'objective' – and the importance of understanding the human experience of growing old.

Bloomsbury Studies in the Humanities, Ageing and Later Life bridges this gap. The series creates a more intellectually diversified gerontology through the perspective of the humanities as well as other interpretive, non-empirical approaches that draw from humanities scholarship. Publishing monographs and edited collections, the series represents the most cutting-edge research in the areas of humanistic gerontology and ageing.

Series editorial board:

Andrew Achenbaum, University of Houston, USA
Thomas Cole, University of Texas Health Science Center, USA
Chris Gilleard, University College London, UK
Ros Jennings, University of Gloucestershire, UK
Ulla Kriebernegg, University of Graz, Austria
Roberta Maierhofer, University of Graz, Austria
Wendy Martin, Brunel University, London, UK

Titles in the series

Ageing Masculinities, Alzheimer's and Dementia Narratives,
edited by Heike Hartung, Rüdiger Kunow and Matthew Sweney
Age and Ageing in Contemporary Speculative and Science Fiction,
edited by Sarah Falcus and Maricel Oró-Piqueras

Forthcoming titles

Ageing and Embodied Time in Modern Literature and Thought,
by Elizabeth Barry

A Poetic Language of Ageing

Edited by Olga V. Lehmann and Oddgeir Synnes

BLOOMSBURY ACADEMIC
LONDON • NEW YORK • OXFORD • NEW DELHI • SYDNEY

BLOOMSBURY ACADEMIC
Bloomsbury Publishing Plc
50 Bedford Square, London, WC1B 3DP, UK
1385 Broadway, New York, NY 10018, USA
29 Earlsfort Terrace, Dublin 2, Ireland

BLOOMSBURY, BLOOMSBURY ACADEMIC and the Diana logo are trademarks of Bloomsbury Publishing Plc

First published in Great Britain 2023
Paperback edition published 2024

Copyright © Olga V. Lehmann, Oddgeir Synnes and contributors, 2023, 2025

The editors and contributors have asserted their rights under the Copyright, Designs and Patents Act, 1988, to be identified as Authors of this work.

For legal purposes the Acknowledgements on p. xv constitute an extension of this copyright page.

Series design by Rebecca Heselton
Cover image: Hilma af Klint, The Ten Largest, No 9 Old Age, 1907, Tempera on lined paper on canvas, 320 × 238 cm © Stiftelsen Hilma af Klints Verk/ artblart.com/ wikimedia commons

All rights reserved. No part of this publication may be reproduced or transmitted in any form or by any means, electronic or mechanical, including photocopying, recording, or any information storage or retrieval system, without prior permission in writing from the publishers.

Bloomsbury Publishing Plc does not have any control over, or responsibility for, any third-party websites referred to or in this book. All internet addresses given in this book were correct at the time of going to press. The author and publisher regret any inconvenience caused if addresses have changed or sites have ceased to exist, but can accept no responsibility for any such changes.

A catalogue record for this book is available from the British Library.

A catalog record for this book is available from the Library of Congress.

ISBN: HB: 978-1-3502-5680-4
PB: 978-1-3502-5684-2
ePDF: 978-1-3502-5681-1
eBook: 978-1-3502-5682-8

Series: Bloomsbury Studies in the Humanities, Ageing and Later Life

Typeset by RefineCatch Limited, Bungay, Suffolk

To find out more about our authors and books visit www.bloomsbury.com and sign up for our newsletters.

To the older generations that inhabit us.
To our own process of ageing to be as poetic as virtuous.

Contents

List of Contributors	viii
Foreword *Gregory Orr*	xi
Acknowledgements	xv
Introduction: A Poetic Language of Ageing *Olga V. Lehmann and Oddgeir Synnes*	1
1 The Mother of Beauty: Notes on the (Possible) Poetry of Dementia *Mark Freeman*	9
2 Poetry and Dementia: Imagining and Shaping More Just Futures *Aagje Swinnen*	27
3 Time and Dignity: A Phenomenological Investigation of Poetry Writing in Dementia Care *Oddgeir Synnes, Eva Gjengedal and Målfrid Råheim*	43
4 Growing Older with Haiku: What Haiku Offers to Japanese Expats in Denmark *Kyoko Murakami*	61
5 Poetry Lasts Forever: Case Study of a 100-year-old Brazilian Poet and His Daughter *Ana Cecilia de Sousa Bastos*	81
6 'An Old Man Can Do Somewhat': Styles of Male Old Age in Shakespeare's *Henry IV, Part 2* *Arthur W. Frank*	99
7 Virtuous Ageing as a Poetic Endeavour: Motivations to Write and Effects of Writing among Older Adults in Norway *Olga V. Lehmann and Svend Brinkmann*	117
8 The Poetics of Growing Old: Metaphoric Competence and the Philosophic Homework of Later Life *William L. Randall*	137
9 Poetry, Science, and a Science of Poetry: With an Illustration of Poetry and Ageing *Steven R. Brown*	155
10 Writing Lives *Merete Mazzarella*	175
11 Other Voices: George Oppen, Dementia, and the Echo of Lyric *Alastair Morrison*	187
Index	207

Contributors

Ana Cecilia de Sousa Bastos is a poet and professor (retired) at the Federal University of Bahia, Brazil. For three decades, she has been studying the developmental poetics of cultural realities, such as those of Brazilian families living in poverty, and the meaning-making processes that women from different generations build around childbirth taken as a marker for understanding developmental transitions. Recently, she has explored developmental transitions adopting collaborative autoethnography as a methodological tool. Besides editing books and writing articles on these subjects, she has also published volumes in poetry and is the grandmother of four lovely children.

Svend Brinkmann, PhD, is a professor of psychology in the Department of Communication and Psychology at the University of Aalborg, Denmark, where he serves as a co-director of the Center for Qualitative Studies. His research is particularly concerned with philosophical, moral, and methodological issues in psychology and other human and social sciences.

Steven R. Brown is Professor Emeritus of Political Science at Kent State University and adjunct instructor in the Program of Research, Measurement, and Statistics in the College of Education, Health, and Human Services. He has published more than 100 articles and chapters on Q methodology applied to politics, psychology, policy sciences, research methodology, education, and literature, and was recently presented with the book *Cultivating Q Methodology: Essays Honoring Steven R. Brown* (2021).

Arthur W. Frank is Professor Emeritus at the University of Calgary, Canada. His books include *The Wounded Storyteller* (1995/2013) and *Letting Stories Breathe: A Socio-narratology* (2010). His most recent book *King Lear: Shakespeare's Dark Consolations* was published in 2022. Among his awards, he is winner of the 2016 Lifetime Achievement Award of the Canadian Bioethics Society.

Mark Freeman is Distinguished Professor of Ethics and Society in the Department of Psychology at the College of the Holy Cross in Worcester, Massachusetts. His research interests include narrative psychology, the psychology of memory and identity, theoretical and philosophical psychology, and the emerging field of the psychological humanities. His most recent books are *Hindsight: The Promise and Peril of Looking Backward* (2010), *The Priority of the Other: Thinking and Living Beyond the Self* (2014), and *Do I Look at You with Love? Reimagining the Story of Dementia* (2021).

Eva Gjengedal is Professor Emerita at the Department of Global Public Health and Primary Care, University of Bergen, Norway. Gjengedal has education as a nurse and in critical care nursing. She has a master's degree in nursing science and her PhD deals with technology and ethics related to patients' and nurses' experiences from intensive care units. She works especially with qualitative research, phenomenology and philosophy of health sciences. Her key areas of empirical research are related to caring and illness experiences (chronic and critical illness), where she has drawn inspiration from various art forms such as theatre, poetry, and fiction. Gjengedal is author of numerous international publications on these topics.

Olga V. Lehmann, PhD, is a researcher, lecturer, and mental health activist. She works as a researcher at The Norwegian Institute of Emotion-Focused Therapy (NIEFT) and she has a private clinical practice. Her main areas of interest involve feelings and emotions, silence, communication, humanistic-existential psychology, grief therapeutic writing, grief and bereavement, poetic instants, and qualitative methods. She has published, among others, *Poetry and Imagined Worlds* (2017) and *Deep Experiencing: Dialogues Within the Self* (2017).

Merete Mazzarella is Professor Emerita in Nordic Literature at the University of Helsinki. Apart from academic work on Swedish and Finland-Swedish literature she has written thirty books of biography, autobiography and essays. She has taught autobiographical writing for forty years and has taken a special interest in medical humanities. In 2006 she was awarded an honorary doctorate in medicine by Uppsala University where she taught literature and creative writing to both students and teachers.

Alastair Morrison is a medical student at McMaster University, Canada. He holds a PhD in English from Columbia University, and his research interests include modern and contemporary poetry, questions of instrumentality and interpretive risk in literary studies, and old age and caregiving as both cultural and clinical phenomena. His work has appeared in journals including *Orbis Literarum*, *Criticism*, and *Age, Culture, Humanities*.

Kyoko Murakami, PhD, is a teaching and honorary research fellow in education at the University of Bath, UK and a visiting researcher at Ritsumeikan University, Japan. Her research focuses on aspects of cognition such as learning, identity and memory from a discursive psychological approach. She has published on international reconciliation practices such as war grave pilgrimages by British veterans, family reminiscence practice and materiality of memory. From a cultural psychological perspective, she has published on dialogic pedagogy and learning in retirement.

Gregory Orr is Professor Emeritus of English at the University of Virginia. He is the author of thirteen collections of poetry, a memoir, and four books about poetry, including *Poetry as Survival* (2002).

Målfrid Råheim is Professor at Department of Global Public Health and Primary Care, University of Bergen, Norway. She is educated as a physiotherapist, holds a master's degree in nursing science and a PhD in health sciences. Råheim works with body experience and lived-through meanings of being ill, with special regard to long-lasting musculoskeletal ailments and life after weight loss surgery. She is author of a number of international publications within these research fields. Qualitative research approaches stand strong in her research with phenomenological and narrative perspectives.

William Randall, EdD, is Professor of Gerontology at St. Thomas University (STU) in New Brunswick, Canada. Educated at Harvard, Cambridge, Princeton Seminary, and the University of Toronto, he has taught at STU since 1995. With Gary Kenyon and others worldwide, he has played a role in developing a unique approach to the study of ageing known as Narrative Gerontology. He has over 60 publications on this and related topics, including such books as *The Stories We Are* (1995/2014), *Reading Our Lives* (2008), and *Storying Later Life* (2011). He is particularly interested in late life spiritual development and the power of 'narrative care' in promoting it.

Aagje Swinnen is Professor with specialized remit in Ageing Studies at the Faculty of Arts and Social Sciences, Maastricht University, NL. Her research interests focus on representations of ageing in literature, film and photography; meanings of participatory literary activities in dementia care settings; and ways in which professional artists give meaning to creativity in the later stages of their career. Her co-edited work includes *Popularizing Dementia: Public Expressions and Representations of Forgetfulness* (with M. Schweda, 2015). Swinnen is co-founder of the European Network in Aging Studies and co-editor of *Age, Culture, Humanities: An Interdisciplinary Journal*.

Oddgeir Synnes is Professor of Health Humanities at the Centre for Diaconia and Professional Practice, VID Specialized University, Oslo, Norway. Synnes has a master's degree in Nordic literature and a PhD in illness narratives and works with applying perspectives from the humanities to healthcare, both through practical projects and in research. His key areas of interest include cultural and narrative gerontology, creative writing (e.g., in cancer care, palliative care, and dementia care), literary representations of illness, and narrative inquiry. His most recent book is *Ways of Home Making in Care for Later Life* (2020), co-edited with Bernike Pasveer and Ingunn Moser.

Foreword

Although this marvellous collection of essays concerns not just poetry but also other forms of expressive writing in the context of ageing, I myself am exclusively a lyric poet and will base my thoughts on that literary form although I sincerely hope that my assertions can be seen as similarly applicable to other forms of shaped literary writing.

Lyric poetry is a remarkable phenomenon in that it is written in every culture on our planet now and has been written or composed in all cultures as far back as the historical record permits us to know. By lyric poetry I mean a brief poem from a personal and individual perspective, though it may or may not make use of the first person pronoun 'I.' Likewise, it makes sense to acknowledge that lyric poetry and song are really so closely linked it's pointless not to recognize their near identity – something the ancient Greeks and Chinese recognized as well as the Nobel committee that recently awarded the Prize in Literature to Bob Dylan. Lyric poetry is not therefore an elitist art form, but a birthright – to read it, to listen to it, to sing it or hear it sung is to participate in a universal human heritage.

If we give it a moment's thought we realize that being a person, being a self in the world brings us two particular awarenesses that can have a deep impact on us. The first awareness is that there is a great deal of disorder in experience. It must be understood that 'disorder' is a conceptual term, it isn't a moral category. Disorder can be good or bad or both. Disorder can take many forms and show many qualities – it can be exhilarating or terrifying, depending. It can be outside us in the world – think of war, or weather, or love, or traumatic violence, or being lost in a city or a forest. Disorder can be in our own bodies – think of pain or illness. It can be in our minds – think of the wild fluctuations in emotion that happen inside us on an almost daily basis, or the bad memories or nostalgic longings that disturb us, or the giddy intoxications we sometimes seek. Or we can think of the future and become anxiously aware of the uncertainty of things, of the unknowability of what next week or next year will bring. The list I've just given can be weighted toward happiness as well as negativity – the disorder of romantic love is often highly prized, and daydreams can be a mind's playfulness with the unknown future. Outdoor adventure or sports can be our body's dynamic encounter with the unpredictable physical world around us. Whether disorder is experienced as exhilarating or life-threatening, it is real. In one form or another, it is absolutely and undeniably present in our daily lives.

Along with the reality of disorder in experience, we have the equally powerful human need for some sense of order. We value it in social and political situations (we want peace, we want civility and good will from neighbours and strangers). But we also crave order in our own lives: we enjoy our private habits immensely, those little rituals that set up reassuring patterns in our day to day lives, whether it's how we brush our teeth or how we arrange our possessions and our rooms. And the cosmic order of nature's cycles has given humans an enduring sense of reassurance from prehistoric times until now: the regular and predictable rising of the sun and moon; the stable rotation of the stars in the night sky.

Lyric poetry exists as a cultural resource to model the self's encounter with disorder and exhibit the ordering powers the poet/self is able to bring to bear on that disorder. Lyric poetry is defined differently in different cultures and at different points in history within a given culture, but it is *always* the most patterned and complex language use in its culture. It is precisely this linguistic and imaginative patterning that give it its power to order the poet's disorder. Lyric poetry orders not by excluding disorder but by incorporating it into the poem itself so that disorder and order exist in a dynamic tension, and both are recognized as forces in human life.

When the poet translates her distress or confusion or delirious joy into words and then orders those words, she has achieved what Robert Frost identified as a main goal for poetry: 'a momentary stay against confusion'. The resulting poem is a model of the poet's experience rendered as an unfolding interplay of disorder and order, both formal and thematic. To have created such a linguistic and imaginative model affirms the self, transforms it even, from someone who has passively endured disorder into an active and responsive shaper. The completed poem, no matter how anguished its subject matter, represents a validation of the power and dignity of the poet's self.

That said, I'll pass on to my own personal experience as an old poet.

Fractured Villanelle on my Seventy-fifth Birthday
   It's a fact that this world is a wild river
   Flowing through time.
                  Never a pause.
   No wonder we respond to it with a shiver.

   What the next moment might deliver
   No one really knows.
                  Wrap that in gauze
   Much as you like, still it gnaws like a sliver.

   It's a fact.
            That this world is a wild river
   Isn't anyone's fault.
                  It's a given without a giver.

   How to respond to it?
                  With wonder and a shiver.

(Orr 2022: 286)

We old cherish the world as much as the young, maybe more so because our mortality is constantly speaking to us through frequent mild or pronounced humiliations of bodily and mental dysfunction. We old cherish the world and yet so much of it exists now only in our minds, in our memories. The bridge of language that connects each of us to other selves around us and to the world – how precious and precarious that bridge is for the old – no longer the huge and solid steel structure conducting heavy traffic of trucks and commuters, but the ragged and dangerous rope bridge above a jungle chasm that is the cliché of adventure movies.

> What connects us to the world?
> What holds us in it?
>
> You'd think: whatever you love.
> Certainly that makes sense,
> Certainly we know that's true.
>
> But for poets, it's also words.
> If you don't believe me
> Listen to Whitman who
> According to his own
> Testimony loved everyone
> And everything.
> And yet
> He felt like an isolated spider
> Letting loose its threads
> In a windy field—"filaments"
> He called them—hoping
> They'd catch hold of some
> Object and become
> "Ductile anchors"
> That secured him to this world:
>
> 'Filament, filament, filament'—
> And what he meant was words.
>
> (Orr 2022: 286)

In my poem, for the purposes of that poem, I claim that language has a special significance and importance for poets as something that links them to the world of things and people ('but for poets it's also words'). But in fact, for *all* of us it is words. Without words we exist in a painful or numb isolation. Without words we have nothing but bodily solitude. To no one is this supreme value of language more apparent than to the old.

We customarily honour the youthful confusions and chaos of romantic love as a source of lyric poetry and popular song, but the power of ordering and meaning-making through poetry and expressive writing can and should attach to all stages of life and all human experiences. I think it's fair to say that ageing in its various manifestations frequently represents an extended crisis of disorder that lyric poetry has, by and large, neglected. And yet, poetry is willing and available for the task of articulating and validating the experiences of the ageing and the old provided it is presented in an alert and sensitive way.

So much of our connection to the rest of the world (of others, of the surrounding environment) is dependent on memory. With ageing and dementia, the sense of self is deeply compromised in part because the forms of memory we use to create a sense of continuity and connection in our lives are no longer available to us or reliable. In these cases, lyric poetry written by people in this circumstance can be significantly restorative of their dignity and identity.

Professional poets in their prime and pride have been known to declare they have no need of an audience, but that bluster has no place in this particular story, which has rightly been expanded into a larger community. In many of the instances considered here, caring guidance is important not only in the poem or story-making phase, but also in what follows – the enactment of some form of social reception of the written piece. To my thinking, a compassionate and responsive audience that validates the writer's achievement is essential. To create a poem or story in itself affirms its writer's individual dignity and identity, but to present that writing to an appropriate and appreciative audience ushers the old author even further out of isolation and back into the human community.

The authors of these humane and lucid essays are to be commended for devising new ways to use poetry and writing and to think about poetry and other expressive forms in relation to ageing and old age. It's a world that awaits each of us – this land where the old live as best they can. If we're lucky we'll live there also, and we will learn to accept its limits and inevitable perils and deteriorations. Then language and memory (that exists as a sharable thing only through language) will no longer be something we take for granted.

>Words, how I loved you
>Then—when I
>Was young
>And you led me
>Out of the dark!
>
>How I love you now
>Even more,
>As the dark approaches.

(Orr 2022: 296)

Gregory Orr
Professor Emeritus of English and Creative Writing
University of Virginia

Acknowledgements

We want to especially thank Ben Doyle for reaching out to Olga years ago expressing his interest in bringing poetic perspectives on ageing forward, later bringing our project all the way to Bloomsbury Academic. He is a very dedicated and kind editor to collaborate with. Thanks to Laura Cope as well, for supporting Ben in the editorial role and being so organized and attentive to our questions along the way. We also want to express our gratitude to the contributors of the volume for their dedication, patience, and perseverance in putting together these chapters during a pandemic. We are also grateful to Gregory Orr for his generous foreword and the permission he gave us to use his poems as part of the book. Finally, we thank VID Specialized University for funding some of the editorial tasks we had to take care of.

Introduction: A Poetic Language of Ageing

Olga V. Lehmann and Oddgeir Synnes

We turn to poetry and poetic language with the aspiration of finding more faithful modalities to express and study the complex – and at times ambiguous – realms of growing old in time, place and culture. Poetic language illuminates, transfigures and enchants our being in the world; it offers insights into the existential questions that are amplified as we age, including the vulnerabilities and losses that humble and connect us. In the words of American poet Stanley Kunitz, 'Poetry ... is ... the telling of the soul's passage through the valley of this life, its adventure in time, in history' (Kunitz 1995: 11).

The title of this book is *A Poetic Language of Ageing*, not *Poetry and Ageing*. The word *poetry* is often used for what literary scholars refer to as lyric poetry or lyric. While poetry can also be narrative and dramatic, lyric poetry (in all its heterogeneity) is traditionally associated with short poems of personal first-person expressions (Jackson and Prins 2014; see also the foreword by Orr in this volume). Theories of poetry, poetic language and lyric are vast, though it is not our aim to present an overview of the multitude of perspectives found predominantly in literary studies. Instead, we generally regard poetic language as broader than lyric poetry, a language also found in narrative and in facets of ordinary language and experiences that represent *poiesis* – a creation, 'bringing form out of a void' (Stewart 2002: 9). Poetic language emerges in the use of metaphors, images and plots to create worlds of meanings, contributing to heightened awareness, reflexivity and wonder. This is a meaning-making language concerned with our possibilities of existence as human beings (Heidegger 1971/2013). Philosopher Paul Ricoeur thus saw poetry and poetic language as connected to Aristotle's *entelecheia*, which concerns our seeing of things in terms of potentialities, not in terms of correspondence but as a re-description of the world (Ricoeur 1991). Poetic language therefore transcends the descriptive language that dominates academic discourses; in capturing the ambiguities and complexities of our human condition, it can help us redefine what ageing is, bringing it closer to a shared sense of dignity.

A poetic language of ageing: A bridge between cultural, literary and narrative gerontology

We consider this book to be a continuation of the evolving fields of humanistic and cultural gerontology, which form efforts to emphasize how ageing needs to be understood as cultural, historical, embodied and discursive (Cole, Ray and Kastenbaum 2010; Twigg and Martin 2019). Cultural and humanistic gerontology turn to the arts as a rich source for the study of ageing, engaging with in-depth explorations of visual arts, movies, and in particular literature and narrative, as found in literary gerontology (DeFalco 2010; Falcus 2015; Falcus and Sako 2019; Maginness 2017; Wyatt-Brown 2000) and narrative gerontology (Bruner 1999; Kenyon, Bohlmeijer and Randall 2010; Randall and McKim 2008; de Medeiros, 2013). Literary and narrative gerontology both highlight the significance of linguistic representations and understandings of ageing but, while the former has primarily been concerned with the analysis of published literary works, the latter has foregrounded the importance of individual and collective meaning-making through narrative resources in old age. However, literary and narrative gerontology share a predominant emphasis on and interest in what Hannah Zeilig (2011: 21) called 'the notion of story'.

Even with its dominant position for human meaning-making in various fields, the importance of narrative has been challenged. Philosopher Galen Strawson (2004) raised a prominent critique in questioning the view that all humans understand themselves narratively, as an unfolding story with a continuity across time and throughout life. Instead, he proposed an episodic way of living which has a closer connection to poetry than narrative. Strawson's perspective has been advocated in medical humanities by Woods (2011) and in literary gerontology by Zeilig (2011: 19), who challenged the usefulness of narrative in understanding lives: 'Our lives and their stories do not have the forward thrust of narratives, they are fractal.' In a similar vein, scholars have argued that the emphasis narrative gives to wholeness and coherence across life must be nuanced by looking at smaller stories (Bamberg 2006; Synnes 2015), considering broken narratives (Hydén and Brockmeier 2008) and going beyond narrative coherence (Hyvärinen et al. 2010).

Despite an increasing problematization and expanding of narrative to understand later life, other genres, like poetry, have rarely been part of the discussion. Still, there are notable exceptions. We would like to highlight three strands where there has been an increasing interest in turning to poetry in later life. The first is the growing interest in the application of poetic practices among older people, both living at home and in nursing homes. The pioneer here was poet Kenneth Koch (1977/1997) and his work on poetry writing in a nursing home in New York City in the 1970s, where he showed how the genre, its directness and imaginative power could open up possibilities, affiliation and wonder among nursing home residents. Several practitioners and researchers have followed with various practices of creative and poetry writing among older people (see e.g., Coberly, McCormick and Updike 2005; de Medeiros 2007; Lehmann and Brinkmann 2019a, 2019b; Synnes, Sætre and Ådlandsvik 2003).

Another context in which forms of poetry practices have been fruitfully applied is dementia care. Poetry involves brevity, rhyme and rhythm, which has been shown to be of particular relevance for the participation of persons with dementia in social oral poetry performances (Glazner 2005; Swinnen 2016a; Swinnen and de Medeiros 2018). Furthermore, the open-ended and associative aspects of poetry might be of particular relevance in shared reading practices (Billington et al. 2013). Finally, several practitioners and researchers have looked into poetry writing with persons living with dementia. Looking at the everyday language of persons with dementia through the lens of poetry might reveal nuances and resources not otherwise attended to (see Aadlandsvik 2008; Killick 1997, 2018; Synnes et al. 2021).

While the field of literary gerontology has predominantly been occupied with prose and narrative, our final strand of interest is in the analysis of published poetry. Among the interested scholars are Woodward (1980), who analysed the later life poetry of Eliot, Pound, Stevens and Williams in light of transcendence, reconciliation and wholeness; Swinnen (2016b), who studied late life creativity in older Dutch poets; and Lund and Simonsen (forthcoming), who investigated contemporary Scandinavian poetry that thematizes ageing in the Nordic welfare states, both from the perspective of older and younger poets. One particular subfield of this interest strand is the representation of dementia in contemporary poetry (Burke 2007; Fürholzer 2022; Guimarães and Jung 2022; Zeilig 2014). Here, it has been argued that poetry can 'bridge the gap between ourselves and the ultimately impenetrable experience of dementia' (Zeilig 2014: 162), though at the same time it can problematize and disturb claims of representing and speaking on behalf of others (Burke 2007). One striking example of how poetry can give voice to experiences of dementia is medical anthropologist Sharon Kaufman's (2017) work on the poetry of her mother, the acclaimed poet Shirley Kaufman, and her life with dementia. Kaufman analysed her mother's late poetry in an intimate ethnography to explore the ways that poetry can capture nuances of identity and experiences that would otherwise be unarticulated, thereby counterbalancing the dominant model of the disease.

A common denominator in the above research is the acknowledgement of poetry as an important, yet underdeveloped genre for giving voice to the experiences and complexities of later life. Lund and Simonsen (forthcoming) have thus called for the need to develop a *lyric gerontology*. This book can be seen as part of a developing lyric gerontology in the way the different chapters engage with poetic practices, as well as close readings of published poetry.

The chapters

The different chapters in this book illuminate how language, in its lyrical and poetic nuances, can open up participation, evocation, reflexivity, and meaning-making and identity making, as well as give older adults expanded possibilities to either promote or recover a sense of dignity. Other aspects that are particularly relevant in light of ageing is poetry's ability to confront, survive and transcend suffering by offering linguistic capacities not found elsewhere (Orr 2002). Dementia is one realm of ageing where some of our authors find poetry and poetic experience to be a resource. For instance, in Chapter 1, Mark Freeman shares a personal account of attending to his mother, who had dementia, and how the mementos that sprout from their encounters shape a crossroads between the narrative and the poetic. Then, in Chapter 2, Aagje Swinnen examines the relation between poetry and dementia through an exploration of the contrasting cases of the Flemish poet Hugo Claus's later life and two poetry interventions in dementia care. While Claus's case underscores a view of dementia as loss of personhood, the poetry interventions challenge a one-sided, negative understanding of dementia as a disease. In Chapter 3, Oddgeir Synnes, Eva Gjengedal and Målfrid Råheim present a poetry-writing project from Norway for persons living with dementia. The authors argue that the engagement with poetry involves a language that invites first-person perspectives that can contribute to discovering capabilities and resources in persons with dementia, and thereby preserve their dignity.

Furthermore, poetry involves rhythm, invocation and musicality, opening towards an enchantment of the world. Poetry should thus not just be treated as an object for interpretation but, like a love song, should be enjoyed (Culler 2015). In Chapter 4, Kyoko Murakami explores the practice of haiku among older Japanese expats in Denmark in terms of three joys – the joy of feeling, the joy of knowing and the joy of thinking. These joys point to a deeper understanding of ageing that delves into the Japanese aesthetics. Also providing a cultural and personal experience to the book, in Chapter 5 Ana Cecilia de Sousa Bastos introduces us to her father, the Brazilian poet José Newton, through empowering storytelling where the fragile meets beauty, spirituality and connection, in spite of solitude, poverty and illness. In a similar vein, in Chapter 6 Arthur W. Frank reads Shakespeare's *King Henry IV, Part 2* with a view to how old age can be enacted differently through the reading of the characters' use of two aspects of poetic language: the narrative and the lyrical. While the dramatic narrative shows how actions and choices have consequences for the characters, the lyrical language stands outside of the play's plot, evoking feelings within us that might open other ways of living in old age.

While many of the chapters and their authors treat poetry primarily as a genre, several others investigate the poetic language of narrative, as well as the intersections between poetry and narrative. For instance, in Chapter 7, Olga V. Lehmann and Svend Brinkmann bring us to a closer understanding of the motivations and experiences to write among older adults in Norway, and what these can tell us about virtuous ageing as a poetic endeavour. In Chapter 8, William L. Randall argues for an understanding of later life as a work of *poiesis* in the way that our self-understanding can be regarded as quasi-literary texts that we are continually composing throughout life. Acknowledging this process, as well as increasing our interpretational repertoire, might expand our tolerance for the ambiguities of later life and encourage wisdom. Then, in Chapter 9, Steven R. Brown applies Stephenson's Q Methodology as an alternative to studying poetry, by means of exploring the impressions of later-life readers of different poems that have older age as a theme. From a different perspective, in Chapter 10, Merete Mazzarella presents the experiences and reflections from her long-standing work as both an autobiographical writer and a teacher for older people on autobiographical writing. Mazzarella sees writing as a process and an exploration of one's life through the tools of literary and poetic language. Writing thus allows novel investigations of oneself and the world, and can be a way of coming to terms with life. Last but not least, in

Chapter 11, Alastair Morrison looks into how different poetic modes can give insight into the experiences of people with dementia. Through a close reading of American poet George Oppen's final collection, *Primitive* (composed together with Oppen's wife Mary, when Oppen himself was faced with the onset of Alzheimer's), the chapter probes into ambiguous questions of bespeaking in dementia care, both how it is at risk of being inappropriate and at the same time necessary to preserve a person's voice.

Closing remarks

The time for approaches that can dignify and empower ageing in academic settings, as well as influence health care interventions and policymaking, is always now. During the COVID-19 pandemic, the needs and wants of older adults was greatly compromised, thus amplifying the vulnerabilities and precarity of many persons in this life phase. Furthermore, the media largely portrays older adults as passive, frail and lacking agency and citizenship. It is our hope that this book can provide other versions of ageing by promoting poetic nuances that might preserve the complexities of later life, as well as point towards hopeful means of participation and contribution between and beyond generations. We therefore argue for engagement with poetry and poetic language that is not only aesthetical and existential but involves an ethical dimension. We end this opening chapter with the words of American poet Adrienne Rich, who reminds us of poetry's transformative power:

> Poetry must recall us to our senses – our bodily sensual life and our sense of other and different human presences.
>
> (Rich 2003: 273)

References

Aadlandsvik, R. (2008), 'The Second Sight: Learning about and with Dementia by Means of Poetry', *Dementia* 7 (3): 321–339.

Bamberg, M. (2006), 'Stories: Big or Small: Why Do We Care?', *Narrative Inquiry* 16 (1): 139–147.

Billington J., J. Carroll, P. Davis, C. Healey and P. Kinderman (2013), 'A Literature-Based Intervention for Older People Living with Dementia', *Perspectives in Public Health* 133 (3): 165–173. https://doi.org/10.1177/1757913912470052.

Bruner, J. (1999), 'Narratives of Ageing', *Journal of Aging Studies* 13 (1): 7–9.

Burke, L. (2007), 'The Poetry of Dementia: Art, Ethics and Alzheimer's Disease in Tony Harrison's *Black Daisies for the Bride*', *Journal of Literary & Cultural Disability Studies* 1 (1): 61–73.

Coberly, L. M., J. McCormick and K. Updike (2005), *Writers Have No Age: Creative Writing for Older Adults*, New York: The Haworth Press.

Cole, T. R., R. E. Ray and R. Kastenbaum, eds (2010), *A Guide to Humanistic Studies in Aging: What Does It Mean to Grow Old?* Baltimore, MD: Johns Hopkins University Press.

Culler, J. (2015), *Theory of the Lyric*, Cambridge, MA: Harvard University Press.

DeFalco, A. (2010), *Uncanny Subjects: Aging in Contemporary Narrative*, Columbus, OH: Ohio State University Press.
de Medeiros, K. (2007), 'Beyond the Memoir: Telling Life Stories Using Multiple Literary Forms', *Journal of Aging, Humanities, and the Arts* 1 (3–4): 159–167.
de Medeiros, K. (2013), *Narrative Gerontology in Research and Practice*, New York: Springer.
Falcus, S. (2015), 'Literature and Ageing', in J. Twigg and W. Martin (eds), *Routledge Handbook of Cultural Gerontology*, 75–82, London: Routledge.
Falcus, S. and K. Sako (2019), *Contemporary Narratives of Dementia: Ethics, Ageing, Politics*, London: Routledge.
Fürholzer, K. (2022), 'Living Oblivion: Poetic Narratives of Dementia and Fatherhood in Pia Tafdrup's *Tarkovsky's Horses*', in H. Hartung, R. Kunow and M. Sweney (eds), *Ageing Masculinities, Alzheimer's and Dementia Narratives*, 73–90, London: Bloomsbury Academic.
Glazner, G. M. (2005), *Sparking Memories: The Alzheimer's Poetry Project Anthology*, Santa Fe, NM: Poem Factory.
Guimarães, J. P. and D. Jung (2022), 'Anne Carson, Dementia and the Negative Self', in H. Hartung, R. Kunow and M. Sweney (eds), *Ageing Masculinities, Alzheimer's and Dementia Narratives*, 91–102, London: Bloomsbury Academic.
Heidegger, M. (1971/2013), *Poetry, Language, Thought*, New York: Harper Perennial.
Hydén, L. C. and J. Brockmeier, eds (2008), *Health, Illness and Culture: Broken Narratives*, Routledge.
Hyvärinen, M., L. C. Hydén, M. Saarenheimo and M. Tamboukou, eds. (2010), *Beyond Narrative Coherence*, Vol. 11, Amsterdam, Netherlands: John Benjamins Publishing.
Jackson, V. and Y. Prins, eds (2014), *The Lyric Theory Reader: A Critical Anthology*, Baltimore, MD: Johns Hopkins University Press.
Kaufman, S. R. (2017), '"Losing My Self": A Poet's Ironies and a Daughter's Reflections on Dementia', *Perspectives in Biology and Medicine* 60 (4): 549–568.
Kenyon, G., E. Bohlmeijer and W. L. Randall, eds (2010), *Storying Later Life: Issues, Investigations, and Interventions in Narrative Gerontology*, Oxford: Oxford University Press.
Killick, J. (1997), *You Are Words*, London: Hawker.
Killick, J. (2018), *Poetry and Dementia: A Practical Guide*, London: Kingsley.
Koch, K. (1977/1997), *I Never Told Anybody: Teaching Poetry Writing to Old People*, New York: Teachers & Writers Collaborative.
Kunitz, S. (1995), *Passing Through*, New York: W. W. Norton & Company.
Lehmann, O. V. and S. Brinkmann (2019a), '"Humbled by Life": Poetic Representations of Existential Pathways and Personal Life Philosophies Among Older Adults in Norway', *Qualitative Inquiry* 27 (1): 102–113. https://doi.org/10.1177/1077800419885414.
Lehmann, O. V. and S. Brinkmann (2019b), '"I'm the One Who Has Written This": Reciprocity and Existential Meaning-Making in Writing Courses for Older Adults in Norway', *International Journal of Qualitative Studies on Health and Well-Being* 14 (1). https://doi.org/10.1080/17482631.2019.1650586.
Lund, N. F. and P. Simonsen (forthcoming), 'Old Songs from the Welfare State: Nordic Gerontological Poetry and Lyric Gerontology', in V. Lipscomb and A. Swinnen (eds), *Palgrave Handbook of Literature and Aging*, London: Palgrave Macmillan.
Maginness, T., ed. (2017), *Dementia and Literature: Interdisciplinary Perspectives*, London: Routledge.
Orr, G. (2002), *Poetry as Survival*, Athens, GA: University of Georgia Press.

Randall, W. L. and McKim, E. (2008), *Reading Our Lives: The Poetics of Growing Old*, Oxford: Oxford University Press.

Rich, A. (2003), *What Is Found There: Notebooks on Poetry and Politics*, New York: W. W. Norton.

Ricoeur, P. (1991), 'Poetry and Possibility', in P. Ricoeur and M. J. Valdés (eds), *A Ricoeur Reader: Reflection and Imagination*, 448–462. Toronto: University of Toronto Press.

Stewart, S. (2002), *Poetry and the Fate of the Senses*, Chicago: University of Chicago Press.

Strawson, G. (2004), 'Against Narrativity', *Ratio* 17 (4): 428–452.

Swinnen, A. (2016a), 'Healing Words: A Study of Poetry Interventions in Dementia Care', *Dementia*, 15 (6): 1377–1404. http://dx.doi.org/10.1177/1471301214560378.

Swinnen, A. (2016b), '"Writing to Make Ageing New": Dutch Poets' Understandings of Late-Life Creativity', *Ageing & Society* 38 (3): 543–567.

Swinnen, A. and K. de Medeiros (2018), '"Play" and People Living with Dementia: A Humanities-Based Inquiry of TimeSlips and the Alzheimer's Poetry Project', *The Gerontologist* 58 (2): 261–269. https://doi.org/10.1093/geront/gnw196.

Synnes, O. (2015), 'Narratives of Nostalgia in the Face of Death: The Importance of Lighter Stories of the Past in Palliative Care', *Journal of Aging Studies* 34: 169–176. https://doi.org/10.1016/j.jaging.2015.02.007.

Synnes, O., M. Råheim, E. Lykkeslet and E. Gjengedal (2021), 'A Complex Reminding: The Ethics of Poetry Writing in Dementia Care', *Dementia* 20 (3): 1025–1043. https://doi.org/10.1177/1471301220922750.

Synnes, O., O. Sætre and R. Ådlandsvik (2003), *Tonen og glaset: pedagogisk arbeid med eldre og verbal kreativitet (The Tone and the Glass: Educational Work with Older People and Verbal Creativity)*, Kristiansand, Norway: Norwegian Academic Press.

Twigg, J. and W. Martin, eds. (2019), *Routledge Handbook of Cultural Gerontology*, London: Routledge.

Woods, A. (2011), 'The Limits of Narrative: Provocations for the Medical Humanities', *Medical Humanities* 37 (2): 73–78.

Woodward, K. M. (1980), *At Last, the Real Distinguished Thing: The Late Poems of Eliot, Pound, Stevens, and Williams*, Columbus, OH: Ohio State University Press.

Wyatt-Brown, A. (2000), 'The Future of Literary Gerontology', *Handbook of the Humanities and Aging* 2: 41–61.

Zeilig, H. (2011), 'The Critical Use of Narrative and Literature in Gerontology', *International Journal of Ageing and Later Life* 6 (2): 7–37.

Zeilig, H. (2014), 'Gaps and Spaces: Representations of Dementia in Contemporary British Poetry', *Dementia* 13 (2): 160–175.

1

The Mother of Beauty: Notes on the (Possible) Poetry of Dementia

Mark Freeman

Introduction: Letting words speak for themselves

The title of this essay refers to Wallace Stevens' (1923) poem 'Sunday Morning,' when he writes of death as 'the mother of beauty'.

> Death is the mother of beauty, mystical,
> Within whose burning bosom we devise
> Our earthly mothers waiting, sleeplessly.
>
> (Stevens 1997 [1923]: 55)

A related idea may be found in Freud's (1957 [1915]) brief meditation, 'On Transience,' when he disputes 'the pessimistic ... view that the transience of what is beautiful involves any loss in its worth' and proclaims, 'On the contrary, an increase! *Transience value is scarcity value in time*.' Contra those who may feel despondent over the fact that life is inevitably 'fated to extinction' (305), therefore, Freud insists that this very fate can intensify our experience of the beauty we behold. In this chapter, I address an instance of such intensification through the life of my mother, whose death in 2016 followed a dozen years of dementia, focusing especially on the way in which bearing witness to her life in her final years allowed theretofore unrealized dimensions of beauty to emerge. In offering this account, I do not seek to elide aspects of her life, and mine, that were painful and stopped well short of being 'beautiful'. Rather, I seek to show that her transience, and the very pain it brought in tow, was the requisite condition for such beauty to become manifest. Indeed, this becoming-manifest was a kind of revelation, one that often emerged in poetic form.

I didn't really see this clearly until I read a blurb for my recent book, *Do I Look at You with Love: Reimagining the Story of Dementia* (Freeman 2021), written by my colleague and friend (and wonderful writer) Leah Hager Cohen.

> Mark Freeman writes of his mother's dementia with a son's sharp wonderment and intimate sorrow. Layered over these, he offers a psychologist's search for

understanding, a search that yields as many questions as answers. What is a self without memory, without narrative? Tracing the progression of his mother's loss, he discovers profound sweetness alongside the pain; moments of startling, salty humor; and eventually a kind of found poetry in their increasingly pared-down verbal exchanges, which read almost like nursery rhymes, full of puzzlement and beauty and love.

Putting aside the fact that the blurb is a lovely one, I greatly appreciated – and found myself thinking more about – her notion of 'found poetry'. I hadn't thought about what I was doing in exactly those terms, but yes; that's what some of it was and aspired to be: the poetry found in quotidian conversation and in the rhythms of everyday life, such as it was. I don't credit myself for having found it. On the contrary, my mother's words found me.

Not too long after receiving Leah's words, I sent another colleague and friend, the poet Robert Cording, a copy of the book. His response, while not as uniformly glowing as Leah's (I've always appreciated Bob's directness and trusted his words; he's about the best reader I know), ended up saying something similar. Here is what he wrote:

> I finished your book today, Mark – a kind of Easter present to myself. I loved reading it (well, everything but the Coda which felt superfluous) and found myself deeply moved, often and consistently. I think – though I loved and felt close to the chapters on 'Presence' and 'the Face of the Divine', my favorite chapter was 'Dislocation'. I know we spoke about your conflicted feelings about taping or transcribing conversations with your mother, but those conversations say more about her (without saying it directly) and you than anything else. They brought your mother alive in ways that simple narration could not, and they made the idea of what it means to be 'commanded' by the other quite real in your case. I was lamenting my near total lack of feeling this Easter until you provided my resurrection. I really mean that. There is so much love in this book as well as the intelligence that only love can provide – in that Murdochian kind of way.

In referring to 'that Murdochian kind of way', Bob was speaking about the extraordinary work of the novelist and philosopher Iris Murdoch (1970, 1993), whose meditations on the abiding connection between art and love inform both of our thinking. I will say more about this connection in due time. For now, I simply wish to highlight his reference to the conversations found in the book and how much they say about my mother and me.

'Yes', I wrote to Bob in response.

> [those conversations] really are central to what I ultimately tried to do in the book – which was to get out of the way and let the tale tell itself. I like how Leah put it in her blurb for the book. Some of it's like found poetry, in a way. As for the 'Dislocation' chapter, I'd be interested to hear more sometime. In some ways, it's surprising that you connected to it as it seems you did; the others you mentioned seemed like more likely candidates. So, I'd be curious to know a bit more about

what you found in it. I'm not seeking more praise, mind you! But it wouldn't surprise me if you found some things that I myself may have missed.

Not one to pass up an invitation of this sort, Bob went on to share the following extraordinary thoughts:

> I didn't read the blurbs – odd, I usually do – but Leah is on the mark – they do read somewhat like prose poems. What I liked especially about the Dislocation chapter is the way everything works by enactment. Meaning, as in a poem or fiction, is being made dramatically through the juxtaposition of your mother's words and yours, without much commentary. And what is remarkable is how much feeling comes through these conversations – from your mother realizing who she is and isn't to you realizing how you can prompt her in ways that can return her to herself, if only briefly. That's what I meant by the command (of Levinas) that you feel towards your mother. When God asks Adam and Eve in the garden after the 'fall' (the question which in my mind the entire Old Testament turns around) 'Where are you?' the reader knows how they have been dislocated, separated from their true natures, and that there will be no return, only wandering, even if that wandering is punctuated by moments of consciousness and lucidity that could not have come without the fall; in your mother's case she cannot find herself again, but she has these moments when love finds her and you both find each other. That's the drama which was for me enacted in that chapter.

In view of these words, I am tempted to ask: Can I just end the chapter here, now? Can I just let a great poet speak to the poetic dimension and leave it at that? I know; I have to move ahead and say some things that might serve to unpack all these ideas. Daunting, though, I must say.

But intriguing too. What *was* I doing in this book? And why was an ostensibly 'narrative person' all but abandoning narrative in much of the book and turning instead to found poetry? One reason was that, in her final years especially, my mother had largely moved beyond narrative owing to her dementia and, limited as she was mainly to the present moment, came to speak the reality of her life in a form much closer to poetry than to narrative. But there is another reason for my moving in this direction as well, and that is that I came to find many of my mother's words fascinating, strange, and, at times, extremely moving – enough that I oftentimes let these words speak for themselves. By degrees, I therefore became more attuned to her utterances and the poetic resonance they often carried. Given this temporal transformation, it might be held that the 'poetry' my mother spoke was accidental, a mere epiphenomenon of the disease. And on one level it was. It certainly didn't have the kind of intentionality that is generally found in poetry, and it didn't have the craft poetry requires. It might also be held that *she* really wasn't the poet in this context, I was; I was the one listening for her words, I was the one selecting which ones were worthy of sharing, and I was the one who decided where they would be located in light of whatever I most wanted to convey. All true. But the most significant words uttered are nevertheless her words, not mine, and they often spoke with a kind of simple clarity and resonance that served to distil and express whole worlds of meaning.

Consider, for instance, the words that comprise the title of the book: 'Do I look at you with love?' That was a question my mother posed upon learning, once again, that I was her son. Advanced though her dementia was by that time, she still knew enough about motherhood to want to know whether she had in fact upheld the role. But there was also something ... ironic about the way she asked that question, something that suggested to me that, through it all, she had a sense of the very strange place where she had landed and that she wanted to speak to it in some way. So, she had essentially been asking during this phase, am I still a person, the kind who says things and does things other persons do? In some ways, she was no one at this point – not, at least, in her own mind. And yet, she was also everyone; she was a site and cypher, an instantiation of a world to which she had once belonged and whose basic properties she still knew. Unwittingly, it seems, she had become a poet. How did she get there?

In what follows, I briefly sketch out four phases marking the movement from narrative to poetry. In speaking of this movement in terms of phases, I want to emphasize that, although they do mark something of a chronological trajectory, there is some substantial 'leakage' between them. I offer them, therefore, not in the name of an ironclad experiential path but in that of a story – a story that, in time, could only be told in a decidedly non-storied way.

Suffocated by story: Narrative and its discontents

As a long-time student of narrative (e.g., Freeman 1993, 2010a), I have generally been committed to the idea that narrative is intrinsic to life itself – which is to say, it is not something that we 'impose' on an ostensibly formless life but is instead woven into its very fabric (Freeman 1998a, 2003). I say 'generally' in this context mainly by way of acknowledging that there is surely a difference between life as lived, in the immediate moment, and life as told, at some present point in time, looking backward (1998b). This difference notwithstanding, I nevertheless remain committed to the idea that life itself – at least as lived by a healthy, well-functioning person – contains an element of narrativity within it (see also Bruner 1987; Carr 1986; Kerby 1991; Ricoeur 1991).

Bearing this commitment in mind, I have generally made another, corollary commitment as well – namely, that narrative is 'good', in the sense that it can give our lives a sense of meaning, purpose, and coherence. This is surely true as well. Accordingly, I sometimes found myself critiquing those who saw it more negatively (e.g., Strawson 2004), even as a kind of prison (Sartwell 2000), a self-constructed box into which we may place ourselves, only to find ourselves living within its too-harsh confines. In this context too, I did acknowledge the ways in which narratives might constrain the movement of life; my own idea of 'narrative foreclosure' (Freeman 2000, 2010b) – the supposition that the story of one's life is essentially over – is very much about this: bereft of the narrative resources that had once served to orient and direct one's life, one may be left in the void, imprisoned by their very absence. 'Sometimes you live too long', my mother said to me at one point. If the story has reached its ending, she seemed to be saying, maybe it was time for her to reach hers. Why go on if there are no more meaningful episodes to be had?

But I am getting ahead of myself. Let me therefore take a step back, share some words about how my mother arrived at sentiments like these, and fill in the picture at hand. Perhaps the most difficult phase of my mother's dementia was the initial one, when she began to find herself coming undone. Even here, at this initial phase, there could be a kind of poetry to her utterances.

'Where am I? Who put me here? Why do I need assisted living?'
'Why do I need help with medicine when I've done it on my own my whole life?'
'I can't find any underwear. It's all gone.'

And so was nearly everything else. How had it come to this? How had the vibrant, competent, self-sufficient woman who had, in recent years, come into her own as a well-respected, highly regarded professional become transformed into this vulnerable, needy being?

When my father died, back in 1975 at the age of 55, my mother had to make some significant changes in her life, including moving into the world of outside-the-home work after some 32 years of being at home. Given her sharp intelligence and strong organizational skills, she would eventually rise to the position of office manager for a school district on Long Island in New York. She would also sell my childhood home and move into an apartment in an upscale area not too far from New York City. Her grief over my father's untimely death remained potent, and for a longer period of time than she had been led to believe would be the case. 'I thought it was supposed to get easier', she said to me one time, around eight years later. And it eventually did, to some degree at least, due to her beginning to date a man whom she had known for some time, who had lost his wife, and who, like she, was eager to return to the world in some way. All of this would eventually change: in time, she left her job for health-related reasons, she moved down to Florida, and she lost her partner to cancer. Through it all, she was able to retain her vitality and sense of know-how.

Difficult and painful though it surely was, my mother knew how to pick herself up from the assaults that came her way, and she had retained much of the strength and fortitude she had acquired. Little wonder that when this profile began to be challenged she would protest, vehemently.

'I know I can still drive just fine.'
'I've always taken care of my own papers.'
'I've never been late for a check.'

I sometimes felt the need to challenge some of these assertions, in the (somewhat foolish) hope that she would look reality squarely in the face and admit her vulnerability and fragility.

'I'm not an imbecile.'
'You're treating me like a child.'

At the recommendation of her neurologist, Mom would eventually move to an assisted living residence; and even though she had been part of the search process and had agreed that this one was her top choice, she had no memory whatsoever of the process and had been convinced that my brothers and I had placed her there against her will. How did she come to find herself with all these old people anyway, with their canes and walkers and wheelchairs? She didn't need any of these! On the contrary, she still moved briskly and gracefully and stood out from the wizened crowd that surrounded her. How frustrating it must have been for her – and how confusing. I was often frustrated during this phase too, because try as I might, there seemed to be precious little I could do to lift her spirits.

'What do you want, ma?' I asked her one day. What can I do? What can anyone do? 'I want to be a person,' she answered.

What did she mean by this? I cannot say for sure. But what I think she meant was: I want to be the person I was, someone who could move about freely, make my own choices, determine my own path through the world. And I want to be a person with a history, and a story. But these are fading away, and with it, it seems, so am I.

> Herein lay her liminal status. Much of the time, she was – subjectively – who she had always been: an office manager and checkbook balancer, able to do just fine, thank you, on her own. ('So buzz off with all your "help!"') This felt sense of identity was sometimes profoundly interrupted, however, and much to her horror, the story she told herself about who and what she was would suddenly explode. At these times, she found herself living a broken narrative and it was made all the more painful by the felt permanence of the break. There would be no fixing it. The disease was marching forward, inexorably; she was hurtling toward the end. She began having more of these desperate moments. But like so many other things in her life, she often forgot having had them. So, she was still looking toward the future, toward the new apartment, the new job, the new *life* that might allow her to recover what had been taken away. Desperate moments were thus frequently replaced by ones that were a curious amalgam of frustration, rage, and hope. I wish these feelings had been distributed more evenly, but there was much more frustration and rage than there was hope.
>
> (Freeman 2021: 47)

In a very real sense, narrative was the culprit. Indeed, I have suggested (Freeman 2008, 2021), there was a dual narrative at work: that of '"the narrative of the vital, self-sufficient Individual", who vigorously resists feelings of fragility, vulnerability, and dependency', and '"the narrative of inexorable decline"' (2021: 48), culminating in the narrative foreclosure referred to earlier. Mom held on doggedly to the former, and rejected, equally doggedly, the latter. 'My mother wasn't ready to go there', I wrote, 'she wasn't ready to join the ranks of [the] non-persons' in her midst, 'and painful though it was, she held fast to what remained of her personhood, her own autobiographical identity' (49). If only she 'could have let go, given herself over to her situation and simply lived her life, unhampered by all the cultural scripts and narratives that permeated her existence (51) … But this is precisely what my mother could not do. She was in too deep' (53). Narrative was too much with her at this stage of her life, and the discontents she suffered were often debilitating and demoralizing. Tough times, all around.

Being let go: The ecstasy of unselfing

Eventually, I began to see a correlation of sorts, one that in its own tragic way promised a measure of reprieve, for my mother as well as for me: the more herself was on the line, her competence and self-sufficiency, the more painful things would be, and the more herself was set aside – listening to music, taking a nice drive, going out for a good meal – the more at home in the world she would be. It was around this time that I realized that as her dementia 'got worse', she herself would likely feel less tortured by her life. And maybe, with the continued loss of self, I had wondered, she would even be able to experience a kind of carefree oneness, an unselfconscious immersion into the world. This is what I would eventually call 'dementia's tragic promise' (Freeman 2008). Here's a passage from the (2021) book that speaks to this:

> It was one of those fall days in New England that demanded your attention. Mom and I decided to take a drive up a country road, toward Mt. Wachusett, which offers vistas of the lush valley below, the mountains of New Hampshire to the north, and on a crystal-clear day like that one, the Boston skyline. I tuned the car stereo to a local classical station. Up we went, climbing the road to the mountain, music playing, the sky blue, the leaves beginning to turn, shaking loose, skittering across the road. She was transfixed (60).
> 'Beautiful.'
> 'It must be peak now.'
> 'Such a pretty road.'
> 'Beautiful, beautiful day.'
> 'What a day.'
> 'Spectacular day for a ride like this.'
> 'What a spectacular, beautiful day.'
> Indeed it was. I felt it too. But not in the way she did:
>
> That day, for a few hours, she was . . . happy. Or something like it. I can't pretend to know exactly where she was, but wherever it was, it did seem to bring her a kind of oneness, a full immersion in the world, untouched by all the chattering stuff inside our heads that keep us from being present to things.
>
> (Freeman 2021: 61)

During this too-brief phase, this is how it was. Truly wondrous at times: dementia's tragic promise, in the form of a kind of ecstatic presence.

At times like these, Murdoch (1970) has written, 'We cease to be in order to attend to the existence of something else, a natural object, a person in need' (58). Ordinarily, the process of moving in this comparatively self-less direction is a demanding one, requiring specific practices, geared toward cultivating and refining one's habits of attention: 'To silence and expel self, to contemplate and delineate nature with a clear eye, is not easy and demands a moral discipline' (63). For Murdoch, we see this process most clearly and compellingly when encountering great works of art: 'Consider what we learn from contemplating the characters of Shakespeare or Tolstoy or the paintings of Velasquez or Titian. What is learnt here is something about the real quality of human nature, when it is envisaged, in the artist's just and compassionate vision, with a clarity which does not belong to the self-centred rush of ordinary life.' (63–4). Great works of art, when truly attended to, openly and unselfconsciously, can arrest us, their very clarity serving to call us beyond ourselves. But this process extends well beyond the domain of art. Murdoch describes this process as entailing a kind of 'detachment', and 'it is difficult and valuable whether the thing contemplated is a human being or the root of a tree or the vibration of a color or sound. Unsentimental contemplation of nature exhibits the same quality of detachment: selfish concerns vanish, nothing exists except the things that are seen.' (64). Mom's dementia gave her a kind of shortcut to this process. She was beyond practising a moral discipline, beyond intentionally cultivating her attentional capacities. But her state of brain and mind, damaged though they were, allowed her to engage in much the same sort of 'unselfing' that Murdoch (82) is considering here.

For the person engaging in this process intentionally, through the kind of discipline Murdoch is speaking of, one could plausibly think of it as 'letting go', in the sense of divesting oneself of those 'selfish concerns' that obstruct our view of what is there, in the world. For my mother, on the other hand, it would be more appropriate to speak of her 'being let go', the divestiture at hand being imposed from without, as it were, by the very dementia that had come her way. Moreover, rather than being a function of her moving beyond selfish concerns, it was instead a function of her moving beyond history and narrative and into a more explicitly poetic realm.

> Life therefore would become most worthwhile for her precisely when *she* – qua autobiographical identity – wasn't there. Or to put the matter somewhat differently, if paradoxically, her healthiest and most life-affirming experiences as a self, a vital self, were precisely when her autobiographical identity and narrative were in abeyance.
>
> (Freeman 2021: 57)

As I went on to note, there does remain a self in ecstatic experiences of this sort: a self still able to experience and enjoy. 'But it is a self that is rooted mainly in the present, in the living moment, in the relation to what is *Other*' (57; see also Freeman 2014).

Why, though, speak of the 'poetic' in this context? Divested of those energies and concerns that conceal the world, my mother had found herself able, temporarily, to encounter the world in such a way that it was *unconcealed* (Heidegger 1971), and *poiesis* entails this very process. As the philosopher Simon Critchley (2015) has written, 'Poetry lets us see things as they are.' But it lets us do so 'as they are anew. Under a new aspect. Transfigured. . . . The poet sings a song that is both beyond us, yet ourselves. Things change when the poet sings them, but they are still our things: recognizable, common, near, low' (8–9). And as a result, 'a whole world becomes available to readers that was not there before' (Parini 2008: 25) – or at least not there in the same way. Octavio Paz (1973), likewise, speaks to this as well in his consideration of the 'strangeness' that may emerge when the familiar has been poetically defamiliarized: 'Strangeness', he writes, 'is wonder at a commonplace reality that is suddenly revealed as that which has never been seen before' (112). It was there, we might say, but not seen, not in the way it is now, the poetry in question serving as the very midwife of the real.

Was my mother a poet when she uttered those words on our drive up that mountain? The answer is clear: yes and no. No; she wasn't crafting poems; she wasn't intentionally marshalling words in the name of poetic resonance. But yes; she was speaking from her heart and soul, simple words, bubbling up from within, to express her sheer delight over what she was encountering without. Yes. Yes. *Yes.*

> Whether wittingly or not, my mother had given herself over to the world at these moments, such that it could appear, and reappear, in all of its bounty and freshness and goodness. She was truly awestruck, and rather than taking pause and reflecting on the spectacle before her, she became awestruck once more, taken aback by what the world could be, by what the world *is*, if we could attend enough to truly encounter it.
>
> (Freeman 2021: 62)

It is possible that I am overvaluing experiences of this sort. But the fact is, 'there were moments during this strange, occasionally wondrous phase, when my mother, largely shorn of ego and desire, became transfixed enough by the spectacle before her as to call out in prayerful joy on the great good fortune of being there to witness it and to let it fill her as it could' (62). Lehmann (2018) has referred to such moments as 'poetic instants' (see also Synnes et al., this volume), while Lehmann and Brinkmann (2019) have written about the 'poetic windows' that sometimes open up in persons with dementia. This is what seems to have happened in my mother's case: In being let go, and thereby experiencing the ecstasy of unselfing, she had become poeticized, as it were, reduced to exaltation, anointed by her very affliction.

Tortured by time: Identity *in absentia*

Would that Mom's ecstatic exaltation could have lasted. What emerged in its wake was vastly different, almost an inversion of this exaltation, filled with confusion, panic, and, at times, sheer terror. I won't pretend to fully understand this turnabout, but it seemed to have something to do with her feeling exiled from reality. With the continued diminishment of her self, and the narrative that supported it, the world became too defamiliarized. And for a time, so did she. So rather than experiencing the kind of unselfconscious belonging that had characterized the previous phase, she had become homeless, in a way, cast out from the recognizable world, left to wander about, not knowing quite where, or who, she was. In place of the ecstasy of unselfing and the bountiful beauty and presence it had brought in tow, therefore, there emerged a desolate, desiccated absence.

At the centre of this extremely disturbing phase was the issue of time – specifically, the felt absence of a knowable past. Mom knew she had a past; she still knew enough about people and places to know what pasts are. There was evidence of her past owing to the presence of the furniture she would see in her apartment, which she had had for a long time, but for the life of her, she couldn't figure out how it got there, in this new, utterly unfamiliar place. 'It's not even a nightmare', she said one time; 'I don't know what it is.' So, there were questions, endless questions:

'Do I live here?'
'Have I ever been here before?'
'How long have I lived here?'
'What town is this?'
'How far away do you live?'
'Do I have another son in Worcester?'
'Where do my other sons live?'

One of the most difficult times for my mother during this phase was when she awoke from a nap, only to look around and find herself completely and utterly lost, unable to find any moorings at all that were recognizable. One day I got a phone call from the main desk: Mom's very confused and wants to speak to you.

'I woke up from a nap, and my mind just went blank. It's never happened before.'

'Well, Ma, actually it has, but you don't remember that it happened, so it feels new to you.'

I went over to her place to see if I could help her get located, and when I arrived, I heard the story again.

'I woke up, and my mind was blank. It's never happened before.'

'Well, it's happened before, Ma. But you've got some memory problems, so you don't remember having been there.'

'I would remember if this had happened before!'

'Ma, all I can tell you is that it has, a number of times.'

'This has happened before?'

'Yes, it has. But you don't remember it due to your memory.'

'I have memory problems?'

'Yes, Ma; you have for quite a while, and you're taking some medicine for them – Namenda and Aricept.'

'I didn't know what they were for.'

'Well, actually you did, but you've forgotten; you've been on them for a couple of years now.'

'So, I have memory problems?'

'Yes, ma, you do.'

'Oh, my God.'

She called herself a 'moron' and apologized repeatedly. Another time she needed me or my wife, Debbie, she said, 'I'm like a child now . . . I have to be put in a nursery, to be watched.'

'No, you're not,' I said; 'you're a full-grown adult.'

'But mindless. Dumb.'

'Brainless', she said another time.

There was confusion too, especially when she asked how long she had been at her assisted living residence.

'Welcome to my new abode,' she said one day.

'What do you mean, Ma?'

'I just moved in today. I don't know how things got here so fast.'

'You've been here for a while, Ma.'

'How long have I been here?'
'About three years.'
'Oh my god. When did I get here?'
'About three years ago, Ma.'
'Huh. How long?'
'It's about three years now, Ma.' It would eventually turn into four years, which brought a new wave of confusion.
'If I've been here four years', she asked, 'why wouldn't I know where I was?'
Not an easy question to answer.
Eventually, things would intensify, such that she had virtually no memory of anything regarding where she was living and not much beyond that either. And so, unlike the ecstatic torrent of 'Beautiful' and 'Spectacular' that she uttered on that fall drive up the mountain, there would be another torrent, equally concise:

'Amazing.'
'Horrifying.'
'Terrifying.'
'My, oh my.'
'Nothing, absolutely nothing.'

Mom would eventually reach the point at which, apart from me, there was virtually nothing left memory-wise. It was pretty clear that I was fading too.
'They don't know what to do with me here,' she said one time.
'What are you talking about, Ma?'
'I don't know where the hell I am. I don't know where I'm going. I don't know *anything*.'
The problem wasn't only hers, though. 'They don't know what's going on here. There's no one around, not a person.'
'There *are* people around', I said.
'So, why am I so completely alone here now, so completely lost?'
The eventual bottom line: 'I can't remember what I can't remember.' And, she might have added, I can't help but speak in a de-narrativized way, either in the form of questions or in the form of clipped, down-to-the-bone responses to my own increasingly futile attempts at dialogue. Was there 'poetry' during this phase of her dementia? It seems like a stretch to call it that; they were just conversations. But maybe it doesn't matter what to call it. What is clear was that Mom had moved beyond narrative during this phase, into a different order of meaning and time. I suppose one could say that she was still living in the moment. But this moment, far from being one of carefree abandon, was instead one of anxiety, dread, and unnameable loss, like being in 'another world'.

Living in verse: The fortunate fall

As I had predicted in the first piece I wrote about my mother, where I addressed 'dementia's tragic promise' (Freeman 2008), things would in fact eventually change for the better, at least subjectively. Mom eventually moved to a nursing home nearby, where she lived for six years. And owing to the progression of her disease, she had moved beyond the abysmal void I have just described. Seen from the outside, her situation was bleak. In addition to dementia, she had Chronic Obstructive Pulmonary Disease, she was in a wheelchair, her paper-thin skin was all mottled and black and blue, and she was virtually blind. For all that, though, she was . . . fine? I still don't know quite how to describe this phase, but here is what I eventually wrote:

> I'm not sure it makes sense to say that she was 'pleased' with where she'd landed, nor was she displeased. Actually, neither of those words seem to apply. That's because there was only the most minimal reflective distance at this time. She was no longer taking stock of things, no longer evaluating, measuring, against some standard of normalcy. She had moved beyond seeing herself as brainless, mindless, dumb, and all the rest. In fact, she seemed to be beyond seeing herself at all. She could still talk about a pain she had, something immediate, but she couldn't – or didn't – talk about her life or her mental state.
>
> (Freeman 2021: 94)

I am quite sure it was 'couldn't'. As for the result, it led to a different kind of relatedness.

So, there she would be as I entered the social room, eyes closed, slumped over, maybe dozing, maybe not; hard to tell. I might walk over and play with her hair a little, at which point she might perk up. If there was no response, I might ask: 'Anybody home?' Then, hopefully, she would know I was there.

'How did you find me?' she would ask.

'I always find you, Ma. Should we take a little spin?'

And then we would go to her room, or, if it was a nice day, go outside, wheel through the parking lot or sit by a nice little garden, try to catch up in whatever way we could. For a time, she would ask questions about me and my life – what I did for a living, whether I was married, whether we had any kids. Sometimes she knew all of this, but generally not; so, some measure of re-acquaintance was needed. One particularly moving conversation happened when I was 57. I responded to all of her questions, of course, but here, I just want to share her words, in the order they were uttered.

> 'So, you're my son?'
> 'Are you married?'
> 'Do you have any children?'
> 'And what is your name?'
> 'So, do you like me as a mother?'
> 'So, how long have I been your mother?'
> 'That's a long time not to know you,' she said, when I told her it's been 57 years.
> 'Wow', she added. 'Look at all the time I've missed with you.'
> 'So, do you call me Ma?'
> 'So, when did I get to know you?'
> 'So, are you nice?'
> 'So, do I look at you with love?'

After she received all the answers and knew the lay of the land, she could only conclude:

'I love being your mom.'

'I love being your son,' I said in response.

'So, it's a good match.'

At this phase, my mother seemed to have a memory of what it meant to be mother – the kind who looks at her children with love – just not the particular one she happened to be.

'Do you know why I'm here?' I asked another time.

'No.'

'I'm here to see you, because you're my mother.'

'Oh, baloney!'

I wasn't quite sure what to do with that one. There could be lighter versions of this too.

'I'm not your mother, am I?'

'Yeah, you are!'

'Oh, for goodness sake.'

'So, do you love me?' she asked after one of these startling revelations.

'Of course I love you,' I said. 'Do you love me?'

'I must!'

The following year brought some additional uncertainty and confusion, as evidenced by this exchange, which emerged when I asked her whether she knew who I was.

'My dear cousin? Brother? Father?'

(Nope.) 'Do you know yet who I am?'

'I love you.'

'But do you know yet who I am?'

'My sweetheart.'

'I'm your son.'

'I'm your son?'

'I'm *your* son.'

'Which one?'

'The best one.'

No wonder she must love me!

I could go on with these exchanges, but there is no need. Diminished though Mom was at this point, she could still play, and much of our time together during this phase was spent doing exactly that. Eventually, this would change, and she would just want to relax in her room or sit outside in the sun near some flowers and . . . be. In some ways, her experiences during the latter part of this phase were reminiscent of the ecstatic transports described earlier. But they were different too. Instead of the ecstatic rhapsodizing over the beauty and bounty of the world, there was a kind of quiescence, a simple state of unencumbered, self-less being, just *there*, in the world.

Simone Weil (1997/1952) once expressed what is – for a healthy, fully functioning person – an impossible wish: 'May I disappear in order that those things that I see become perfect in their beauty from the very fact that they are no longer things I see.' She herself knew it was impossible. 'When I am in any place, I disturb the silence of heaven and earth by my breathing and the beating of my heart.' But the aim still remains: 'To see a landscape as it is when I am not there' (37). Earlier on, my mother had approached the state Weil describes. There had been unselfing, but it had been incomplete – which is precisely why there would be a measure of enjoyment; as noted earlier, there still remained an 'I' who could look, feel, appreciate. At this later phase, though, the 'I' had diminished to a point of virtual non-existence, with the result that all that existed was 'world'.

I don't know that Mom was ever a poet, poetically charged though many of her utterances were. But she certainly wasn't one at this late time. She was all but speechless as she neared the end of her life, her existence, such as it was, essentially having devolved (evolved?) to a state of pure unselfed being. Then again, maybe she was the ultimate poet? For there would no longer be any gap, any slippage, between language and world, no effort to say what cannot be said. She had finally arrived at the seemingly impossible destination Weil had spoken of, and with this arrival, she had essentially become the world, its sunlight filtering through her, its sultry summer winds breathing in her, until it was all gone.

Whose words do we speak and write? On poetic repurposing

I have stated several times that I am unsure whether to call my mother's words 'poetry'. Or at least they weren't when she uttered them. In a way, though, I suggested, they *became* poetry through my telling of her story (see also Synnes et al., this volume; Synnes et al. 2021; Swinnen in this volume). They became transmuted, as it were, from conversational entries to poetically charged semantic beings whose resonances spilled beyond their ordinary roles. Was the resultant poetry mine, then? Another clear answer: yes and no. Her words didn't become poetically charged until they became part of the story I sought to tell. But again, these words were not mine; they were hers. And they were what incited me to tell the story in the first place. They had carried poetic potential; all they needed was a home where this potential could be realized. Mom and I built this home together. Whatever poetry there may be in the story at hand is therefore ours.

Maybe Mom should have been a co-author of 'my' book. Would she have been second-author or first-? Mark Freeman with the help of Marian? No; that's not quite right. Marian Freeman with the help of Mark? That doesn't work either. Let's not linger here in this inconclusive territory. It's quite pointless.

What is not pointless is to wonder, a bit more, about what is involved in the kind of poetic 'repurposing' this work entails. The issue here is not unrelated to the kind of artistic repurposing the philosopher and art critic Arthur Danto discussed in his important book *The Transfiguration of the Commonplace* (1983), when he addressed the work of Duchamp, Warhol, and others who sought to transform ordinary objects – urinals, bicycle wheels, Brillo boxes – into artworks by placing them in artful contexts like museums. Danto's work was more about the art world and the importance of theory than it was artistic repurposing and the kinds of resonances it might generate, but the idea of transmutation or transfiguration cuts across the two. What had initially been quite ordinary becomes extra-ordinary. What had initially been in the service of something else – peeing, shovelling, scrubbing – becomes 'autonomized,' such that we, the viewers, come to treat these theretofore functional objects as nonfunctional artistic works, perhaps even notable for their theretofore ignored aesthetic properties. So, it was with many of the dialogues I shared with my mother: what had initially been in the service of 'checking in' or 'catching up' became transfigured through repurposing, the very same words now being the vehicles of expressive meaning, located in the space between her and me.

Philosopher James Edwards (1997) has suggested that poetry allows us to see and feel 'the continual possibility of the familiar's sacramental transformation into the alien' (212). Needless to say, Edwards is speaking of the 'good' alien here – that is, that form of emergent, wondrous strangeness entailed in beholding reality anew. Perhaps 'alien' is the wrong word, though. For this experience has a curious, and seemingly contradictory, feature to it – namely that the alienness in question bears within it a new familiarity and a sense of recognition, such that we may be brought to a mode of seeing felt to be more real and more true than the mode employed before (Freeman, 2018). *Yes, that's who she is. I see her now, more clearly.*

Simone Weil's work, which I referred to earlier, is useful in this context too:

> We live in a world of unreality and dreams. To give up our imaginary position as the center, to renounce it, not only intellectually but in the imaginative part of our soul, that means to awaken to what is real and eternal, to see the true light and hear the true silence. A transformation then takes place at the very root of our sensibility, in our immediate reception of sense impressions and psychological impressions. It is a transformation analogous to that which takes place in the dusk of evening on a road, where we suddenly discern as a tree what we had at first seen as a stooping man; or where we suddenly recognize as a rustling of leaves what we thought at first was whispering voices. We see the same colors; we hear the same sounds, but not in the same way.
>
> (Weil 1997/1952: 159)

Here, then, is one way of thinking about what Octavio Paz (1967) calls 'the poetic experience'. It is about giving up 'our imaginary position as the center', as Weil put it, renouncing it, defeating it, thereby allowing us 'to awaken to what is real and eternal, to see the true light and hear the true silence'. There was still more to be done, however. For as a writer, I had to find language more adequate to who and what my mother was, language that might allow others to see her – and the phenomenon of dementia – anew too. Writing about the tragic element of dementia was certainly part of what needed to happen. That was one feature of the challenge. But I had to let beauty enter the picture too, such that others might be moved beyond their ossified images of what a person with dementia, as well as dementia itself, was all about. What was for some 'a palpable ugliness' eventually emerged for me and my family as 'the beauty of nature, stark and real'. We would learn 'to be present, literally and figuratively, to my mother's changing face, with its creases and folds, its caverns and abysses, its profound thereness, not to be sidestepped or elided but to be *seen*' (Freeman 2021: 110) – an afflicted human being, in inexorable decline, living the reality of transience. I had to try to show that face and that mode of being, so often hidden or denied, so that the images at hand could be challenged and reimagined. The challenge was large, indeed.

'Poetry', Czeslaw Milosz (1968) has said, 'is a constant self-negation' (280). With this self-negation, there can emerge the real. Poetic language takes this process to another level by showing the process of emergence itself, thereby disclosing the hidden potential of reality. As Heidegger (1971) puts the matter, 'The work holds open the open of the world' (45). The poet and critic Yves Bonnefoy (1989) does well to capture the paradoxical nature of this process. Somehow, he writes, 'this world which cuts itself off from the world seems to the person who creates it not only more satisfying than the first but also more real' (164). This does not of course mean that the words found in a book are more real than the flesh and blood human being standing, or sitting, before me. What it does mean is that, through writing, one can sometimes clarify and purify reality, such that its extraordinariness can be made manifest in its ordinariness, the two held together in a metaphorical tension, bleeding into one another, in a way that allows the world to be seen in fuller measure (Ricoeur 1977, 1981).

There may be no more suitable site for this repurposing and reimagining than the process of ageing. This is because the ossified images referred to above – of decline, deterioration, and, not least, death – are too often the default images. And being the default images, they too often come to be construed as the realities they depict. There is no eliding the harsh reality of aspects of dementia, and there is no eliding the reality of human demise. But that's not the aim in any case. The aim, again, is to see reality anew, in a way that it can embody and contain more of what it is than we are customarily able to see. If this is what my mother's words were able to do, I will be more than happy to call it poetry – 'found poetry', as my friend Leah had called it. Given its unintended and uncrafted nature, some may think of such poetry as being 'lesser'. In a way, though, I see it as being more – precisely *because* of its unintended, uncrafted nature. Oftentimes, sitting with Mom, trying to connect in some way, was like walking along the shore and coming across a beautiful shell or stone, of the sort I might pick up, put in my pocket, and set down on a shelf at home, where it would carry the weight of its being and its history. That's what her words were like for me: mementos, and gifts, unsought and unbidden, there to be preserved in some way, through writing.

References

Bonnefoy, Y. (1989), *The Act and Place of Poetry*, Chicago: University of Chicago Press.
Bruner, J. (1987), 'Life as Narrative', *Social Research* 54 (1), 11–22.
Carr, D. (1986), *Time, Narrative, and History*, Bloomington, IN: Indiana University Press.
Critchley, S. (2015), *Memory Theater*, New York: Other Press.
Danto, A. C. (1983), *The Transfiguration of the Commonplace: A Philosophy of Art*, Cambridge, MA: Harvard University Press.
Edwards, J. C. (1997), *The Plain Sense of Things: The Fate of Religion in an Age of Normal Nihilism*, University Park, PA: The Pennsylvania State University Press.
Freeman, M. (1993), *Rewriting the Self: History, Memory, Narrative*, London: Routledge.

Freeman, M. (1998a), 'Mythical Time, Historical Time, and the Narrative Fabric of the Self', *Narrative Inquiry* 8 (1): 27–50.
Freeman, M. (1998b), 'Experience, Narrative, and the Relationship between Them', *Narrative Inquiry* 8 (2): 455–466.
Freeman, M. (2000), 'When the Story's over: Narrative Foreclosure and the Possibility of Self-renewal', in M. Andrews, S. D. Sclater, C. Squire and A. Treacher (eds), *Lines of Narrative: Psychosocial Perspectives*, 81–91, London: Routledge.
Freeman, M. (2003), 'Rethinking the Fictive, Reclaiming the Real: Autobiography, Narrative Time, and the Burden of Truth', in G. Fireman, T. McVay, & O. Flanagan (eds), *Narrative and Consciousness: Literature, Psychology, and the Brain*, 115–128, New York: Oxford University Press.
Freeman, M. (2008), 'Beyond narrative: Dementia's Tragic Promise', in L.-C. Hydén and J. Brockmeier (eds), *Health, Illness, and Culture: Broken Narratives*, 169–184, London: Routledge.
Freeman, M. (2010a), *Hindsight: The Promise and Peril of Looking Backward*, New York: Oxford University Press.
Freeman, M. (2010b), 'Narrative foreclosure in later life: Possibilities and limits', in G. Kenyon, E. Bohlmeijer and W. Randall (eds), *Storying Later Life: Issues, Investigations, and Interventions in Narrative Gerontology*, 3–19, New York: Oxford University Press.
Freeman, M. (2014), *The Priority of the Other: Thinking and Living Beyond the Self*, New York: Oxford University Press.
Freeman, M. (2018), 'Living in verse: Sites of the poetic imagination', in O. V. Lehmann, N. Chaudhary, A. C. Bastos and E. Abbey (eds), *Poetry and Imagined Worlds*, 139–154, London: Palgrave Macmillan.
Freeman, M. (2021), *Do I Look at You with Love? Reimagining the Story of Dementia*, Leiden, The Netherlands: Brill | Sense.
Freud, S. (1957), 'On Transience'. *Standard Edition*, *14*, 305–307. London: Hogarth. (Originally published in 1915)
Heidegger, M. (1971), *Poetry, Language, Thought*, New York: Harper Colophon.
Kerby, A. (1991), *Narrative and the Self*, Bloomington, IN: Indiana University Press.
Lehmann, O. V. (2018), 'The Cultural Psychology of Silence: Treasuring the Poetics of Affect at the Core of Human Existence' (Unpublished doctoral dissertation), NTNU Norwegian University of Science and Technology, Trondheim, Norway.
Lehmann, O. V. and S. Brinkmann (2019), '"I'm the One Who Has Written This": Reciprocity and Existential Meaning-Making in Writing Courses for Older Adults in Norway', *International Journal of Qualitative Studies on Health and Well-Being* 14 (1). https://doi.org/10.1080/17482631.2019.1650586.
Milosz, C. (1968), *Native Realm: A Search for Self-Definition*, New York: Farrar, Straus and Giroux.
Murdoch, I. (1970), *The Sovereignty of Good*, London: Routledge.
Murdoch, I. (1993), *Metaphysics as a Guide to Morals*, New York: Penguin.
Parini, J. (2008), *Why Poetry Matters*, New Haven, CT: Yale University Press.
Paz, O. (1973), *The Bow and the Lyre: The Poem, the Poetic Revelation, Poetry and History*, Austin, TX: University of Texas Press.
Ricoeur, P. (1977), *The Rule of Metaphor: Multidisciplinary Studies of the Creation of Meaning in Language*, Toronto, CA: University of Toronto Press.
Ricoeur, P. (1981), 'The Metaphorical Process as Imagination, Cognition, and Feeling', in M. Johnson (ed), *Philosophical Perspectives on Metaphor*, 228–247, Minneapolis, MN: University of Minnesota Press.

Ricoeur, P. (1991), 'Life in Quest of Narrative', in D. Wood (ed), *On Paul Ricoeur: Narrative and Interpretation*, 20–33, London: Routledge.

Sartwell, C. (2000), *End of Story: Toward an Annihilation of Language and History*, Albany, NY: SUNY Press.

Stevens, W. (1997), *Collected Poetry and Prose*, New York: The Library of America. (Poem "Sunday morning" originally published 1923)

Strawson, G. (2004), 'Against Narrativity', *Ratio* 17 (4): 428–452.

Synnes, O., M. Råheim, E. Lykkeslet, and E. Gjengedal (2021), A Complex Reminding: The Ethics of Poetry Writing in Dementia Care. *Dementia* 20 (3): 1025–1043. https://journals.sagepub.com/doi/10.1177/1471301220922750

Weil, S. (1997), *Gravity and Grace*, London: Routledge. (Originally published 1952)

2

Poetry and Dementia: Imagining and Shaping More Just Futures

Aagje Swinnen

In 2015, I interviewed the established Dutch poet Leo Herberghs (1924–2019) about the ways in which he experienced creativity in the final stage of his career. Herberghs was 91 years old at the time and lived with his wife in their home in the South of the Netherlands. While I was initiating contact with the poet, some of his colleagues wondered if he would agree to an interview given that his health was declining. They cautiously implied that they were worried about his cognitive abilities. When I subsequently met the couple at their place, in passing, Herberghs's wife Ciska mentioned the poet's forgetfulness and suggested she sat in on the interview for his comfort. Herberghs himself never used the word 'forgetful' during my visit except when his wife subtly referred to it. He did, however, ask me whether there were many poets living with dementia. He was also adamant that, without Ciska's help, he would have to relocate to a care facility immediately. Re-reading the interview transcript today, I realize that the pace of this interview was significantly slower when compared to the conversations with the other poets in my study on experiences of late-life creativity (Swinnen 2018) and that Herberghs had not provided lengthy answers to my questions. Moreover, he often repeated certain statements and phrasings. Still, the author and I engaged in a meaningful exchange on his working routines, his motives for writing poetry, his position in the literary field and his literary legacy.

Herberghs noticed that his poems had become shorter and more impression-like in recent years, possibly due to 'a lack of breath' (his words).[1] He had also spent more time on editing and ordering his earlier work than on creating new work. Nevertheless, Herberghs strongly emphasized the continuity in his career and called his life 'an existence in words, written words'. He felt surrounded by people who helped him sustain this preferred 'existence in words' – for instance, Bert van Melick who read and commented on his writings – even though Herberghs was becoming increasingly frail. In Herberghs's view, age in terms of life experiences had little effect on the nature of his poetry: 'When I write poetry, I am a 10-year-old child. I believe that [age]

---

[1] All translations from Dutch to English in this chapter are mine.

does not play a role in poetry. You may come to a more profound insight [as you age] but that does not result in new poetry, I believe'. He even went so far as to pose the rhetorical question that 'maybe one has to be "demented" to write good poems'. Herberghs was not only able to continue his literary practice in an adjusted form in the context of his private home at the end of his life, but he also remained visible in the literary field as a professional poet through the instalment of the Leo Herberghs Poetry Prize in 2014 to recognize poetic talent.

Interestingly, for Herberghs, poetry and forgetfulness/dementia were not a contradiction in terms. This may be surprising at first because the illness often comes with word-finding and comprehension problems and poetry is regarded as the most semantically dense and difficult literary genre. In this chapter, I will argue that, perhaps counterintuitively, the aesthetic and pragmatic affordances of poetry enable people who live with dementia to express themselves. That is, if they find themselves in a context that is open to their contributions. If not, the stigma of dementia is almost impossible to overcome for them, which results in the silencing of their creativity and personhood. I will demonstrate this by means of two further case studies: the first, relates to the Flemish poet Hugo Claus, and the second, to two participatory literary activities – the Alzheimer's Poetry Project and Shared Reading. Before presenting and analysing these case studies, I will introduce my theoretical approach.

Theoretical approach: Dementia as a disability

Since the 2010 project 'Beyond Autonomy and Language', awarded in the ZonMw funding scheme Disability Studies in the Netherlands, I have conceptualized Alzheimer's disease and related dementias (from now on referred to as dementia) as a disability together with my Maastricht colleagues Ruud Hendriks, Annette Hendrikx and Ike Kamphof (Hendriks et al. 2016). In recent years, this approach has gained momentum (e.g., Shakespeare, Zeilig and Mittler 2019), not least because it helps us understand dementia as a social justice issue rather than as just a dreadful illness in need of a cure. In her book *Feminist Queer Crip* (2013), Alison Kafer differentiates between the medical/individual model of disease and the political/relational model, a distinction that I find helpful in rethinking dementia as a disability.

The medical/individual conceptualization of dementia is predominant both within health care and among the general public. Following this model, dementia is considered a disease of the brain that implies a progressive decline in cognition and difficulties in functioning. Dementia is understood to signify a loss of personhood and self, which makes it almost unthinkable that one could have a full, meaningful and dignified life with the illness – an assumption that Kafer calls ableist (2013: 3). This concept of dementia has resulted in the stigmatization and Othering of people living with dementia (Hughes, Louw and Sabat 2006). Dementia conceptualized as a purely medical and individual affliction has established a hierarchical binary between *us*, neurotypical people, and *them*, neurodivergent people who have failed to comply to the neoliberal idea of ageing successfully, i.e., independently and in good health. Consequently, the affects that come with a dementia diagnosis include fear (of losing one's self and one's dignity), shame (about becoming dependent), disgust (at losing decorum and autonomy) and guilt (for becoming a burden to others).

By contrast, the political/relational model suggests that 'the problem of disability no longer resides in the minds or bodies of individuals but inbuilt environments and social patterns that exclude or stigmatize particular kinds of bodies, minds, and ways of being' (Kafer 2013: 6). According to this model, dementia is 'experienced in and through relationships' (8) and subjectivity emerges from interactions with other people (Gilliard et al. 2005). Hence, when people are confronted with memory loss that starts interfering with their daily activities, their surroundings need to help them uphold who they were and support the person they will become. The political/relational model goes beyond the stimulation of the participation of people who live with dementia through different types of activities and the improvement of accessibility. It aims to honour their voices and empower them to advocate for themselves. The model also serves to acknowledge and fight against the many injustices and micro-aggressions that people living with dementia are confronted with because they depart from the norm of able-mindedness. In this sense, Kafer's political/relational model – which is not specific to dementia – resonates with what Tom Shakespeare, Hannah Zeilig and Peter Mittler argue: 'what is required is a stronger response, an equalities-based approach, that recognizes that people with dementia are a minority group in society, who are poorly served in many environments, and who consequently face exclusion, even oppression' (2019: 1080). In the words of Dragana Lukić and Anne Therese Lotherington, we must start 'appreciating life together in difference' (2019: 119).

In this chapter, I first present the case of Hugo Claus, a renowned Flemish poet who opted for euthanasia a few years into his Alzheimer's diagnosis. I show how the medical/individual conceptualization of dementia made it hard for the poet to imagine a meaningful future with the disease. I then contrast this case with two participatory cultural arts activities for people who live with dementia that are based on the spoken word, namely the approaches of the Alzheimer's Poetry Project (APP) and Shared Reading (SR). I have selected these uses of literature because they are still underexamined in comparison to other activities in dementia care settings that include singing, dancing and arts and crafts. I argue that both approaches are inspired by the political/relational model of dementia. In an ideal scenario, the activities of APP and SR do not only facilitate participation but engender inclusion by destabilizing the hierarchical binary between neurotypical and neurodivergent people.

The case of Hugo Claus

A mediatized death

Hugo Claus (1929–2008) was an acclaimed Flemish writer, painter and theatre and film maker. In his rich oeuvre, he advocated liberties such as sexual freedom, abortion, secularization and euthanasia. As such, it is not surprising that Claus, with support of the organization 'Recht op waardig sterven' (The right to die with dignity), opted for a self-chosen death two years into his diagnosis of Alzheimer's disease and after seven years of living with memory loss.[2] Claus passed away on 19 March 2008, a few days before his 79th birthday. His death became mediatized in an unprecedented way. The cultural elite of Flanders and the Netherlands attended Claus's funeral at the Bourla Theatre in Antwerp on 29 March 2008. Flemish and Dutch television broadcasted the ceremony in which actors read from Claus's poetry and selected acquaintances painted a picture of him. The general tone was one of admiration for Claus as a literary phenomenon and for the death he had chosen. The remarkable public interest in Claus' passing not only stemmed from the fact that he was Flanders' most renowned writer, often tipped for the Nobel Prize in Literature, but also because the Belgian law that enables people with dementia to opt for euthanasia when they are competent to decide autonomously had only recently been adopted. Proponents of euthanasia have introduced the term 'Claus-effect' to suggest that the mediatized death of the writer increased public awareness of euthanasia, also in relation to dementia (Rogiers and Claeys 2017).

The speech Erwin Mortier gave at Claus's funeral (2008) has left a lasting impression on the Flemish collective memory. Mortier (a friend and a colleague of Claus) presented him as the last representative of the generation of artists born before and shaped by WWII that advanced the cultural, social and philosophical emancipation of Flanders. Mortier called on his fellow writers to honour the master by writing in the service of 'radical freedom and equality, and to expose all powers that want to gag or enslave them' (2008: 20). He then sneered at agents of these 'powers' who questioned Claus's choice of euthanasia. Many interpreted this as an attack on cardinal Godfried Danneels who, in his 2008 Easter homily, disapproved of the disproportionate media attention that euthanasia was receiving compared to the disregard for people in need of care who decided to face their vulnerabilities until the very end (De Dijn 2008).

Mortier and Danneels represent two opposing ideological sides in the Flemish euthanasia discussion. Mortier believes it to be factually true that dementia equals unbearable suffering and presents euthanasia as the ultimate act of agency and triumph of autonomy and a commonsensical solution to this suffering. Following a debatable progress narrative, he positions people who question euthanasia as religious torment-worshipping bigots who are stuck in the past, incapable of showing empathy (De Dijn 2008: 158). Despite initiatives such as the campaign *Vergeet dementie onthou mens* (Forget dementia, remember the person/Mensch), developed by the Expertisecentrum Dementie Vlaanderen, Mortier's view has come to dominate public discourse in Flanders. There is little room in this discourse for the many ways in which the lives of people with dementia are entangled with their surroundings and the impact of this entanglement on how the disease is experienced, how the person behind it is valued and how care is organized (De Lepeleire et al. 2008: 179). It is in this social context that Claus was confronted with Alzheimer's disease and chose to die.

---

[2] I refer to the timeline in Claus's 'Biography' on the website of the Hugo Claus Centre at the University of Antwerp (https://clauscentrum.be/biografie2000.html).

Anticipating later life with cognitive decline

Our knowledge of the final years of Claus's life, when he lived with Alzheimer's disease up to the day he died, is hardly based on biographical information. This is partially because the author was never keen to reveal much about himself, about the man behind the work. Claus did not believe in the notion of a fixed and coherent self; he compared himself to a chameleon (Schaevers 2004: 187). This explains the subtitle of the abecedarium *Hugo Claus: Een groepsportret* (Hugo Claus: A Group Portrait; Schaevers 2004), a compilation of his most pertinent quotes from the period 1951–2004. The quotes present Claus as a postmodern subject with different faces. They also show, however, great consistency in Claus's views on the meaning of writing, his fear of decline, the comfort of a self-chosen death and the relative significance of an artistic legacy. These views are informative for our understanding of how the poet anticipated cognitive decline in later life and its impact on his creativity.

Writing had no therapeutic effect for Claus, but it did give meaning to his existence (Schaevers 2004: 88). He turned Descartes's 'cogito ergo sum' into 'I write, therefore I am' (414). This does not imply, however, that he experienced writing as an easy task: 'Writing is a torment but also a delight' (335). Poetry was at the core of Claus's literary practice, and, in his later years, he felt it should become his sole priority (293–94). He was adamant that writers do not retire and, in a 2000 interview, foresaw that he would work to his very end (288). In his view, ageing is a natural part of life (280). He did not fear death; he feared the possible decline preceding it. As early as 1978, he stressed in an interview the importance of having control over his life's end. Claus recounts approvingly how Hemingway committed suicide when he experienced early symptoms of forgetfulness after he had watched his father 'become senile' (430). In a 1986 interview, Claus remembers how his own father begged his general practitioner to help him die because he was suffering immensely (11). Just like him, Claus would have wanted to have a suicide pill at hand. In another interview, he characterizes a self-chosen death as 'very festive and comforting' (431). Long before his own diagnosis of Alzheimer's disease, Claus is firm in his statement that 'If I start to "get demented", they have to kill me soon' (11). In 1999, he admitted that he was experiencing word-finding problems when talking about the novel *Elegy for Iris* (John Bayley's memoir about his marriage to the writer and philosopher Iris Murdoch) that portrays 'one of the most glorious intelligences of England' as less competent than a three-year-old child (11). About the motivations underlying his particular fear of cognitive decline, we learn that Claus did not want to become a burden on others (430) and that he wished to preserve his dignity (95).

These quotes from interviews with Claus show how he envisaged writing poetry in his final years unless he would be affected with dementia. Following the rationale of the medical/individual model of the disease, Claus is unable to imagine that a life with dementia could be meaningful and that he would be able to adapt and enjoy his literary practice as a result. Fear of an undignified and dependent life is the emotion behind the quotes above. It is not caused by lived experience but based on his observation of people such as Hemingway, Murdoch and his own father. His reaction is to locate the responsibility for the problem of dementia in the individual and he views euthanasia, portrayed as a dignified and joyful death, as the only answer to his fear. What is presented as a logical 'solution', however, is characteristic of a neoliberal masculinist and rational order that presents death as preferable to becoming the fearful Other (Shildrick 2015). As Lukić and Lotherington write: 'Suicide [in relation to dementia] is a fatal act of agency, while at the same time an effect of the us-them binary that powerfully stigmatizes "them"' (2019: 118). This resonates with what Margaret Gullette (2011) has called 'the duty to die' for all older people who are unable to live up to the ableist ideal of successful ageing.

There are some elements in the collection of quotes, though, that offer a glimpse of a counter narrative. Claus hints at a notion of a relational self when acknowledging that 'Others resonate. [They function as a] soundboard. You only live through others' (Schaevers 2004: 22). In addition, he recognizes the importance of being in the present rather than in the past or in the future (260, 269). He also acknowledges that no one knows whether Murdoch was happy or unhappy when living with Alzheimer's (11). *Hugo Claus: Een groepsportret* includes quotes up to 2004. The question is what happened to Claus and his literary practice between 2004 and the day he died?

Final words?

In 2011, *De wolken: Uit de geheime laden van Hugo Claus* (The Clouds: From the Secret Drawers of Hugo Claus; Schaevers 2011) was published posthumously. It is a collection of work from Claus's archive, containing photographs, manuscripts, letters, notes and more, in anticipation of scholarly editions to follow in the years after Claus's death. In the last chapter, also entitled 'The Clouds', editor Mark Schaevers explains that Claus's archive includes a large package of 'scribbled paper' with the 'vague contours' of what the writer envisioned would become his final work. According to Schaevers, the papers contain ideas for characters, scenes and plot development but he also suggests that they mainly illustrate Claus's writing struggle. There is, indeed, a difference between these notebooks and the earlier handwritten texts by Claus included in the book. His handwriting is less firm. The pages remain largely empty and the text that is there is fragmentary and testifies to word-finding problems. The pages also include drawings that hook together. This seems to confirm the account of Claus's final years by his last wife Veerle de Wit: 'he suffered unbearably when he found he could no longer write. He had been trying it for a long time. But the sentences no longer went smoothly from left to right; they ran right off the page' (Rogiers and Claeys 2017: n.p.).

Some reviewers found it incomprehensible and painful that Schaevers decided to include evidence of Claus's decline in the posthumous publication (Gerreway 2011). I would argue, however, that the final chapter of *The Clouds* shows us first-hand that Claus kept writing despite what was happening to him, which both confirms and denies what he predicted all along (as shown above). What does the so-called pack of 'scribbled paper' tell us about his late-life experiences? Schaevers gives readers a clue by including notes, selected from workbooks, diaries or loose pages from the period 1960–2008 and printed in red, at the bottom of the final chapter's pages. I suspect that they were chosen because of their poetic potential – they seem to be showing some continuity in who Claus was as a personality and an artist. The first note is: 'The silences when he is invited to visit friends. / Vanriet: "And what do you think about that, Maestro?"/ He is less invited. / (Which is not true, too much awe, staring at, various symptoms. Very personal.)' (Schaevers 2011: 322). Assuming that this note is, indeed, from Claus's final years, it relates to his feelings about the ways in which he is positioned by friends and colleagues. They still address him playfully and collegially with 'maestro' while asking him for his opinion. However, simultaneously, the note suggests that Claus felt scrutinized for behaviour that departs from what is expected and could be attributed to his Alzheimer's diagnosis. It is difficult for Claus to navigate between the star persona of the maestro that puts him on a pedestal and the stare that separates him from neurotypical people when he blunders. The second note reads like a rhetorical question: 'The doctor said you have the heart of a horse / the rectum / the lungs of the late Stan Ockers [famous Belgian cyclist] / the tail / but what don't I have' (342)? Some readers may easily fill in the blanks with 'a healthy functioning brain' or 'a good working memory' – hereby locating the problem in the body, symmetrically following the structure of the other lines. By withholding an answer, though, Claus leaves open the suggestion that he may lack something of an entirely different order. (The companionship of people who accept him for the person he has become? The ability to imagine a meaningful life with dementia?)

If it is true that Claus co-staged his funeral himself as many news items asserted, it is worth having a closer look at his (re)appearance on stage in the form of a pre-recorded video. In this video, Claus reads his 'Sonnet XV' (1986) above the coffin with his mortal remains (Claus 2008: 140). According to Dirk van Hulle (2005), 'Sonnet XV' is an adaptation of William Shakespeare's 'Sonnet 107'. This poem starts off with the sentiment of love's uncertainty and ends with the realization that the lyrical I and his true love, the Fair Youth, will outsmart death by means of the poem that testifies to their love ('My love looks fresh, and Death to me subscribes / Since, spite of him, I'll live in this poor rhyme'). Claus does not only change the form, rhyme and meter of Shakespeare's sonnet but also turns its meaning upside down. Van Hulle argues that, while Shakespeare's poem describes the development from insecurity to certainty, Claus sings the praises of uncertainty itself and renounces the confidence that he associates with youth ('Now the world is mortal as I / and that's it. / Only uncertainty gives me a kick, / I don't believe a thing'). As such, 'Sonnet XV' disavows a profound belief in the power of poetry to leave an eternal mark on earth. Yet, it is significant that Claus recites this poem from beyond the grave and that his words were supplemented by actors who read his other work at the funeral. Thus, Claus's words could still be heard even after his passing. The overall effect of this particular staging is as ambiguous as the ultimate answer of the chosen death itself.

The Alzheimer's Poetry Project and Shared Reading

I now turn from the sobering case of Claus to two ways in which poetry making and reading have been successfully implemented in activities for people who live with dementia. This move is characteristic of what has been called 'post-critique' in literary and cultural studies (Felski 2015), which implies a renewed interest in literary practices by lay persons in everyday settings since the rise of reader response criticism and the sociology of literature in the 1960s. The practices under focus are The Alzheimer's Poetry Project and Shared Reading.

The Alzheimer's Poetry Project (APP) is an oral poetry method developed by the slam poet Gary Glazner. It has been implemented in several dementia care settings in New York (http://www.alzpoetry.com). Glazner's workshops include both poetry recitations and improvisations. In the poetry recitations, Glazner (2005) as Poetry Facilitator[3] starts from a corpus of existing poems and invites participants who live with dementia to join him through call-and-response. Body movements such as motoric gestures (e.g., hand clapping, feet tapping) and illustrative gestures (i.e., showing the meaning of a phrase) may accompany the recitations. Poetry improvisations start from open questions on topics such as love, autumn, or ice cream to which the participants respond. Glazner collects these responses and turns them into poems suited to poetry recitations. In 2014, I went to Brooklyn, New York, to observe and learn about Glazner's work in The Brooklyn Memory Center for five months through a participatory ethnographic approach (Swinnen 2016). Back in the Netherlands, I organized 20 workshops ('Poetry and Storytelling Cabinet' project) that introduced the oral poetry method[4] to the closed dementia wards of De Beyart and Scharwyerveld (Swinnen & de Medeiros 2018) in Maastricht. I took on the role of Poetry Facilitator and kept a research diary. Student assistant Helen Verploegen helped organize the sessions, recorded them and made field notes.

Shared Reading (SR) is an approach established by a British organization called The Reader (https://www.thereader.org.uk). It entails reading sessions in which literary texts – excerpts from novels and short stories as well as poems – are read aloud by a Reader Leader who invites participants to engage in an open discussion. In the Netherlands and Belgium, SR has been adopted by *De Culturele Apotheek* (The Cultural Pharmacy, https://www.cultureleapotheek.nl) and *Bond zonder Naam* (Union Without Name, https://www.bzn.be/nl/home) respectively. These organizations aim to contribute to the wellbeing of participants and to improve social connectivity through literature as a shared experience. From June until October 2021, I studied the practice of SR in the Dutch-speaking context during the COVID-19 pandemic when people, after a longer period of lockdown, gradually started to return to life as it used to be ('Shared Reading in Times of Lockdown' project). Student assistant Maike Brinkman and I were able to observe 12 SR sessions in the Netherlands and Flanders. SR was not specifically developed to cater to people who live with dementia, but it has been successfully integrated in health and social care (Billington et al. 2013; Gray et al. 2016). In the Netherlands, De Culturele Apotheek has introduced SR in Odense Houses, i.e., walk-in-centres that were originally established in Denmark that focus on the empowerment and wellbeing of people who live with dementia and their caregivers.

---

[3] Glazner does not use the term Poetry Facilitator. I introduce it here to draw a parallel with the Reader Leader of SR.

[4] I combined the approach developed by Glazner with the storytelling method TimeSlips (Swinnen and de Medeiros 2018), which falls beyond the scope of this chapter.

For this chapter, I focus on two sessions that were observed, recorded and transcribed verbatim by Maike Brinkman in Odense House Amsterdam and Odense House Haarlem. The Reader Leaders in these sessions were two volunteers of *De Culturele Apotheek*.

Close reading and listening (cf. Bernstein 1998) approaches served to analyse the data with particular attention to the interactions among the participants, the input of the Poetry Facilitator/Reader Leader, responses to individual literary texts, procedures of the participatory literary activity, expressions of personhood and evidence of inclusion. When possible, cross-coding (with the student assistant or the co-author) helped to increase the validity of the interpretation. For all projects, informed consent was secured, and the data have been anonymized for this chapter.

What a poetic form entails and what distinguishes it from prose has been up for debate for decades in literary scholarship (Wolf 2005). In what follows, rather than focusing on distinct features of poetry both semantically and syntactically, I will address how they function in the APP and SR as specific literary practices (thus pragmatically). What is it that makes both APP and SR meaningful approaches when collaborating with people who live with dementia? Following the political/relational model of dementia, with meaningfulness, I refer to opportunities for them to interact and connect with other people, to express themselves creatively without restriction or reprimand and to appear as individuals with their own unique characters and preferences.

The comfort of repetition

In one of my earlier pieces on the APP, I argue that to value poetry as a meaningful 'intervention' in dementia care, we must approach it as literary performance rather than as a printed text that remains unchanged over time (Swinnen 2016: 5). When literature is performed, repetition becomes 'the ultimate vehicle for meaning and artistry' (5). The approach behind the APP capitalizes on this characteristic of oral poetry to include people who live with dementia in the activity. Call-and-response builds on the possibility of participants to repeat poetic lines after the Poetry Facilitator. The lines are short enough for people to remember and to recite them – sometimes by only moving their lips. The integration of the accompanying gestures also has an element of repetition in it as they repeat the rhythm or the content of the poem in other systems of signification. In addition, the chosen poems themselves may include an element of repetition. One example is 'Polonaise' (1927), a poem by Paul van Ostaijen from which I used the first eight lines for call-and-response sessions in the Dutch context:

> I saw Cecilia coming
> on a summer night
> two ears to hear
> two eyes to see
> two hands to grab
> and ten fingers far

I saw Cecilia coming
On a summer night

The composition of this excerpt relies on the repetition of words and the symmetry of phrases: 'two' in combination with body parts connected to the senses. The poem also builds on circularity. Even though new lines follow on the second 'one summer night' in the original, I chose to start over again as if the poem contained a loop. Furthermore, recording the participants' contributions in the rounds of poetry improvisation and literally giving the words back to them is illustrative of how important repetition is to make the activity work. For an outsider, the different layers of repetition may seem excessive but, for the target group of people who live with dementia, it turns so-called shortcomings associated with their disease into something fun and empowering. There is no need to generate words autonomously or understand them cognitively. Instead, words can resonate for what they are, i.e., a relational tool in a conversational turn taking or even mere sound.

Although SR as an oral literature practice differs greatly from the APP and the Reader Leader is less of a performer than the Poetry Facilitator, the analysis of the sessions in the Odense Houses confirm the importance of repetition. SR starts with the Reader Leader reading a text aloud. If this does not immediately generate responses from the participants, she reads the text once more. When the group discussion has reached a point of saturation, the Reader Leader invites a participant to read the text once more. As such, the same short text can be repeated up to three times in a time span of approximately 20 minutes. The fact that the participants get a copy of each text so they can follow it on paper also empowers them to repeat some words and lines verbatim, even though this is not explicitly anticipated by the design of the cultural activity as is the case in the APP call-and-response sequences. In addition, participants also literally repeat what other participants, or the Reader Leader, say and, in her turn, the Reader Leader validates the input of contributors by replicating it:

SP4   You can't walk much on a ship.
SP5   On a ship...
SP4   So it takes place, if I understand correctly, this is someone who is on a ship.
SP5   Yeah, a ship? Yes.
SP4   But the ship, yeah, that can never be very big.
SP5   It's not a rowboat, hey? A ship you can walk on, yes.
RL   But what kind of ship could this be?

(Odense House Amsterdam, July 2, 2021)

This exchange was inspired by a passage from Toni Morrison's *Beloved* (1987) that starts with the phrase 'there is a loneliness that you can cradle'. Speaker 5 says after Speaker 4 that the text concerns a ship and pairs the noun with the verb 'walking' as initiated by Speaker 4. The Poetry Facilitator invites both speakers to continue the conversation on the type of ship, thereby welcoming them to reiterate that it could be a rowboat. Again, what for neurotypical people could come across as an unusual, perhaps inefficient way of interacting through the spoken word, is here a tool to participate, connect and receive affirmation.

From mono-perspectival poetic fragment to collective experience

For literature to be successfully included in APP and SR activities, it must be short. In the call-and-response sessions of the APP, poems that are already brief in themselves are further condensed. 'The Tyger' (1794) by William Blake, for instance, becomes little more than its famous lines 'Tyger Tyger, burning bright / In the forests of the night'. SR makes use of poems and excerpts from novels and short stories. Without introducing the literary context of these excerpts, they become more poetic in the sense that their degree of narrativity declines (Billington et al. 2013: 166). Werner Wolf writes that the lyric offers a 'mono-perspectival point of view of consciousness' that is used 'not as a means of shedding light on elements of external reality but on revealing itself, its thoughts and in particular its emotions' (2005: 36). Shorter texts are automatically lower in narrativity than longer texts because they include fewer characters, events and temporal and spatial changes.[5] Instead, they offer a glimpse of a scene, an experience, an emotion, which is oppositional to chronology and causality. A passage from Vonne van der Meer's novel *De vrouw met de sleutel* (The Woman with the Key, 2011), for example, discloses only that a lonely woman starts writing an ad in which she offers to tuck people in and read aloud to them at bedtime.

Neither in APP nor in SR sessions is there an exclusive invitation for participants to fill in the gaps of the literary texts and turn the scarce information that they are given into an interpretative whole. Call-and-response does not require the participants to comment on the meaning of the poems. And, although SR is based on open questions that invite participants to respond to a text cognitively, the method is open to emotional and experiential responses as well. Indeed, the questions are not only focused on what the literature is about but also on what it means to the participants who are encouraged to make connections between the text and their personal lives. Often, the Reader Leader asks whether some aspects of the reading are familiar to the participants or whether they recognize themselves in the text (which differs from reminiscing):

RL	Do you ever stand waiting at an exit?
SP1	Yes.
RL	And do you also experience doubt whether it is this exit?
SP1	Yes, I have that a lot.
RL	And do you recognize that a bit here in the text?
SP1	Well, I was then waiting for a region [taxi] that dropped me off there and I was waiting in a different place. So, I was also at that exit, exactly what you say. Yes, I remember that very well.
RL	Yes, do other people recognise this?
SP2	Yes, because, when you get to the station, you have two entrances, in the front and back side. You can get out through both.
RL	Oh yeah.
SP2	Yes, I sometimes wonder sometimes where she will come from.

(Odense House Haarlem, 15 June 2021)

---

[5] It is, for this reason, that Synnes et al. (2021) suggest using Orr's term 'lyric stories' to value the poetic contributions of people who live with dementia.

This type of prompting – here in relation to the poem 'Vier manieren om op iemand te wachten' (Four Ways to Wait for Someone, 2001) by Joke van Leeuwen – is somewhat comparable to the open questions[6] that the Poetry Facilitator asks in the poetry improvisation sessions, although in the APP approach there is less emphasis on recognition and a new poem created on the spot is the foreseen result.

Every response to a literary text is coloured by the background and experiences of the reader/participant. As Maurice Hamington and Ce Rosenow write, 'A reading ... its performance, if you will, is a relationship with a singularity: an interplay between the words/form and the audience (which can be as few as one) who brings to the event a history and disposition that shape the experience' (2019: 75). Characteristic of the APP and SR is that there is ample room for voicing and sharing these experiences in the group. The poem 'Vier manieren om op iemand te wachten', which offers a mono-perspectival point of view on waiting, resulted in a conversation of approximately 18 minutes about possible misunderstandings over where and when to meet that started with the example above. The participants talked both about their fear of getting this wrong and the self-doubt resulting from it. They validated each other's input, built on each other's stories and encouraged each other to contribute to the conversation. In this way, a single-voiced poem turned into a polyphonic exchange of experiences, a multi-voiced social event.

The beauty of this SR session lay in the fact that, even though the setting was an Odense House, the participants did not suggest a causal relationship between their forgetfulness on the one hand and anxiety over making mistakes in planning and organization on the other hand. Fears and moments of panic were presented as things that anyone could overcome. Therefore, there was no need for shame. Instead of zooming in on an individual illness experience and its detriments, the notion of commonality prevailed. The key is that both text and responses do not have to be upbeat and happy to be meaningful; the APP and SR activities make it possible to share all kinds of vulnerabilities.

Poetry as a portal to the imagination

Poetry theorists argue that poetic language differs from prosaic and everyday language in the way it signifies (Wolf 2005). As such, ordinary meaning-making processes do not suffice to fully understand it. Because of the delay in and complication of signification, we associate reading poetry with intricate deciphering processes. Surprisingly, this hermeneutic stance may create space for neurotypical people to accept the unanticipated everyday language of people who live with dementia (Synnes et al. 2021, see also Synnes et al., this volume). Creative activities such as the APP and SR offer failure-free zones in which participants are safe to contribute according to their capabilities and without standing corrected. This implies that it is no longer relevant whether the input of a participant is indicative of an immediate creative outburst or of word-finding and comprehension problems that are characteristic of some types of dementia.

Verbal input that departs from the expected can become a portal to an imaginative excursion that others may join. An example of this dynamic from the SR sessions can

---

[6] The RL starts with yes/no questions in this example but then introduces open questions, as the SR approach envisions.

be found in the responses to the poem *Nu en straks* (Now and Later) by Tsaed Bruinja that was published on 15 December 2020 at the beginning of a second lockdown in the Netherlands. The poem imagines what life could be like after the COVID-19 pandemic without explicitly mentioning the words lockdown, pandemic or corona. Remarkably, the poem gave rise to an exchange between participants about a man who decides to leave his wife and family for another love interest from a different gender (Odense House Amsterdam, 2 July 2021). This narrative was triggered by the poetic start of the text 'in the new soon/near future' that, in the view of four participants, referred to 'a new boyfriend', 'a new relation' and a 'new partner'. They continued to connect the successive lines of the poem to their alternative narrative for almost 10 minutes.

While the dialogue evolved, the Reader Leader was slightly taken aback. On the one hand, she kept on positively acknowledging the input of the participants. On the other hand, she tried to direct the participants' attention to specific parts of the poem to make their interpretation more in line with her own. When this did not work out, she threw the pandemic into the conversation: 'What I like is how you can read it in different ways. As a personal love history or indeed as a, as a society, how we get out of the corona crisis. I think you mean that or not? That that's the change?' The participants validated her input but circled back to their own interpretation unruffled:

SP5   It can be anything.
RL   It could be anything. Yes, yes.
SP3   It was, of course, a big mess.
RL   Yes, yes.
SP6   Well, I'm also making up my experience [interpretation] here on the spot, so, I don't know what the real background is either.
RL   That's what we're here for.
SP6   So, it's very good that you throw in corona, I think.
SP3   Yes, also for just the kids.
SP6   Yes, also.
RL   What's it like for the kids?
SP6   Yes, in a new hetero relationship, this can of course also prevent a new partner from again distancing himself from that past, from that family, and from those old friendships, I think.

The participants mirrored the Reader Leader's role by acknowledging her input and complementing her ('it's very good that') but did not approach her intervention as decisively significant. Thus, it was the reading of the neurotypical Reader Leader that did not match the collective interpretative process rather than the other way around.

What happens in this instance goes beyond what is usually understood by participation and inclusion of people who live with dementia. Rather than participants having to conform to an interpretative standard set by neurotypical people, the literary text now serves as a vehicle for playful exchange that does not remain limited to the semantic and syntactic parameters of the poetic words. While, in the example of the previous section, the conversation still focused on recognition and experience, here the poem becomes a portal to the imagination. This imaginative space is an alternative for the reality where participants are constantly confronted with the fact that their medical condition sets them apart from people who do not have it, which is much in line with Anne Basting's (2009) well-known credo 'forget memory, try imagination'. The SR approach turned the poem *Nu en straks* into a means for the temporary upheaval of power differences among neurotypical and neurodivergent people. When the participatory arts are recommended for their transformative potential, this is exactly what people hope to achieve. It also explains why I argue that APP and SR are exemplary not just of the relational model of dementia but also of the political. Although the Reader Leader in this example was not entirely comfortable with the direction taken in the group discussion, she did have the sensitivity not to position herself as the expert with the power of the ultimate interpretation.

Conclusion

In this chapter, I have examined the relation between poetry and dementia by contrasting two conceptualizations of the illness and by showing how they play out in two case studies: the case of the Flemish poet Hugo Claus and the case of two literary practices in dementia care, the Alzheimer's Poetry Project and Shared Reading. The first case illustrates how poetry and dementia become irreconcilable when the latter is solely understood as a dreadful disease that implies the loss of personhood and of creative talent. At the beginning of this chapter, I referred to the poet Leo Herberghs who acknowledged change, relativized the significance of able-mindedness for his literary practice and surrounded himself with people who helped him sustain what he called his 'existence in words'. Claus, on the other hand, had a writer's persona to live up to and was hyper visible in a societal and artistic context that prioritizes the medical/individual model of dementia. This left little room for him to appreciate poetry as an existential tool – even in times of cognitive vulnerability – instead of as an aesthetic accomplishment and a profession. The tragic outcome of this logic is the perception of euthanasia, a so-called dignified death, as an ultimate remedy to the threat of an anticipated undignified life. By contrast, APP and SR activities are 'potential site[s] for collective reimagining' (Kafer 2013: 9) through the engagement with and the lived experiences of people with dementia who join these activities. The aesthetic and pragmatic affordances of poetic language as a live event offer participants opportunities to contribute and connect and, in doing so, encourage the formation of new bonds and the strengthening of self-worth. The political/relational conceptualization of dementia that underpins these activities, furthermore, helps us think the future differently – Kafer calls this 'a politics of crip futurity' (3). It stimulates us to reflect on what a good life with dementia could mean and how it implies a destabilizing of the boundaries between neurotypical and neurodivergent people.

Acknowledgements

I would like to thank Oddgeir Synnes and Olga Lehmann for inviting me to contribute to this volume. My gratitude also goes to everyone involved in the APP and SR sessions that I was able to observe and/or participate in. A special thanks goes to the student assistants Helen Verploegen and Maike Brinkman. Furthermore, I am grateful to Peter Simonsen and Nicklas Freisleben Lund for bringing the work of Werner Wolf to my attention and to Christien Franken for copy-editing the chapter.

References

Basting, A. (2009), *Forget Memory: Creating Better Lives for People with Dementia*, Baltimore: Johns Hopkins University Press.
Bernstein, C. (1998), *Close Listening: Poetry and the Performed Word*, Oxford: Oxford University Press.
Billington, J., J. Carroll, P. Davis, C. Healey, and P. Kinderman (2013), 'A Literature-Based Intervention for Older People Living with Dementia', *Perspectives in Public Health* 133 (3): 165–173.
Claus, H. (2008), 'Sonnet XV', in *De laatste van mijn demonen: Voor Hugo Claus*, 140, Amsterdam: De Bezige Bij.
De Dijn, H. (2008), 'Frustraties en miseries van/in een postchristelijke cultuur: Beschouwingen bij de mediastorm rond euthanasie in maart 2008', *Ethische perspectieven* 18 (2): 152–160.
De Lepeleire, J., A. Beyen, M. Burin, L. Ceulemans, R. Fabri, G. Ghijsebrechts, J. Lisaerde, T. Temmerman, B. Van Den Eynden, and N. Van Den Noortgate. (2008), 'Euthanasie bij personen met dementie', *Ethische perspectieven* 18 (2): 175–181.
Felski, R. (2015), *The Limits of Critique*, Chicago: University of Chicago Press.
Gerreway, C. (2011), 'Tien redenen waarom dit boek voor ergernis kan zorgen', *De Reactor: Vlaams-Nederlands platform voor literatuurkritiek*, 6 June. Available online: https://dereactor.org/teksten/tien-redenen-waarom-dit-boek-voor-ergernis-kan-zorgen (accessed 19 October 2021)
Gilliard, J., R. Means, A. Beattie and G. Daker-White (2005), 'Dementia Care in England and the Social Model of Disability', *Dementia* 4 (4): 571–586.
Glazner, G. (2005), *Sparking Memories: The Alzheimer's Poetry Project Anthology*, Santa Fe: Poem Factory.
Gray, E., G. Kiemle, P. Davis, and J. Billington (2016), 'Making Sense of Mental Health Difficulties through Live Reading: An Interpretative Phenomenological Analysis of the Experience of Being in a Reader Group', *Arts & Health* 8 (3): 248–261.
Gullette, M. M. (2011), 'The Mystery of Carolyn Heilbrun's Suicide', in *Agewise: Fighting the New Ageism in America*, 42–61, Chicago: The University of Chicago Press.
Hamington, M. and C. Rosenow (2019), *Care Ethics and Poetry*, Cham: Springer Nature.
Hendriks, R.P.J., A. Hendrikx, I. Kamphof and A. Swinnen (2016), 'Goede verstaanders; Wederzijdse articulatie en de stem van mensen met dementie', in G. Van Hove, A. Schippers, M. Cardol and E. de Schauwer (eds), *Disability Studies in de lage landen*, 81–99, Antwerpen: Garant.
Hughes, J. C., S. J. Louw, and S. R. Sabat, eds (2006), *Dementia: Mind, Meaning, and the Person*, Oxford: Oxford University Press.
Kafer, A. (2013), *Feminist Queer Crip*, Bloomington: Indiana University Press.
Lukić, D. and A. T. Lotherington (2019), 'Fighting Symbolic Violence through Artistic Encounters: Searching for feminist Answers to the Question of Life and Death with Dementia', in C. Confortini, and T. Vaittinen (eds), *Gender, Global Health, and Violence:*

Feminist Perspectives on Peace and Disease, 117–138, Washington: Rowman & Littlefield.

Mortier, E. (2008), 'Heel ons verdriet', in *De laatste van mijn demonen: Voor Hugo Claus*, 20–25, Amsterdam: De Bezige Bij.

Rogiers, F. and G. Claeys (2017), 'Zullen we het dan nu over het leven hebben', *De Standaard*, 19 August.

Schaevers, M., ed. (2004), *Hugo Claus: Groepsportret. Een leven in citaten*, Amsterdam: De Bezige Bij.

Schaevers, M., ed. (2011), *De wolken: Uit de geheime laden van Hugo Claus*, Amsterdam: De Bezige Bij.

Shakespeare, T., H. Zeilig and P. Mittler (2019), 'Rights in Mind: Think Differently about Dementia and Disability', *Dementia* 18 (3): 1075–1086.

Shildrick, M. (2015), 'Death, Debility and Disability', *Feminism & Psychology* 25 (1): 155–160.

Swinnen, A. and K. de Medeiros (2018), '"Play" and People Living with Dementia: A Humanities-based Inquiry of TimeSlips and the Alzheimer's Poetry Project', *The Gerontologist* 58 (2): 261–268.

Swinnen, A. (2018), '"Writing to Make Ageing New": Dutch Poets' Understandings of Late-life Creativity', *Ageing and Society* 38 (3): 543–567.

Swinnen, A. (2016), 'Healing Words: Critical Inquiry of Poetry Interventions in Dementia Care', *Dementia* 15 (6): 1377–1404.

Synnes, O., M. Råheim, E. Lykkeslet, and E. Gjengedal (2021), 'A Complex Reminding: The Ethics of Poetry Writing in Dementia Care', *Dementia* 20 (3): 1025–1049.

Van Hulle, D. (2005), 'Bloemlezingen en vertaalnormen: Shakespeare à la flamande', *Filter: Tijdschrift over vertalen* 12 (2): 41–50.

Wolf, W. (2005), 'The Lyric: Problems of Definition and a Proposal for Reconceptualisation', in E. Müller-Zettelman and M. Rubik (eds), *Theory into Poetry: New Approaches for the Lyric*, 59–91, Amsterdam: Rodopi.

3

Time and Dignity: A Phenomenological Investigation of Poetry Writing in Dementia Care

Oddgeir Synnes, Eva Gjengedal and Målfrid Råheim

The setting is one of Norway's most renowned literary festivals, Bjørnsonfestivalen, in the city of Molde in September 2018. On the stage, a professional actor is reciting poems of persons with dementia who have been part of a poetry-writing project in the city. A full auditorium listens attentively. The first two rows are made up of most of the participants. As the poems are read aloud, several of the participants can be seen laughing, commenting on their own poems and being touched by the recitations. During the festival, the local city buses had poems of the participants printed at the rear end, making the poems part of the everyday life of the community and the festival. Being central in this poetry-writing project, we found it important that the poems were given a larger audience at a literary festival that is concerned with marginalized voices and freedom of speech. The voices of persons with dementia are rarely heard in today's society. And when they are, it is predominantly through a tragic narrative of loss of memory and language (Dupuis et al. 2016; Kontos et al. 2020). While not wishing to underscore the losses and difficulties that dementia entails, the poetry project showed linguistic capabilities among the participants that both enthralled the participants themselves and a larger audience. We also found it fitting that the poems were brought into a *literary* festival with an emphasis on the word literary. Experiences from the project underscored that an opening towards a poetic language can be liberating when living with a condition of increasing difficulties related to memory and communication. We claim that working with poetry involves a language emphasizing sensual details, episodic memories and associations, more than coherent and elaborate narrations. Many of the texts produced during the project contain evocative images, details and expressions that have poetic qualities deserving an enhanced attention, which we also will argue can be important ways of preserving dignity for persons with dementia.

Background

Dementia is defined as 'an umbrella term for several diseases that are mostly progressive, affecting memory, other cognitive abilities, and behaviour that interfere significantly with a person's ability to maintain their activities of daily living' (WHO 2017: 2). Consequently, a dementia diagnosis means impaired memory and accordingly, reduced ability to store and recall previous experiences. According to The World Health Organization's *Global Action Plan on the Public Health Response to Dementia 2017–2025*, long-term care for persons with dementia should cover a great variety of activities in health and social care and facilitate a dementia-friendly society. Offering poetry-writing groups to persons with dementia can contribute to achieving this goal. We have previously argued that participating in such groups can be a complex reminder of important events in the lives of people with dementia, and thus has the potential to shed light on aspects of their identity despite memory impairment (Synnes et al. 2021). We referred to the Swedish psychologist Lars-Christer Hydén (2018a), who claims that persons with dementia tend to express themselves by giving linguistic glimpses of important events in life rather than telling long autobiographical stories (198). We further argued that this may be in line with American poet Gregory Orr's (2002: 98) view of *lyric stories*, meaning small poems centred on significant events or images in the poet's life. Poems based on expressions from persons with dementia participating in poetry-writing groups may be regarded as such lyric stories, which are different but still close to narratives. Furthermore, we also saw poems without narrative elements. Certain elements and memories may be captured in poetic form, underscoring a perspective on dementia as opening towards possibilities. To capture this potential, special attention and sensitivity are required.

Through a presentation of the above-mentioned poetry project and through a close reading of some of the poems, we will investigate how a practice of poetry writing might open different dimensions in the everyday language of persons with dementia, and how poetry might offer glimpses into aspects of the *episodic self*. Hence, the aim of the chapter is to investigate how a poetic practice in dementia care can preserve aspects of self-experience and dignity.

Theoretical perspectives

A phenomenological perspective of the episodic sense of the self in dementia

Considering the presumed strong bond between creating one's life story and the forming of identity, it has been argued that identity deteriorates as dementia progresses (Caddell and Clare 2010). Consequently, questions related to impact on self-experience and identity are highly debated (Summa 2014) and researched (Caddell and Clare 2010) in the field of experiential consequences of dementia diseases. Standpoints differ – from seeing dementia as leading to total loss of self to arguing for maintenance of the self on more levels (Caddell and Clare 2010: 113), which also influences dementia care.

According to a narrative account of self, the life story has a time structure where significant events and experiences in life from birth to one's death are united in an overarching narrative (Zahavi 2007: 180–1). The Danish philosopher Dan Zahavi elaborates on this by saying that: 'the narrative approach is mainly concerned with the issues of long-term diachronic identity and persistency and insists that the experience of a self as unified across a lifetime relies upon one's ability to situate one's memories, personality traits, goals, and values within a coherent narrative structure' (2014: 56). Although narratives are obviously of great importance in developing one's self-understanding, a one-sided emphasis on this perspective is subject to criticism. Zahavi calls this view 'an unacceptable oversimplification'. Supported by a phenomenological perspective, he argues for operating 'with a different level of selfhood than the one addressed by a narrative account' (Zahavi 2007: 185).

In phenomenology, a distinction is made between different levels of structuring self-experience: a pre-reflective and a reflective level (Summa and Fuchs 2015). The pre-reflective self refers to the most basic form of self-awareness, where practical skills, habits, immediate self-reference, immediate recognition of situations and other forms of competences are sedimented in the body, also called the minimal or core self. The reflective parts of the self are associated with the autobiographical or narrative self. However, it is significant to note that these different layers are not strictly separated (Summa 2014). Recognizing the existence of the more basic layers of self-experience may nuance the understanding of persons with dementia (Summa and Fuchs 2015; Zahavi 2007). However, this also presupposes a nuanced understanding of time that does not unilaterally regard time as linear (diachronic).

Instead of diachronically structuring time by a beginning, middle and end, phenomenological time is characterized synchronously by temporal unfolding or duration where context and wholeness are essential. An experience of duration is made possible by a threefold structure of inner time consciousness. Zahavi (2014: 64) refers to Husserl, who describes this structure as 'a "duration-block," that is, a temporal field that comprises all three temporal modes of present, past, and future'. This may be illustrated by the perception of time-objects, which are objects that are not experienced in isolation. The present experience (primal impression) contains aspects of previous experiences (retention) and expectations for the future (protention) (Husserl 1954/1970: 168; Zahavi 2014: 64). Retention or implicit memory differs from recollection or explicit memory, which means that previous experiences are integrated into the present experience and not something one remembers explicitly. Past and future create horizons for the present. A melody, for instance, is an example of a time-object. We do not experience the melody as isolated points along a timeline, but rather as an 'inseparable unit' (Toombs 1990: 229), which applies to many experiences in life.

This time structure allows for an understanding of the temporal self as *episodic*, meaning that a situational experience does not necessarily belong to a coherent overriding life story, which presupposes an explicit memory. The memory may be *implicit*, 'embodied in habits and other kinds of bodily and situation-related associative memories' (Summa and Fuchs 2015: 392; Merleau-Ponty, 1945/2014: 139–43). According to Summa (2014: 483), 'the centrality of the self is displayed by the experience and the reference to the lived body'. It refers to a pre-reflective and bodily-based sphere of knowing and acting in the world as intentional subjects (Zahavi 2007). People have a non-reflective understanding of the self in the world. This does not mean that people are not able to think and reflect, but this is not the primary way of being in the world. 'Reflective self-consciousness is a possibility, but not a necessary condition of being oneself' (Fuchs 2020: 667). On the contrary, people are always situated in a meaningful context and hence can grasp the meaning directly (Benner and Wrubel 1989: 41).

The phenomenological time perspective has particular significance for the view of people with reduced memory, such as people with dementia. In this context, the notion of *episodic sense* of self is particularly relevant. The episodic self is preserved and performed as embodied and through smaller linguistic means like indexical self-reference (Summa and Fuchs 2015). Both Kontos (2005) and Hydén (2018a, 2018b) show with empirical examples how people with dementia, despite their inability to tell stories due to cognitive impairment, are still able to communicate an episodic sense of self in specific situations through bodily gestures and habits. Kontos describes how residents with dementia in a nursing home express a sense of themselves by small meaningful bodily movements, such as their different ways of walking, eating, dressing etc. Hydén (2018b) writes about a woman with impaired verbal language skills, who during an interview still was able to tell about important events in her life with a few words and body gestures. In situations like this the storytelling can be supported by a person close to the storyteller (Hydén 2018a, 2018b).

In dementia conditions, the pre-reflective dimension of self seems less or not afflicted compared to dimensions of the self-reflective self and, hence, narrative construction of self (Summa and Fuchs 2015). Consequently, the quality of experiences as *mine* is not necessarily affected on a pre-reflective level. This means that familiarity and competence remain in many situations in which incorporated habits and practices are actualized, and in situations where spontaneous self-reference concerning emotional experiences is still working adequately. Bodily-based implicit memory is at play. Examples may be spontaneous familiarity with a melody or wording in well-known songs and poems, playing a familiar instrument or when invited to dance by the rhythm of appealing music and movements of others. Examples may also be the experience of pain, discomfort or joy in concrete situations, embodied in phrases such as 'my pain', 'my discomfort', 'my joy'. However, according to Summa (2014), the relation between these layers or dimensions of self-experience and agency is not to be understood as static. Referring to Husserl, the stream of conscious experience is *holistic*, inferring that the narrative and the core self would tap into each other. Pre-reflective self-awareness and reflective moments can exist side by side (Summa and Fuchs 2015). It is exactly here, where the minimal experiential sense of self and the narrative self would meet, where the episodic sense of self belongs.

Poetic language as possible openings towards understandings of time and self

Above, we have argued for an *episodic sense of self* in dementia that positions itself on a continuum between a minimal self and a narrative self. Here, we would like to expand this perspective with some theoretical elaborations on *poetic language*. While Summa and Fuchs (2015) argue for the preservation of an episodic self in embodied memory and non-narrative language, e.g., indexical referencing, we will argue that poetry and poetic language might offer linguistic meaning-making that might be seen in light of an episodic sense of self.

A characteristic feature of much poetry is its insistence on a specific moment that is made the focal point. As poet Mark Doty explains: 'One of poetry's great powers is its preservative ability to take a moment in time and attempt to hold it ... That's an extraordinary thing, that something as small as a poem extends our lives' (quoted in Moyers 2000: 59).

In the following, we suggest three perspectives that will further inform our analysis of poetry writing in dementia care and how poetry might 'extend our lives' through its preservative ability: 'poetry as form-making engagement with the senses and facilitator of intersubjectivity'; 'poetry as lyric story' emphasizing the close connection between narrative and poetry'; and 'poetry as poetic instants', underlining poetry's connectedness to the emotional intensity of the moment.

Poetry as form-making engagement with the senses and facilitator of intersubjectivity

In her book *Poetry and the Fate of the Senses* (2002), poet and literary scholar Susan Stewart presents an argument for poetry's centrality for consciousness and engagement with the senses. For Stewart, the form-giving capacity of poetry has been crucial in the historical shaping of our notion of the first-person perspective and continues to be a vast repertoire today. Central to her argument is how poetry brings form to consciousness: 'As first person expression ... in measured language, lyric poetry lends significant – that is, shared and memorable – form to inner consciousness that is time itself' (2002: 42). The poetic form gives permanence and extension to consciousness and individual sense experience. Furthermore, by naming and summoning experience into continuing existence, poetry opens up an intersubjectivity for individuals and society: 'As metered language, language that retains and projects the force of individual sense experience and yet reaches toward intersubjective meaning, poetry sustains and transforms the threshold between individual and social existence' (2002: 2). For Stewart, poetry as *poiesis*, as creative figuration thus creates a potential recognition between persons by reaching out and making our inner experience intelligible to other people. Through poetic form, this potential recognition extends beyond the context of production or utterance; the practice of reception opens up a plethora of interpretive possibilities. In Stewart's argument, how the poetry's form-giving leads to materiality is crucial to counter the oblivion of darkness we might face as human beings and as society: 'it is precisely in material ways that poetry is a force against effacement – not merely for individuals but for communities through time as well' (2002: 2). Inspired by Stewart, we will investigate how the practice of crafting poetry out of the words of persons with dementia might be seen as form-giving of sense experiences that opens for intersubjectivity.

Poetry as lyric story

The concept of *lyric story* is taken from poet Gregory Orr. In his book *Poetry as Survival* (2002), Orr is concerned with how personal lyric poetry can be important for healing processes when faced with suffering and hardship through life. By personal lyric poetry, Orr means 'a poem that usually features an "I" and that focuses on autobiographical experience' (2002: 22). Orr describes how poems are located on a continuum between lyric stories and lyric poems. While the lyric poem is centred around images and emotions, the lyric story in addition has narrative elements (Orr 2018). However, in contrast to larger narratives, which often have multiple scenes, images and characters, lyric stories will only have two to three characters and be centred around a single scene, image or object (2002). Considering an episodic sense of the self in dementia, it is worth noting how lyric story offers one version of narrative that is more episodic without involving a full-fledged and coherent account of oneself. Poems from our project might be fruitfully read as lyric stories while not being considered fully developed narratives.

Poetry as poetic instants

Several philosophers have emphasized that poetry might offer an alternative to or a critique of a one-sided narrative understanding. In his criticism of narrative's hegemonic status for identity and meaning-making, Strawson (2004) advocates for poetry and an episodic understanding of self that might be just as crucial for many people in contrast with the diachronic perspective offered by narrative. To exemplify an episodic experience of the past, Strawson refers to how the German poet Rainer Maria Rilke commented on poetry and memory: 'the Episodic attitude to the past may have an advantage over the Diachronic: "For the sake of a single poem . . . you have . . . many . . . memories . . . And yet it is not enough to have memories . . . For the memories themselves are not important."' They give rise to a good poem 'only when they have changed into our very blood, into glance and gesture, and are nameless, no longer to be distinguished from ourselves' (2004: 432).

Poetry as connected to the moment can be found in French philosopher Gaston Bachelard's emphasis on *poetic instants* (1939/2013). For Bachelard, poetry is the opposite of prose, as it involves a stopping of clock time and an introduction of *vertical time* (Kearney 2008: 38). While clock time is continuous and horizontal, vertical poetic time for Bachelard is tied to lived experiences of emotional intensity (Lehmann and Klempe 2016; Lehmann 2019). Poetry involves an experience of time that spurs an examination of the instant. Thus, for Bachelard, the poetic instant also implies an ethics, a 'morality of the instantaneous' that is an emancipatory power manifested in the poetic moment: 'it is this vertical time that the poet discovers when he rejects horizontal time – namely, the becoming of others, the becoming of life, the becoming of the world'. (Bachelard 1939/2013: 59). Poetry and the instant thus require an ethics of attention, of vigilance and receptivity to the moment and to the other. In our reading of poems from the poetry project, we will also look at them from the perspective of poetic instants, which implies a heightened awareness towards moments of emotional intensity, both of the here and now in the production of the poems as well as moments from the past.

The poetry project and the crafting of the poems

The poetry-writing project took place at a day care centre for people with dementia living at home, located in the city of Molde on the west coast of Norway. The practice consisted of group sessions led by the first author of this chapter, who has worked for many years on the use of creative writing in health care settings (see Synnes 2015, 2016). Two employees at the day care centre and one health science researcher participated as observers. The groups consisted of the group leader inviting responses to the reading of poems and by looking at various pictures, as well as attending to spontaneous comments from the participants. At the start, several of the participants were sceptical and anxious of saying something wrong or not remembering something. The group leader thus spent considerable time making the participants feel safe and downplaying the result, focusing on the process and having a good time together.

According to poet Jane Hirshfield, 'Poems can be found, if they're looked for' (2018). In the project, the poems were sometimes found in the expressions of the participants during the group meetings, written down on the spot and introduced to the group and read aloud by the group leader. However, most poems were found in the transcriptions from the tape-recorded conversations. Later the same day, as the meeting took place, the group leader and Arne Ruset, who is both a poet and geriatric psychiatrist, sat down 'listening' and reading the transcripts looking for poetic expressions, such as evocative details, captivating phrases, choices of words that stood out, etc. As such, these poems are not the deliberate work of the participants; rather, they are the result of an interpretational frame, looking at the everyday language of persons with dementia as potential poetic expressions. In the classic essay 'How to recognize a poem when you see one', literary theorist Stanley Fish argues that 'the paying of a certain kind of attention results in the emergence of poetic qualities' (1980/2014: 79). By paying close attention to the various transcripts, we were surprised how many poems could be found there, often vivid expressions or details that had escaped our attention during the group meetings. Inspired by John Killick's long-standing work on poetry writing among persons with dementia (1997, 2018), we opted for his principle of never adding words, omitting only, for instance, unclear sentences or false starts, sometimes dividing longer statements or narrations into smaller poems, or dividing sentences into stanzas and using line shifts to enhance the rhythm of the spoken words of the participants. This is minor editing when it comes to words, but the presentation of the poems sometimes required more major editing. However, all the words and expressions of the poems are the participants' own.[1] Thus, the group leader and Ruset call themselves editors, while the participants are the authors.

At the next meeting, the poems were brought back to the group, read aloud and handed out to the participants. The interpretational frame of looking at the verbal expressions of the participants as poems created enthusiasm and astonishment among the participants. They became enthralled and visibly touched hearing the poems and seeing them in print. While they recognized their words and expressions, they also clearly realized that the end products were different, that they had somehow been enhanced through the poetic presentation. One aspect was obviously the careful editing which highlighted words, certain expressions, and details; another aspect was how the words

---

[1] Naturally, in an English-language article the original poems in Norwegian had to be translated. We have strived to maintain the wordings, images, and rhythms in the poems to make them appear as close to the Norwegian poems as possible.

were presented as poetry in print and through declamation. Poet Howard Nemerov (2020) highlights how the appearance of poetry on the page demands a different *tone* and *pace* when reading, either loud or in silence, compared to prose. Together, this way of looking at the expressions of persons with dementia allowed a heightened awareness of each line and word. In total, 66 poems were created during the project.

Two groups, each consisting of three participants, met over two days in autumn 2017. In spring 2018, two other groups, with four participants in each group, met twice. Altogether, eleven persons with dementia participated, six women and five men, ranging in age from 75 to 98 years.[2] The health care workers, who knew the participants well, invited users they thought would get pleasure out of attending such groups. Although the dementia diagnoses varied, all participants were living relatively early in the course of the disease and were able to communicate verbally.

Poetry, time and dignity: A close reading of selected poems

As we have argued above, even though the narrative self is put at risk or made vulnerable, it does not mean that the self has been lost. Other parts of the self, such as embodied memory and what has been termed the episodic self, remain. By looking at the everyday language of persons with dementia through the lens of poetry and poetic language, we want to show in the following how this might spark a nuanced understanding of self and agency.

We will start with a poem of Torvald,[3] a retired man in his seventies, who at the first meeting told the following story that became the poem 'The Lieutenant':

<u>The Lieutenant</u>
I was a little farm boy from Vik[4]
That was who I was

What changed my life
was a lieutenant from the army
at a draft session
He was the first person I know of
who asked if I had intended
to take any education

I who hardly remember anything
will never forget the time
I had to make a decision
that made me end up here

---

[2] Three of the participants from autumn 2017 also participated in spring 2018.
[3] The names of the participants in the chapter are pseudonyms, in accordance with the informed consent given.
[4] Fictional name.

> Because then I got a choice
> Had gotten a job at Svalbard[5]
> But at the same time I had applied
> For a preliminary course at a technical school
>
> But this I still know
> no matter how old I might have become
> I know and remember that I thought:
> I can always travel to Svalbard
> But I will never again apply to any school
> And so I chose the school
> And never got to Svalbard

This poem is representative of several poems from the writing group that can be labelled lyric story, like Orr (2002) suggests. The poem is concentrated around one scene or image and with only two characters. The lieutenant asks Torvald about his thoughts of further schooling, something no one else had done before, which made him opt for an education. Furthermore, the narrative element of the poem is obvious in its retrospective reflexivity: Torvald is looking back from the present perspective at a significant event that has altered his life course and made him end up in this particular place ('that made me end up here'). Looking at the poem (and revisiting the transcript as well), it is a remarkably well-crafted story that required close to no editing, apart from dividing it into stanzas and introducing line breaks at appropriate places. While we could always speculate if this might be a well-rehearsed story that has been central in Torvald's narrative repertoire in life, what we find particularly striking is Torvald's metacommentary on the importance of the episode and how this is something he will never forget despite his present condition, something that displays a creative use of language that is much more than a repetition of a previous story. Consider the quite eloquent and humorous commentary that is displayed: 'I who hardly remember anything', 'But this I still know / no matter how old I might have become.' In addition, the poem ends with the funny punchline: 'And never got to Svalbard', which becomes a surprising twist to the story and the preceding reflections of the narrator. We were surprised by how central humour was, not just in Torvald's poem, but in many of the poems in this project, underscoring the continuing ability to use language in an engaging way.

The lucidity of the story and the explicit articulate remarks of his condition became particularly forceful when we realized that Torvald, no more than a minute after the telling, could not remember a word of what he had told. When he heard the poem read aloud at the next group meeting, he started laughing, recognizing the story, while at the same time following the reading with suspense towards the climax, where he

---

[5] The Svalbard Islands is a Norwegian archipelago located in the Arctic Ocean, halfway between the northern coast of Norway and the North Pole.

laughed at the point of the story and said: 'That's right! That's how it was. I never got to Svalbard... but how did you know?'

Reflecting on Torvald's lyric story, we are reminded of American poet Robert Frost, who claimed that poetry is 'a momentary stay against confusion' (1939: 235). When Torvald told this small story, he was in total command of his words, joking with his condition and setting up the telling towards the punchline. And, during the reading of the poem, Torvald listened attentively, immersing himself in the poem, noticing each word and expression. Considering Frost's remark, we wonder if the telling and the revisiting of the poem through reading can be seen as a momentary stay against the confusion of the everyday world of living with dementia.

We found it striking that we received so many stories and poems through these meetings, something that surprised the participants and the attending staff. We believe that a foundational element for this was the atmosphere in the room and among the participants and the group leader, a setting where nothing was deemed wrong, and which encouraged the participants to express their thoughts and free associations. Could one also think of the group as a momentary stay against confusion in how it created a supportive and playful atmosphere based on what the participants told and remembered? Related to a phenomenological understanding of implicit memory in dementia as situation-related associative memories (Summa and Fuchs 2015: 392), one might regard many of the expressions of the participants as implicit memory that was activated through various associative connections during the group setting. Even though the lyric story of Torvald in many ways can be seen as an explicit memory (e.g., the reflective nature of the memory, the link between the significant event and the present situation), it was not a memory that was the result of a deliberate recall, but something that spontaneously appeared during the open-ended associations in the group.

Torvald's story is representative for many other similar lyric stories from this project that we regard as expressions of the self where the episodic and narrative selves merge. The lyric story of Torvald clearly displays a narrative self in this story, but it is not told as part of a larger coherent life story, something that Torvald would have struggled to do. Besides, Torvald also forgot about his telling just after sharing this story in the group. This is also something we saw among many of the participants: smaller narrations and lyric stories that were coherent were difficult to locate within a larger narrative. Thus, most of the lyric stories in the material are not incorporated into the larger life stories of the participants. They are snapshots, stories more akin to an episodic sense of the self, presented through narrative.

One last aspect of Torvald's poem that we would like to highlight is what is gained by naming this as a lyric story. While one might think of these as smaller narrations, considering the poem of Torvald and similar stories as a lyric story emphasizes how we read them, adding weight to each line, noticing and highlighting evocative details and expressions. As editors, looking at the narrations as poetry changed our interpretational frame, and we were surprised how many 'poetic expressions' could be found there, enhanced by the stanzas, something we believe would not have stood out for us if we had treated the stories as running texts. The close reading of the stories as poems also reveals strong expressions of the self and personal agency. Reading Torvald's poem is stepping into a miniature coming-of-age story: beginning with who he once was ('a little farm boy') to what he became. We argue that reading smaller narrations as poems might open other forms of agency, where the interpretational frame gives enhanced focus on possible first-person expressions that are preserved through the lyric form (Stewart 2002).

The next poem, of Dagny, a woman in her eighties, gives us a short glimpse into life as a child on an islet on the Northwest coast of Norway:

<u>Row Inlander</u>
I grew up on an islet
We were the only ones who grew up there
Learned to row long before we started school
even when the weather was rough!
But those times it was adults rowing
putting us ashore
Afraid to row? Oh, no!
It was the most natural thing in the world

A funny thing was when someone came
from the meadow, further inland
We rocked the boat, and they got terrified

'Inlander, let's row inlander!' we said
and then we lifted the oars high
They were not used to rowing, you know
so they held the oars high up in the air
before they dropped them into the sea

While the poem 'The Lieutenant' clearly is a lyric story with obvious narrative elements, this poem is closer to a lyric poem as the episode is not seen considering the whole life history, nor from the situation of its telling. Still, it is a poem with a strong sense of the self in how it depicts the first-person perspective of a small girl in a specific environment. The poem starts with placing the girl on the islet together with her siblings (the word 'we' underlines that they were several other children in her family) and how they learned to row from a very early age. This is then followed by an anecdote of how they used to make fun of people who came out to the islet and were not used to rowing by parodying their helpless style.

This poem is representative of many other poems of the participants in the way that it portrays a close connection between a childhood environment and the poet. Inspired by phenomenological theories of the self, we consider how this poem shows an *enworlded* and *embodied* sense of self (Carel 2008: 16). Although Dagny may have lost much of her explicit memory, her implicit or bodily memory is intact and will remain in situations where incorporated habits from her childhood's world are activated. The poetry group did not invite practical action; it may nevertheless have inspired her to express herself in a poetic language that provides an opportunity to implicitly recognize past experiences. The poem also shows that Dagny can still give concrete descriptions of her rowing skills. We can imagine how Dagny almost felt in her body what it was like to row the boat fluently and efficiently, in contrast to the clumsy, helpless inlanders' way of rowing.

The lyrical self in Dagny's poem is clearly grounded in (and on) the islet, displaying an intimacy with the world on this particular islet ('We were the only ones who grew up there'); living close to the ocean, learning to row boats, and the need to step into the boats even in rough weather ('it was the most natural thing in the world'). Thus, the poem displays a clear sense of connectedness to the islet, the environments and the boats, in contrast with the people from inland who were easily scared of being in a boat or did not know how to handle the oars when rowing. According to Stewart, lyric language involves an engagement with the senses, making form out of sense experience (2002, ix). The poem of Dagny gets its vivid poetic images from the description of the sensuous and embodied experiences of rocking the boat and the lifting of the oars in the mock interpretation of the inlanders.

Contemplating the phenomenological aspects of the poem we notice how the poem is a world-making phenomenon, or as French philosopher Paul Ricoeur puts it: poetic images are verbs more than portraits of the world (Helenius 2013: 63). The poem of Dagny (and similar poems in the material) can be considered a world-making enterprise in how aspects of the poem are an evocation of episodic snapshots from the past based on sensual details that Dagny recalled. According to literary scholar Jonathan Culler (2017), the main importance of the lyric 'is not the representation of a past event but its evocation in the lyric present'. As such, poems are happenings in the world; they make something here and now. This poem, like several of Dagny's other poems that brought forth memories from the islet, is an episodic glimpse of the self. In light of Bachelard, we might regard them as *poetic instants* (Bachelard 1939/2013) or *poetic windows* (Lehmann and Brinkmann 2019), opening towards a vertical time of lived experiences of emotional intensity that are actualized in the author's telling.

Furthermore, poetry as a world-making phenomenon is tied to the reception in the writing group and potential readers. Dagny's poem (together with so many of the other poems) achieved something. A salient aspect of the poem, in addition to the sensual and embodied details, is the naming in the poem, something that unfortunately largely goes missing due to the anonymization process. Many poems consist of specific (and exotic) names of places, fjords, siblings, significant characters and animals. American poet Adrienne Rich ponders how reading a book on the creatures and plants of the Pacific coastline of North America involved a heightened awareness: 'these names work as poetry works, enlivening a sensuous reality through recognition or through the play of sounds ... to evoke other worlds of meaning ... These names work as poetry works in another sense as well: they make something unforgettable' (Rich 2003: 5–6). In the poem, the expression 'row inlander', the details, along with the names of the islet and the surrounding archipelago, evokes a world of meaning that enters the mind of the listener and reader of the poem. In the writing groups, we experienced how listening to the poems made them see the other group members and themselves in a different light, turning the sessions into moments of solemnity where they thanked each other for the sharing.

The following poem by Leif is a good example of how poems are happenings into this world. One question that we pondered during the group session was: 'What have you learnt from life?' Some utterances from Leif ended up as this poem:

<u>What I Have Learnt from Life</u>
I have never thought much about it
There was always something to do
summer as winter
Skiing in the winter
And ice skates that we made
out of an old scythe!
We just took a block of wood
and rammed it down
And then we had to be careful
that it had the right angle
Yep, it went well
When I think of it
it was original

Leif was one of the members that struggled most with language and he was often quite hard to understand, but sometimes there were glimpses of stories or reflections like this poem above. Hearing his poem read out loud visibly touched Leif, and when speaking to the staff afterwards he expressed how significant it was by raising his arms, explaining the magnitude of the event. Leif mentioned to staff and relatives several times the impact of the group. This poem illustrates our point of why we find it fruitful to turn to poetry as a genre. This poem works precisely as a glimpse into a first-person experience that would easily be overlooked if we did not preserve it through the poetic form. Leif's verbal expressions were rarely successful as stories, but here we see how his small reflections really come to life through the poetic form (see also Freeman; Lehmann and Brinkmann, this volume).

We find a feasible relatedness between Leif's poem and Stewart's argument on how poetic language both retains and projects an individual's experience while at the same time creating intersubjectivity (Stewart 2002: 2). In dementia care, we believe that the episodic sense of self can sometimes be better captured by poetry's possible preservation of sense experiences and reflections that we might pay less attention to in the busy flow of everyday life. Leif's poem can be regarded both as a preservation of some sense experiences, practical know-how and reflections that otherwise would be mute or unrecognized. As such, we believe the poem can be a way to acknowledge and honour Leif's voice in the group and thus preserve his dignity. In an interview, one of Leif's sons expressed how much it meant for his father that his stories were written down – Leif was immensely proud of the poems. At the same time, we experienced how the poems also became important in sharing in the group. Even though some were better storytellers than others, everyone experienced that their participation resulted in poems that became vital parts of the group. This underscores poetry's preservative ability. As poet Mark Doty explains: 'What the poem makes is a version of a moment, a replica, a touchstone – something to keep and to give away' (quoted in Moyers 2000: 59).

An example of how poetry in its very form can act as something to keep and to give away is the following poem by Dagny, who once again takes us back to the islet at the northwest coast of Norway:

The Willow and the Sea
The only tree I had
was a little willow
It rose up against the garden fence
and then it bowed to the wind
Could not climb it
One of the sturdiest trees that exists
Nothing else could manage out there
in the sea

According to Stewart (2002), the form-giving capacity of poetry opens an understanding of first-person perspective as shared and memorable. Reading 'The Willow and the Sea', we experienced how this poem made an immediate impression on us, even the ones who were not present in the writing group. In its condensed form, the poem not only gives an impression of Dagny's childhood experience, but also offers a portrait of the harsh conditions of life on a small islet along the rugged coastline of Norway. At the centre of the poem is the willow, this small tree that could never grow tall and which you could not climb. Still, the poem presents the willow as one of the sturdiest trees that ever was. We might read the willow as a symbol of the historic conditions at the islet and how the forces of nature formed the life of the inhabitants on this rough coastline. But we also may read the poem as a portrait of Dagny herself and her poetic capabilities despite her present condition. The greatness present even in the tiniest willow underlines how strength might manifest itself in the fragility of life.

The intersubjective quality of the poem manifested itself also in how it made a lasting impression on us. Having read this poem together with other of Dagny's poems from the islet, we (the authors of this article) decided to visit this islet. On a dark November morning we drove to the coastline. We spotted the islet on the other side of a small bay. After balancing on a pier that recently had been overflowed by the tide, we found ourselves on Dagny's islet. The wind was blowing, and while searching for the willow, the sun broke through the clouds. Even though we could not find the willow, the beauty and the roughness of the landscape made a lasting impression on us. In line with Bachelard, we also regard Dagny's poem as a poetic instant, both for Dagny and us as readers, in how the poetic moment might open for 'the becoming of others, the becoming of life, the becoming of the world' (1939/2013: 59).

Poems as possible openings towards intersubjectivity was demonstrated at the literature festival (Bjørnsonfestivalen). According to the audience's response, it was obvious that the poems made strong impressions. The leader of the day care centre told of feedback she received afterwards on how people had been touched by the poems and recitations. The project still lives on at the day care centre, and in 2021 a collection of the poems was published (Synnes and Ruset 2021) where several of the participants read their poems at the book launch. Additionally, one poem from this project has been published in a well-known yearly nationwide poetry collection of established poets (Wisløff 2021). Giving persons with dementia and their poems public attention can be an important way to enhance their cultural and narrative citizenship. According to Baldwin (2008), a narrative citizenship for persons with dementia must acknowledge that stories can be told in multiple ways, meaning that narrative can also involve dance, movement and alternative expressions. Baldwin does not mention poetry, but we highlight how poetry as a genre can be an important part of narrative citizenship. Another point in Baldwin's argument for narrative citizenship is how persons with dementia can play vital parts in our stories. We strongly believe that the poems have the potential to affect the people who read or hear them. From our perspective, it is apparent that the poems have now become part of our story and our understanding of persons with dementia.

Closing remarks

The aim of this chapter was to investigate how a poetic practice in dementia care can preserve aspects of self-experience and dignity. By combining theoretical insights from phenomenology and theoretical perspectives on poetry, we have argued for how an episodic sense of self can be captured by poetry. In our close reading of selected poems from persons with dementia, we have shown how poetry can give nuanced representations of the first-person perspective, on a continuum from poems containing narrative elements (lyric story) to lyric poems concentrated around a single image and/or emotion. In a phenomenological understanding of time, poetry may be regarded as time-objects, which honour implicit memory and the power of shared moments. We argue that the practice of poetry-writing groups can contribute to discovering capabilities and resources in persons with dementia and thereby preserve their dignity. Furthermore, we have highlighted that this practice and the poems of persons with dementia have the potential to challenge the one-sided negative representation of these persons and thus enrich the intersubjective understanding of a shared world. We would like to close this chapter with an anecdote from the book launch of the poetry collection of our participants in the city of Molde in September 2021. Dagny, who at that time had moved into a nursing home, was accompanied to the happening. Having many poems present in the collection, among them the title poem, we wanted her to read a poem at the very start. Being seated on the stage and presented with her poem and a microphone, Dagny needed some time. But then we heard her mutter to herself: 'Oh, yes, I know this poem.' And then she read it, slowly and steady. And once again we were taken to Dagny's islet.

Acknowledgements

We thank Olga V. Lehmann, Gregory Orr, Alicja Rosé and Aagje Swinnen for valuable comments during the writing of the chapter. We would also like to thank project partners poet Arne Ruset and professor Else Lykkeslet and the staff at the day care setting where the poetry project took place. Our greatest gratitude goes to all the participants and their family members who gave permission to the use of the poems.

References

Bachelard, G. (1939/2013), 'Poetic instant and metaphysical instant', in G. Bachelard, *Intuition of the Instant*, 58–63, Evanston, IL: Northwestern University Press.

Baldwin, C. (2008), 'Narrative Citizenship and Dementia: The Personal and the Political', *Journal of Aging Studies* 22 (3): 222–228.

Benner, P. and J. Wrubel (1989), *The Primacy of Caring: Stress and Coping in Health and Illness*, Menlo Park, CA: Addison-Wesley Publishing Company.

Caddell, L. S. and L. Clare (2010), 'The Impact of Dementia on Self and Identity: A Systematic Review', *Clinical Psychology Review* 30 (1): 113–126.

Carel, H. (2008), *Illness: The Cry of the Flesh*, London: Routledge.

Culler, J. (2017), *Theory of the Lyric*, Boston, MA: Harvard University Press.

Dupuis, S. L., P. Kontos, G. Mitchell, C. Jonas-Simpson and J. Gray (2016), 'Re-claiming Citizenship Through the Arts', *Dementia* 15 (3): 358–380.

Fish, S. (1980/2014), 'How to Recognize a Poem When You See One', in V. Jackson and Y. Prins (eds), *The Lyric Theory Reader: A Critical Anthology*, 77–84, Baltimore, MD: Johns Hopkins University Press.

Frost, R. (1939/2004), 'The Figure a Poem Makes', in J. Cook (ed), *Poetry in Theory: An Anthology 1900–2000*, 234–236, Malden, MA: Blackwell Publishing.

Fuchs, T. (2020), 'Embodiment and Personal Identity in Dementia', *Medicine, Health Care and Philosophy* 23 (4): 665–676.

Helenius, T. (2013), 'Reflections on Poetic Work: Heidegger and Ricoeur', *Studia Philosophiae Christianae*, 49 (4): 41–67.

Hirschfield, J. (2018), 'Poetry, Permeability, and Healing', Available online: https://poets.org/text/poetry-permeability-and-healing (accessed 20 March 2021).

Husserl, E. (1954/1970), *The Crisis of European Sciences and Transcendental Phenomenology: An Introduction to Phenomenological Philosophy*, Evanston, IL: Northwestern University Press.

Hydén, L. C. (2018a), *Entangled Narratives: Collaborative Storytelling and the Re-Imagining of Dementia*, Oxford: Oxford University Press.

Hydén, L. C. (2018b), 'Dementia, Embodied Memories, and the Self', *Journal of Consciousness Studies* 25 (7): 225–241.

Kearney, R. (2008), 'Bachelard and the Epiphanic Instant', *Philosophy Today* 52 (Supplement): 38–45.

Killick, J. (1997), *You Are Words*, London: Hawker.

Killick, J. (2018), *Poetry and Dementia: A Practical Guide*, London: Kingsley.

Kontos, P. (2005), 'Embodied Selfhood in Alzheimer's Disease: Rethinking Person-centered Care', *Dementia* 4 (4): 553–570.

Kontos, P., A. Grigorovich, S. Dupuis, C. Jonas-Simpson, G. Mitchell and J. Gray (2020), 'Raising the Curtain on Stigma Associated with Dementia: Fostering a New Cultural Imaginary for a More Inclusive Society', *Critical Public Health* 30 (1): 91–102.

Lehmann, O. V. (2019), 'The Poetic Resonance of an Instant: Making Sense of Experience and Existence Through the Emotional Value of Encounters', In P. Marsico and L. Tateo (eds), *Ordinary Things and Their Extraordinary Meanings*, 53–75, Charlotte, NC: Information Age Publishing.

Lehmann, O. V. and S. H. Klempe (2016), 'The Centrality of Aesthetics for Psychology: Sciences and Arts United Through Poetic Instants', in J. Valsiner, G. Marsico, N. Chaudhary, T. Sato and V. Dazzani (eds), *Psychology as the Science of Human Being*, 51–66, New York: Springer.

Lehmann, O. V. and S. Brinkmann (2019), 'I'm the One Who Has Written This': Reciprocity in Writing Courses for Older Adults in Norway, *International Journal of Qualitative Studies on Health and Well-being* 14 (1).

Merleau-Ponty, M. (1945/2012), *Phenomenology of Perception*, London: Routledge.

Moyers, B. (2000), *Fooling with Words: A Celebration of Poems and Their Craft*, New York: Perennial.

Nemerov, H. (2020), 'Poetry', in *Encyclopedia Britannica*, 5 November, Available online: https://www.britannica.com/art/poetry (accessed 24 May 2021).

Orr, G. (2002), *Poetry as Survival*, Athens, Georgia: The University of Georgia Press.

Orr, G. (2018), *A Primer for Poets & Readers of Poetry*, New York: W. W. Norton.

Rich, A. (2003), *What Is Found There: Notebooks on Poetry and Politics (Expanded Edition)*, New York: W. W. Norton & Company.

Stewart, S. (2002), *Poetry and the Fate of the Senses*, Chicago: The University of Chicago Press.

Strawson, G. (2004), 'Against Narrativity', *Ratio XVII* 17 (4): 428–452.

Summa, M. (2014), 'The Disoriented Self: Layers and Dynamics of Self-Experience in Dementia and Schizophrenia', *Phenomenology and the Cognitive Sciences* 13: 477–496.

Summa, M. and T. Fuchs (2015), 'Self-experience in Dementia', *Rivista internazionale di Filosofia e Psicologia* 6 (2): 387–405.

Synnes, O. (2015), 'Narratives of Nostalgia in the Face of Death: The Importance of Lighter Stories of the Past in Palliative Care', *Journal of Aging Studies* 34: 169–176.

Synnes, O. (2016), 'Storytelling as a Dignity-Preserving Practice in Palliative Care', in O. Tranvåg, O. Synnes and W. McSherry (eds), *Stories of Dignity Within Healthcare: Research, Narratives and Theories*, 61–74. Keswick, UK: M&K Publishing.

Synnes, O., M. Råheim, E. Lykkeslet and E. Gjengedal (2021), 'A Complex Reminding: The Ethics of Poetry Writing in Dementia Care', *Dementia* 20 (3): 1025–1043.

Synnes, O. and A. Ruset, eds. (2021), *Tellagulla: Dikt av personar som lever med ein demenssjukdom. (Tellagulla: Poems by Persons Living with Dementia)*, Molde, Norway: Råkhaugen Day Care Centre for Persons with Dementia and Molde University College.

Toombs, S. K. (1990), 'The Temporality of Illness: Four levels of Experience', *Theoretical Medicine* 11 (3): 227–241.

Wisløff, E., ed. (2021), *Ren poesi julehefte (Pure Poetry Christmas Booklet)*, Oslo, Norway: Aschehoug.

World Health Organization, (2017), *Global Action Plan on the Public Health Response to Dementia*, 2017–2025. https://apps.who.int/iris/bitstream/hand le/10665/259615/9789241513487-eng.pdf?sequence=1 (accessed 12 July 2021).

Zahavi, D. (2014), *Self & Other: Exploring Subjectivity, Empathy, and Shame*, Oxford: Oxford University Press.

Zahavi, D. (2007), 'Self and Other: The Limits of Narrative Understanding', *Royal Institute of Philosophy Supplements, 60: Narrative and Understanding Persons*, 179–202.

4

Growing Older with Haiku: What Haiku Offers to Japanese Expats in Denmark

Kyoko Murakami

Haiku scholars and practitioners in Japan and around the world take various approaches to define or describe what haiku is and how it should be read and written. Here is what Roland Barthes says on haiku:

> You are entitled, says the haiku, to be trivial, short, ordinary: enclose what you see, what you feel, in a slender horizon of words, and you will be interesting; you yourself (and starting from yourself) are entitled to establish your own notability; your sentence, whatever it may be, will enunciate a moral, will liberate symbol, you will be profound at the least possible cost, your writing will be filled.
>
> (Barthes 1982: 70)

As a Japanese native and non-expert of haiku and literary studies, this quote seems to commend haiku for its simplicity, brevity and mundaneness. The creative practice of haiku is being grounded in the everyday experiences of the haiku poet, not aiming at conveying abstract thoughts or transcendental philosophical ideas. Haiku is a symbolic practice that resists meaning (Barthes 1982). This initial observation compels me to grapple with and stay curious as to what haiku offers to people from all walks of life. Haiku is 'a poetic form that generally concerns itself with the world outside the self, the world of nature, and the possibility of experiencing oneness with all that' (Marshall and Simpson, 2016: 126). In haiku we make observations about the world outside ourselves, using quick descriptions of it. In contrast to Western literary art, Barthes seems to be pointing to the haiku's unique character, as a literary practice that suspends meaning, using language without a definitive meaning, exempt from analysing its meaning and interpretation:

> The haiku's task is to achieve exemption from meaning within a perfectly readerly discourse (a contradiction denied to Western art, which can contest meaning only by rendering its discourse incomprehensible), so that to our eyes the haiku is neither eccentric nor familiar: it resembles nothing at all: readerly, it seems to us simple, close, known, delectable, delicate, 'poetic'—in a word, offered to a whole range of reassuring predicates; insignificant nonetheless, it resists us, finally loses

the adjectives which a moment before we had bestowed upon it, and enters into that suspension of meaning which to us is the strangest thing of all, since it makes impossible the most ordinary exercise of our language, which is commentary.

(Barthes 1982: 81)

Is haiku a form of poetry without meaning-making? What is left in haiku as a literary practice if we take out meaning-making? Apart from being the shortest fixed form in poetry, haiku has only two rules: it must follow a rhythm of '5-7-5' (17 syllables in total),[1] and include "seasonal words" (*kigo* in Japanese). But in fact, there is something more important than these required forms and elements. The real appeal is to capture the momentary movement of the mind, or what is called 'the Haiku moment' (Epstein 2014; Louis 2017; Marshall and Simpson 2016). The amount of information that can be packed into a short phrase of only 17 syllables is not large. Therefore, when you compose a haiku, you need to focus on something that moved you and explore the way you feel.

Beyond its global appeal and popularity, haiku is associated with mindfulness, therapy, healing. Research on older adults attending the University of the Third Age[2] reports that reading and writing haiku improved their self-efficacy (Creely and Southcott 2020). In the medical and therapeutic community, Haiku therapy, or intervention using haiku, is practised (Hiltunen 2005; Stephenson and Rosen 2015; Stork 2020). Robert Epstein, a well-known writer and psychologist at Harvard, has written books such as *The Sacred in Contemporary Haiku* and there are many articles suggesting the benefits of haiku as therapy (2014). The research confirms that haiku as a therapeutic tool is effective for older adults, as reading and writing haiku is seen to be beneficial in battling mental health issues including promoting emotional health (Massey 1998). Haiku has been applied to mindfulness (e.g., Kempton 2018), to effective learning as a pedagogical tool (Minagawa and Yokoyama 2013; Pflaum 2017), and as a mental health intervention tool that is useful and beneficial to those who suffer from mental health issues (e.g., Epstein 2014; Welch 2020). The research on ageing in Japan has reported that haiku is beneficial for older adults as it enhances the sense of happiness. Haiku is a popular hobby and meaningful leisure activity for older adults in Japan (Hashimoto and Atsumi 2015).

Haiku has established its prominence to literary scholars (Barthes 1982; Paz, 1981). In addition, haiku as an art of living (Veenhoven 2003) is considered a transformative tool for gaining insight, enlightenment and learning through aesthetic experience. However, haiku's relevance and possible efficacy for older adults is not well documented. I myself dived into the practice of haiku as a leisure activity with two research participants as part of the research for this chapter and found that it expanded my perspective in life – addressing and answering existential questions such as what

---

[1] An English-language haiku is typically written in 3 short lines. The first line is 5 syllables; the second, 7 syllables; and the third, 5 syllables.
[2] It is also known as U3A, which is a UK-wide 'network of learning groups aimed at encouraging older people to share their knowledge, skills and interests in a friendly environment' (https://www.ageuk.org.uk/information-advice/work-learning/education-training/university-of-the-third-age/).

matters in life and how we can enjoy living our lives as we grow older. These questions were particularly relevant and poignant during lockdowns due to the COVID-19 pandemic. In this chapter, I will explore the question of what haiku practice (reading and writing haiku) offers to older adults, using a small case study of two Japanese older adult expats living in Denmark. I will consider haiku as an everyday hobby or leisure activity and capture the experience of composing haiku poems and the process of haiku practice to illustrate the three joys of feeling, knowing and thinking (Minagawa 2017). Haiku is not just an elite literary art; it also offers much to, and is enjoyed by, older adults, as part of their everyday activities. It gives them an opportunity to express the way they feel, the moments when something touches their hearts and arouses their emotions. I will explore the notion that haiku can be regarded as 'art-of-living' (Veenhoven 2003),[3] which enables them to lead a good life.

A case study of haiku for older adult Japanese expats in Denmark

The present research was motivated and prompted by my interest in language use, in particular, a creative aspect of the way in which older people use language practice to face life's adversities with resilience and meaning (Murakami 2021). My knowledge, experience and understanding of haiku were rudimentary, being formed from my formal education in Japan. So, I started my ageing and haiku research by getting to know someone who writes haiku in my circle of friends and acquaintances. Through a Japanese friend S,[4] who had supported me in moving to Copenhagen, Denmark and during my stay and work there (2014–2019), I was introduced to A, who is a friend of S and lives in Denmark. A is in her eighties and S in her seventies. They both live in the suburbs of Copenhagen as retirees. A has been practising haiku since her retirement for over 20 years. S, like me, is familiar with haiku through her formal education in Japan but never composed haiku poems during her adulthood. They do not suffer from known illnesses, being healthy apart from general wear-and-tear issues of being in old age.

A, S and I met for the first time online[5] on 7th October 2020. This was a meeting for me to explain my research in terms of its aims, scope, questions and rationale and for me to obtain informed consent. In this initial meeting, S stayed online during the entire session. As she was listening to our conversation, S became interested in learning about haiku from A and asked to remain in the meeting and take part in the research. A and I welcomed her to remain. In hindsight, this constituted an interesting interactional dynamic, a community of practice (Lave and Wenger 1991; Wenger 1998),

---

[3] Veenhoven (2003) further clarifies what is meant by 'leading a good life.' There are different views on what a good life is and what capabilities are called for. He specifies that, in the hedonistic view, life is better the more we enjoy it. Art-of-living is then 'the capability to take pleasure from life' (2003: 373). In this chapter, I adopt this notion and the 'enjoyable' life. This does not mean that people do not have problems and difficulties in life. In the context of ageing, it is important to set this as a primary goal for older adults.
[4] The participants in this research chose to be called with the initial of their given names.
[5] All the research communication was done via internet (via email or Zoom and Skype or its equivalent online video conference app called LINE).

in which A, being an experienced practitioner of haiku teaching, was showing the ropes of how to read and compose haiku to novices, S and me.

In the semi-structured, audio-recorded interview, I asked questions in Japanese including what it is about haiku that A liked and what haiku-related project she is currently working on has brought her joy. A responded to my questions, explaining how she started haiku and what the main appeal of haiku was for her. At the end of the first meeting, I asked if the three of us could meet again soon. After the second meeting, A encouraged S and me to have a go at composing haiku poems. So, we decided to meet online regularly to discuss our experience of composing haiku and share the haiku poems we created. S and I were novices in haiku practice; we learned from A by seeking feedback and advice from her. Together in a group, we have been composing and sharing haiku in our regular monthly meetings since October 2020. We have been experimenting with all kinds of haiku writing prompts, starting with photos, to mimic the *ginko* experience. *Ginko* is a Japanese word that refers to walks to seek inspiration for haiku composition. We also have tried to compose haiku to mark special days and events (e.g., birthdays, anniversaries, memorial events, death and funerals, Christmas and New Year's holidays). Each month we email our haiku poems in advance and then meet online to share and discuss them. We named our group '*Haiku-kai*' (English equivalent of the haiku meeting). The encounter via a research interview serendipitously turned into a special-interest group. Later in the chapter, I will mull over the significance of a community for older adults, whilst reflecting on this process of research that gave birth to a community for people having a shared interest in haiku. In the haiku practitioner community, there is a tradition of having a regular meeting called '*kukai*'[6] (tr. A haiku gathering), where haiku poets share their own haiku poems. This is a formal meeting, involving some critiquing of each other's haiku. So far, up to the time of finalizing this chapter, we have met 14 times online, including 3 research interviews and 11 *kukai* meetings. I audio-recorded the interviews and *kukai* meetings.

My research question of what haiku offers to older adults became more relevant as my research coincided with the sudden lifestyle change necessitated by the COVID lockdowns. Social distancing, for instance, was proven to be a challenge for all. Once a day for an hour to an hour-and-a-half, I have been taking a walk, recommended by the government for maintaining health during lockdowns. I decided to take this as doing a *ginko* i.e., taking haiku walks in local parks, riverside paths and wooded areas in the local area where I live. Having the opportunity to enjoy outdoor natural areas inspired me and my research participants, A and S, to compose haiku and research specific haiku-related topics, especially seasonal words in Japanese. The *ginko* walks have immensely helped both myself and the participants to have a clear headspace in our otherwise stressful, anxiety-laden times during lockdown. A is in her eighties and has lived in Denmark in her adulthood. After a divorce, she has lived alone. Her grown-up children and her grandchildren, who now live in Denmark and Germany, visit A regularly. She has been writing haiku since the time of her retirement from a full-time job in Copenhagen. S is in her early eighties and was widowed in her mid thirties. She

---

[6] A meeting to create and present haiku and to critique the haiku.

retired from her full-time job several years ago and, like A, lives alone. She keeps in close contact with her grown-up children and her grandchildren, who live in Denmark and the UK.

What led older adults to take up haiku as a hobby

Unlike some other hobbies that require expensive tools and space, everyone can compose haiku, as many haiku experts say (e.g., Itsuki Natsui [Mori 2021]). A's answer as to how she started haiku about 20 years ago when facing her retirement echoes this:

> Around 2000, my friend in Tokyo, who has been retired, made me realise that I had no hobbies. She said I should try writing haiku because I didn't need any tools, so I had a go. I was not sure what to do so I asked her to show me how to write haiku poems. She said I need to put a word about the season in haiku.
> (Interview 1 with A, 20 October 2020)[7]

As the opening quotes suggest, all one needs is a perspective to see nature as it comes (Barthes 1982). Anyone can get into composing haiku without much preparation or money to buy tools (you only need a pen and notebook) or having to hire or set up a physical space. Listening to A, both S and I also felt that we could start reading and composing haiku immediately. A's relationship with haiku deepened upon retirement:

> It was in 2002 when I retired. I had vaguely thought about it as my hobby. Then the friend asked me if I would like to join a haiku group[8] she is a member of, so I joined. At first, I was glad to read various haiku poems written by other members. I did not know much then. I didn't know what and how, but I started posting my own haiku poems. We posted our 5 or 6 haiku poems to a haiku magazine every month for about 10 years. My haiku poems were corrected and received feedback. I met a good teacher. I totally absorbed myself in the world of haiku.
> (Interview 1 with A, October 2020)

As an experienced haiku practitioner, A shared many episodes as to what the most important thing in her haiku practice is. As a novice, S also spoke enthusiastically about the process of learning to write haiku and how she became hooked on writing her own haiku. As I listened to the recordings of the interviews and *kukai* meetings, it became clear that they 'enjoy' composing haiku as well as reading other peoples'. My question of what haiku offers to older adults became more focused around the joys of practising haiku as we continued to meet and share our haiku. I transcribed the interviews and *kukai* interactions and thematically analysed them, using Minagawa's categorization of

---

[7] All the extracts from the interviews and meetings were conducted in Japanese. They were transcribed in Japanese first, and the chosen extracts were translated into English by the author.
[8] Typically, haiku practitioners join a group to learn from a kind of a teacher how to write haiku. The group is a place where they can share their own haiku with other members and receive feedback from the teacher.

the three joys of haiku (2017). Drawing on Vygotsky's concept of symbolic tool, Minagawa explored adolescents' use of haiku as symbolic tool in the classroom and analysed the process of creating and appreciating haiku in late adolescence and late childhood (Minagawa and Yokoyama 2013). Minagawa argues that haiku brings 'joy to feel', 'joy to know', and 'joy to think' to the creator/recipient (2017). In the process of creating and appreciating haiku, each person learns and judges by himself/herself and has his/her own thoughts. It was suggested that there are abundant elements that lead to the development of 'the ability to discuss with others, compare and scrutinize ideas, create better solutions and new knowledge, and find the next question' (2017: 25).

Practice of haiku: Three joys of the everyday

Many people recognize that haiku is a short poem that puts a 'seasonal word' in the rhythm of '5, 7, 5' moras (or syllables). There is also something more important than counting syllables and fitting the words into the form. It means 'capturing the momentary movement of the mind' (Sunaba 2019). The amount of information that can be packed into short phrases of only 17 characters/syllables is limited and, therefore, one needs to focus on "something that moved him/her" and explore the way she/he feels. These feelings, the felt sense of the experience with the world around, is expanded by Minagawa (2017) as three joys of the Everyday:

> Haiku has three joys. The first is 'joy of feeling' and enjoying the activities of the season with all five senses will enrich your life. The second is 'joy of knowing,' and you can become smarter little by little just by reading the wisdom and thoughtful *Sai'jiki*[9] of your ancestors and knowing the meaning of seasonal words that accurately represent seasonal features. The third is 'joy of thinking,' and the experience of condensing and expressing what you have received in your heart into seventeen sounds is also utilized in your life and work. And, in the background of the three joys, there is always contact with people, and by talking with each other, each one deepens. 'Feeling,' 'knowing,' and 'thinking' are the cognitive processes of human beings, and human beings live by being supported by touching and talking.
>
> (Minagawa 2017: 22, translation by Murakami)

In the following, I will discuss further the three joys of the everyday as applied to the haiku practice of my research participants.

Joy of feeling through nature

One may ask when the opportune time is to compose haiku. The answer is unanimous amongst haiku experts and enthusiasts. The moment you 'notice' (or become 'aware' of

---

[9] *Sai'jiki* is a 'literary calendar' in a literal translation. It is a lexicon containing words referring to seasons. Haiku poets look up words referring to a particular season or month.

something; *kidzuki* in Japanese) and 'feel' something at home or outside is the opportune moment of composing haiku (Pflaum 2017). Such moments are ubiquitous, and sometimes you do not realize such moments are passing by.

Haiku gives 'joy to feel' as a primary way of being in and experiencing nature (Minagawa 2017). Haiku does not need any particular preparation or training, as A says. The most important preparation is *ginko*.[10] *Ginko* in Japanese means an act of seeking inspiration for haiku. Some haiku scholars and experts call it 'haiku writing walk' or simply 'haiku walk' (Caiola-Musacchia 2013) or 'foraging for haiku' (Summers 2018). *Ginko* can be done alone or with others. Marshall points out a communal aspect of haiku practice due to *ginko* as a collective activity. 'To this day, community-building remains a notable feature of haiku. In Japan haiku enthusiasts may join one another on a *ginko*, or communal haiku walk. The social dimension of haiku practice is evident as well in the haiku contests called *kukai*, where the participants themselves serve as judges in selecting the best haiku' (Marshall 2013: 99).

Answering the interview question of 'what kind of activity do you need for seeking haiku inspiration?' A says she walks for about an hour. In her *ginko* walk, she tries to capture whatever the image is that comes to her and often records it in a notebook, on the spot, if she can (Interview 1). The most essential element in haiku composition is to be at one with nature and to feel it without analysing the experience of nature (Pflaum 2017; Ross 2002). A says that there is no single way to be at one with nature when she goes on a *ginko*. She says it is intuitive as to when she feels inspiration from the scenery. In response to my question of whether she takes pictures with a camera when she goes on a *ginko* walk. She elaborates on the joy of feeling nature as follows:

> I don't take pictures of the scenery. I don't do [that] at all, and I burn [the image of the scenery] in my eyes and [jotting down] words in my notebook. Taking a photo makes me feel different.
>
> (Interview 1 with A, October 2020)

The intuition of her haiku writing is serendipitous, an unexpected, accidental joy of seeing and feeling some natural elements:

> When I want to get something, I end up not getting it. There are times when I am just walking along, and something makes me feel suddenly different ... It feels like a fish gets caught [without having to try or by accident] when I do not think about it.
>
> I think it's better to let your shoulders relax and leave it to you naturally. I can say this freely because at that time I was not a member of a haiku circle, but for example, if you are a circle member, you have to scrutinize and select your haiku poems and submit them, don't you? So, I can't say such a careless thing [it does not apply to all haiku practitioners].
>
> (Interview 1 with A, October 2020)

---

[10] *Ginko* is a noun in Japanese. Gin (吟) refers to an act of making a poem; ko (行), an act of walking. In this chapter, I use 'go on a *ginko*' or 'do *ginko*'.

A implies that those haiku enthusiasts or professional haiku poets, who have deadlines for submitting haiku to haiku journals and receiving feedback from reviewers, may have motives other than enjoying haiku. Her relationship with haiku is admittedly, relaxed, stress-free and free-spirited, which allows her to be at one with nature and to capture freely whatever comes to her eyes and other senses, and to her mind. It is a very sensory, sensuous and creative experience. After the first meeting with A online, S and I also started going on *ginko* walks – S in Denmark and I in England. It was at the time of COVID-19-related restrictions for gathering in Europe being tightened. People were permitted to exercise outdoor once a day, so we used our daily allowance to go for *ginko* walks.

Ginko: A haiku walk

I must admit that I had not heard of the word *ginko* until A mentioned it in the interview. I did not even know how to spell the word in Chinese characters. It struck me that haiku poets go for a walk seeking inspiration. *Ginko* walk may sound unique to only haiku poets. However, it seems to resemble what Henry David Thoreau says, 'Walking with a purpose is . . . SAUNTERING' in contrast to a walk to seek the shortest course to the sea' (Thoreau 1862: 657). Ingold's characterization of the act of reading, similar to that of walking, is worth noting: 'The reader, "seeing" his reading as he "walks" through it, is constantly in motion, all senses continually in play, slowing down and speeding up, like a craftsman using his various instruments' (Carruthers 1998, cited in Ingold 2010: 17). He also compares the reading to a pilgrimage: 'in the liturgical procession or pilgrimage, one could walk through a landscape as scripture' (17). He suggests that 'to walk is to journey in the mind as much as on the land: it is a deeply meditative practice' (2010: 18). Based on these ideas, *ginko* can be seen as the haiku poet walks the landscape as the haiku text. *Ginko* can be considered as meditative and touches deeply at the spirit level.

Ginko is an essential element of haiku practice. Through the walk, haiku composition is made possible, particularly in the dynamic movement of immersing oneself in nature and capturing what appeals to the heart/mind in an instant. This is what Joan Giroux calls 'the haiku moment' (cited in Louis 2017). 'The haiku moment [is] both evocative and relational, a moment of potential in which the impulse to capture or freeze presence finally yields to movement, across time and space. Presence is constructed through a web of spatio-temporal relations: metonymic, intertextual, and imaginative' (Louis 2017: 36).

It is an intriguing act and seems to underline interesting concepts as expressed in the following interview extracts:

Me: You said 'nothing', but what kind of feeling is it? What kind of feeling is nothing?
A: Don't think about anything. For example, say I may go for a *ginko* walk, just because I will walk on a route that has shops along the way, I should not plan to shop after this *ginko*. I don't think of anything, just walk and look at the scenery. Yeah, it's like that.

The experience of *ginko* is further elaborated in the interview with S and the subsequent online meeting in which I recorded S's actual *ginko* walk in August 2021. I followed S's *ginko* online as she broadcast live using her smartphone and recorded the *ginko* experience as she narrated live on her experience, or her lifeworld of *ginko*. Here are the extracts from the analytical commentary of the *ginko* walk that S made. It was written in December 2021 as a reflection. The following extracts illustrate the haiku moment and the joy of feeling nature, the oneness:

> When we begin our *kukai*, the first time we met as a haiku group, I learned the word "*ginko*". I thought that only a *ginko* would get me started with making haiku, so I decided to take my own trot and a leisurely walk. In the *ginko* walk, the joy of entering my own world swelled. I have no sense of direction, so I'm always worried about not being able to come home. I have a fear of getting lost and am not good at walking alone. Therefore, I invited someone for a walk, but it did not last as it involves the other person to be available.
>
> However, when I started going on a *ginko* walk, beyond my anxiety, I was immensely attracted to being able to experience another world. When Kyoko suggested that we communicate over the phone whilst I was on a *ginko* walk, I agreed to do so.
>
> It was raining cats and dogs on the day we agreed to talk. In my mind, I was close to cancel [*sic*] the *ginko* walk. After a while, the torrential rain turned into drizzle. I think you can see the state of our *ginko* in the series of haiku that followed. The wonderful world I experienced during just over an hour of *ginko* became mine.
>
> (Email from S, 13 December 2021, translated by Murakami)

The above extract on the *ginko* walk on 17 August 2021 was followed by six haiku poems. On the topic of rain in the summer, she composed a series of haiku capturing the constant change of her embodied experience of rain. Some haiku capture her feeling sensuous in and with the rain; others express her determination to continue walking, experiencing rain, as it were, at one with rain, with nature. S shared her reflection on the *ginko* later in the email:

> It rains in Denmark for a short time. During this time, the rain is only for about an hour. It was a truly happy event for me to be able to experience the change throughout my body in that time-space. [When it rains,] going out is a hassle, and the desire to quit [the *ginko* walk] grows greatly. In such a situation, the promise with the friend, Kyoko, who pushes my back [i.e., to go on a *ginko*], and putting a little load on myself gives me a bit of a pressure. With these streams of thoughts and complex feelings, *everyday life comes alive again.* [The *ginko*] evokes various feelings and sharpens [my senses]. *Ginko is best for anti-ageing.* Moreover, the fact that words pop out from my mind is evidence that the brain is working actively. The joy of knowing the world of haiku swells within me and enriches me. This is a joy from the inside and my facial expression naturally shows it. I had eye contact with many people on the street. How nice it was that they smiled back to me! I'm

looking forward to going on a *ginko* walk tomorrow and what experience it will bring.

(Email from S, 13 December 2021, translated by Murakami)

S acknowledges a benefit of *ginko* for anti-ageing and emphasizes the joy of feeling nature as the crucial element of haiku practice. She also points out a social benefit as a consequence of the joy of feeling, which affects her behaviour (smile) and extends her joy through the others' smiling back, which is an added benefit of haiku practice as she overcomes the fear of going on a walk alone and learned to communicate with passers-by. In the liminality of *ginko*, S's haiku above captures the constant changes of the environment and feelings which she was experiencing. The haiku written by S on this ginko will be discussed later in the chapter.

Joy of knowing

The second joy that Minagawa suggests is that haiku involves a joy of knowing, coming to learn new seasonal words referring to a month, by looking up poetic words in *Sai'jiki* and learning new words and their evocative effect through 'wisdom and the words of ancestors' (2017: 22). A explains how she experiences 'the joy of knowing':

For example, if you want to write a haiku using the word *tanabata* [the Festival of the Weaver (the star Vega), the Star Festival on 7th July], you need to check *tanabata* with *Sai'jiki* to find out what season it signifies. We may think it is a term for summer. But *tanabata* is in fact the term that signifies autumn, not summer.

(Interview with A, October 2020)

Using the right seasonal word for the haiku can be difficult, especially for a beginner expat like S, who has no *Sai'jiki* at hand. However, contemporary haiku made in non-Japanese speaking countries is more lenient about this rule of having to include the right seasonal word. A had bought a copy of *Sai'jiki* as soon as she realized that not looking up words in *Sai'jiki* would compromise her haiku quality. From that point on, she found another joy, 'the joy of knowing' new words that signify the same meaning (Minagawa 2017), expanding her knowledge of words that can be used in haiku. She further explained how appealing it is for her to use the seasonal words that spark literary beauty in Japanese words:

Well, I was interested in Japanese culture and the Japanese language since I left Japan and moved to Denmark many years ago. I didn't want to forget Japanese as my mother tongue as I got older. When I was in Japan, I hadn't really thought about the Japanese language. When I started living abroad, I realised that Japanese was a beautiful language.

One of the reasons that A started writing haiku was to stay abreast with traditional Japanese culture and Japanese language as a literary art. Being an expat and getting older, she said that she had felt strongly about her roots in Japan. In the first and second interviews, she said she became aware that her native language has a calming effect, no matter how much and how well she could speak Danish and English. The older she gets, the more important it is for her to use Japanese language. Since starting her haiku practice, she sees differently the traditional Japanese culture such as haiku as she senses the beauty of Japanese language. This may sound like she is nationalistic, ethnocentric or even nostalgic about her own culture, but I do not think she was praising Japanese language as if it were more beautiful than other languages, say English or Danish, in which she is also proficient with. It is through her practice of haiku that her awareness and appreciation of the beauty of Japanese language grew. In particular, with the rule of haiku having to include a seasonal word, she learned various seasonal words referring to a particular period or a day of the year. She said, 'it is a good way for me to learn wisdom and the words of the ancestors. I find out what I didn't know. As in the words of the old and new, I began to think that it was important to rekindle the old and know the new' (Interview 1 with A, October 2020). Likewise, S said that she had been enchanted by the power of words and enthused with learning new words, since she listened to A in the first interview. Both experience 'the joy of knowing' whilst writing haiku. S said that she wakes up every morning these days with the exciting prospect of writing new haiku. She underlined, 'my mind is packed with words to be used and they are to be shaped in the form of haiku, which I find enriching' (S, Interview 2, 2020).

The participants' 'joy of knowing' through their haiku practice is further linked to seeing and experiencing ageing. A said that she gradually became aware of the concept of haiku and the principal aesthetic sense of Japanese culture, *wabi-sabi*.[11] 'The Japanese aesthetic of *wabi-sabi* refers to 'the imperfect and temporary nature of things' (English 2016: 7). According to Kempton (2018: 30), *wabi-sabi* is elaborated threefold: 'an intuitive response to beauty that reflects the true nature of life'; 'an acceptance and appreciation of the impermanent, imperfect and incomplete nature of everything' and 'a recognition of the gifts of simple, slow and natural living'. A explained the way ageing is seen from *wabi-sabi* as follows:

> when you think about life and getting old, in particular things aren't perfect. By coming into contact with imperfections, you come to know yourself and get to know yourself better. Nature and human activities are imperfect, and in the process of ageing, especially, the notion of people and their lives being imperfect, impermanent and feeling has become apparent. To me, writing haiku poems about the imperfections of humanity and nature through observing nature helps me understand a bit more about this idea of wabi-sabi and what haiku is about.
>
> (Interview 1 with A, 8 October 2020)

The extract above illustrates that haiku enables A to know herself deeply and see her own ageing in light of *wabi-sabi*, that is, to see beauty in changing things, impermanence

---

[11] Etymologically, *Wabi sabi* originated as two separate words, both imbued with aesthetic value, with roots in literature, culture and religion. '*Wabi* is about finding beauty in simplicity, and a spiritual richness and serenity in detaching from the material world. *Sabi* is more concerned with the passage of time, with the way that all things grow and decay and how ageing alters the visual nature of those things' (Kempton 2018: 300).

and imperfections. There is a sense of humility and acceptance toward ageing in her account above. From the perspective of a haiku practitioner, A sees a sense of beauty in ageing as a natural phenomenon of decay, impermanence of body and a transient nature of who we are.

Joy of thinking

The third category of joy in the practice of haiku is the joy of thinking. What counts as a joy of thinking for older adult expats, such as A and S? The restrictive form of haiku forces us to be creative and think about, sometimes grappling with, the choices of words and the word form. Haiku poets are faced with various challenges, for example, not being able to find the appropriate words, missing words, missing or surplus letters (or characters or syllables), or problems with arranging the words. S in particular seems to enjoy this challenge as she jots down words that come to her mind every morning and asks herself how to expand one word into the 17-syllalble haiku form (Email, 13 December 2021). However difficult it may sound to wrestle with words, meaning and form, A said that 'through touching nature and feeling it, I can think with reason and use analytical skills, as well as sharpen my instinct to feel, that is, improve my sensitivity' (Interview 2, October 2020). It seems that the joy of thinking is integral to the joys of feeling and knowing.

Since starting haiku, both A and S have been able to use Japanese language more frequently. They both emphasize that they see the importance of using their native language as they grow older. A says, 'I live on my own, and most of the time, thinking is done in Japanese. I want to make sure that I remember to use Japanese more as I get older.' This concern is reflected in the research on the linguist development of older adults. For instance, Dutch and German researchers examined a linguistic reversion of immigrants, who tend to use the first language in old age more than they did in middle age (Schmid and Keijzer 2009). A local council in the area in Japan where there is a large migrant population has produced a manual to support older adult migrants, who experience the reversion to the first language and the culture of their home country and find it difficult go about daily businesses and communicate in Japanese language (Office of Aichi Prefecture n.d.).

It seems that the problem depends on where you reach your old age. As in the case of A and S, the quality of life in old age will change drastically when it comes to their ageing life in Denmark. They juggle with different cultural and linguistic backgrounds and having a life base in Denmark, reaching old age in their foreign land. Older adult expats can encounter many obstacles, such as the linguistic reversion to their native language, making life in old age even more difficult. Both A and S are aware of this scenario of not being able to maintain their second/foreign language in order to function in Danish society. This issue is reflected in the burgeoning studies on ageing and migration (e.g., Pot, Keijzer and De Bot 2020). Pot et al. note a 'language barrier' for older migrants when communicating medical issues in a second language (L2) context. Yet how a limited L2 proficiency impacts on the ageing process of migrant adults has, so far, not been systematically investigated. This question is important, given that having a limited L2 proficiency may pose immediate drawbacks on their ability to maintain independence and a quality of life as they age.

As the interview account shows, A and S are mindful of experiencing the linguistic reversion to the mother tongue and culture as a possible barrier to their quality of life in their ageing process. They seem to use haiku practice as a way of accepting the reversion to Japanese language in order to maintain and even enhance their quality of ageing life, instead of treating it as a detriment to their daily communicative functioning.

Polyphony in haiku

As with many literary forms, haiku can be said to be dialogic, drawing on Bakhtin's notion of dialogism (1984 [1929]). Haiku prompts internal dialogues (e.g., the writer and his/her other selves on nature whilst experiencing it). Many of the haiku that A and S have written may be seen as a form of dialogue between an older adult and their other selves. For example, A's relationship with haiku is dialogic as she insists that she is not lonely and 'haiku is a friend to those who live alone' including herself (Interview 2). She even calls haiku 'a friend of her heart'. She continues, '[e]ven if you talk to yourself at home or wherever, aloud or silently, you can use haiku as a way of keeping my thoughts and ideas. Haku is 'in lieu of a personal diary' (Interview 1, 2020). When composing haiku, she doesn't just put her own voice and perspective in a haiku, but also the voice of others, which is brought in to depict the very gap, contrasting between the past and the present, or the future. The haiku practice keeps her being engaged with noticing, in which she expresses her feeling of the haiku moment freely. She said that she preferred to go on a *ginko* walk by herself as she can sharpen her gaze, totally dedicate her attention to nature and immerse herself in it.

Similarly, S's haiku is deemed to be dialogic. It is evident in the following example haiku poems, which are composed based on her *ginko* walk and reflective accounts; S is not by herself in the walk:

> Stop the rain stops,
> decide now and off I go
> on a *ginko* walk

> The sound of rain,
> is gentle on my ears,
> splashing my body

> The sound of rain
> wraps around me refreshingly

> For eight seconds,
> rain ceases to stop,
> hurry up

> When the rain stopped,
> I suddenly looked up,
> red-purple sky

> The rain stops,
> the sky looks as if it dyed the surroundings
> (translated from Japanese to English by Murakami)

In these six haiku poems she composed during the ginko walk, S is totally immersed in speaking her voice on nature, in this case, the rain on that afternoon in the summer of 2021. Despite the fear of taking a walk alone and possibly getting lost on the way home, which her reflective account shows (see above), different voices about the rain are revealed in the haiku poems. She was *feeling* the rain as if it embraced her refreshingly (Haiku 3) and with splashes, almost conveying a sensuous sensation (Haiku 2), or listening to the rain as if it were lyrical music to her ear (Haiku 2). The rain has been described in polyphony,[12] in multiple ways, depicting an ephemeral experience of the walk lasting less than an hour. All six poems on the rain, with composition based on that *ginko*, convey the impermanence of the phenomenon of her being with the rain. She was at one with nature, being focused on the here-and-now, using haiku's brevity and simplicity.

Haiku on ageing

As another way of illustrating the way in which the participants experience ageing through haiku, I would like to share haiku poems on ageing, composed by the participants, A and S. For this chapter, I asked them to choose their haiku poems on ageing, growing older, which were shared in our monthly *kukai* meetings. English translations were added by the participants themselves. Haiku marked with (A) at the end of haiku are by A, (S) by S.

The following three haiku poems address the participants embracing ageing in terms of the *wabi-sabi*: decay, impermanence and simplicity aligned with nature. Ageing is considered as the passing of time through metaphor of nature and living creatures:

1) 色あせた　我が人生に　咲くバラか (S)

> Is it a rose
> That blooms in my faded life?

2) 老ひ重ね　枯葉を重く　感じけり (A)

> Getting older
> Feeling heavy dead leaves

---

[12] It refers to many-voicedness, 'a plurality of independent and unmerged voices and consciousness' (Bakhtin 1984 [1929]: 6).

3) 厳寒の　屋根鳥一羽　風の立つ　(A)

In the freezing cold
A bird on a roof,
The wind rises up

Still with the theme of passing of time, ageing is anthropomorphized and presented as a challenge, a learning goal expressed in a humorous tone:

4) 老いなんて　駆け足で来る　追いつかぬ　(S)

Age is chasing me
I can't keep up with ageing

5) 年老いて　負けてたまるか　テクノロジー　(S)

Getting older,
I cannot bear losing the battle with technologies.

Whilst ageing as passing of the time is a consistent theme, the participants' subjective experiences are expressed within the embodied time. Their acceptance of the time passing is clear, as well as impermanence.

6) 急ぐこと　なしゆっくりと　年歩む　(A)

No hurry,
slowly
I walk the year
[A's comment: As you get older, you come to understand the proverb, 'if you are in a hurry, make a detour'.]

7) 年重ね　無常流るる　師走かな　(A)

Getting older
Feeling more emptiness
in December
[A's comment: At the end of the year, things are easy to change, and I feel the fragility and emptiness as I get older.]

8) 聖樹の灯　道しるべ役　兼ねており　(A)

The sacred tree
lighting on a road
as well as a road to departure

In the following three haiku, ageing is seen as gaps between past and present (e.g., generational). Haiku captures the participants' dialogue with themselves.

9) 重ね　想いはつのり　子は知らず (S)

Getting older,
my longing increases, my children don't know.

10) 着ぶくれて　鏡の我に　達磨負け (A)

Dressed in layers,
myself in a mirror
Daruma loses a battle
[A's comment: Even Daruma (i.e., a symbol of perseverance and staying the path) gave up my bloating.]

11) 私みて　恥ずかしげにか　薄化粧 (S)

Looking at myself,
Embarrassed, putting on light makeup.

The next two haiku capture the simple pleasure experienced with a family member or a pet.

12) 春の日に　大大好きと　孫がいう (S)

On a spring day
My grandson says he loves me very very much

13) 冬うらら　老ひの一日　老猫と (A)

Relaxed in a winter a day
Looking back the old days
with an old cat
[A's comment: As I get older, I often remember old times and often indulge in recollections.]

Lastly, ageing makes them think about their homeland; the haiku expresses the yearning for the homeland:

14) 半生記　今も生きてる　異国の地 (S)

Half of my lifetime,
the foreign land, where I still live.

Conclusion

In this chapter, I have explored the question of what haiku practice offers to older adults with the exploratory case study of Japanese older adult expats living in Denmark. I applied the categorization of the three joys of feeling, knowing and thinking in haiku practice by older adults to the data gathered, using online semi-structured interviews, *kukai* meetings online and reflective comments sent via email. As for the joy of feeling, we can see older adults being at one with nature during *ginko* walks, experiencing that they are at one with nature. They also come to have a deeper understanding of ageing as they see it, from the aesthetic concept of *wabi-sabi*, in which they accept and appreciate the perspective that everything is impermanent, imperfect and incomplete, and recognize the gifts of living simply, slowly and naturally. The joy of knowing pertains to their learning of new seasonal words as wisdom and the words from their ancestors, as they praise the beauty of Japanese language through haiku practice. As for the joy of thinking, they consider having to think carefully as to how their word choices fit into the short form of haiku. This challenge forces them to be innovative with words and syllables and to learn new words, deepening their appreciation of the language (i.e., the joy of knowing). The haiku poems on ageing they have shared with me since October 2020 are polyphonic, reflecting their dialogic relationship with nature – with selves and voices emerging as they go on a *ginko*. I have illustrated the enriched life they have led with haiku and that haiku can be a powerful 'art of living'. What I have presented here is only a small-scale exploratory inquiry, which has room to widen its scope to other older adults in multicultural contexts. To build on the analysis presented and to explore this direction for future research, I suggest that it is worth looking further at haiku from Bakhtin's dialogism. Methodologically, a phenomenological analysis seems plausible to expand the analysis of the experience, using concepts such as 'lifeworld' and 'lived experience' (Langdridge 2007). With a caveat for applying uncritically a notion of positive or successful ageing drawing from positive psychology of ageing (Ranzijn 2002), I envisage that the current research contributes to the advancement of positive psychology (Seligman and Csikszentmihalyi 2000) on older adults and their ageing process.

References

Bakhtin, M. M. (1984 [1929]), *Problems of Dostoevsky's Poetics* (ed. and trans. C. Emerson), Oxford: Blackwell.

Barthes, R. (1982), *Empire of Signs*, New York: Hill and Wang, The Noonday Press.

Caiola-Musacchia, R. (2013, 30 November 2013), 'Rewrite Your Day with a Haiku Walk'. https://www.rewireme.com/happiness/rewire-your-day-with-a-haiku-walk/.

Creely, E. and J. Southcott (2020), 'Developing Perceived Self-efficacy in Later Life through Poetry Writing: An Analysis of a U3A Poetry Group of Older Australians', *International Journal of Lifelong Education* 39 (2): 191–204.

English, P. (2016), 'Imperfection: Embracing Wabi-Sabi', *Liminalities* 12 (4): 1–9.

Epstein, R. (2014), *The Sacred in Contemporary Haiku*, CreateSpace Independent Publishing Platform.

橋本 Hashimoto, S. 成. and 尚. 厚海 Atsumi, N. (2015), '高齢者の余暇活動と主観的幸福感に関する研究', 土木学会論文集D3 土木計画学 ('A Study on Leisure Activities and Subjective Happiness of the Elderly', *Journal of Japan Society of Civil Engineers D3 Civil Engineering Planning*) 71 (5): I_567–I_576.

Hiltunen, S. M. S. (2005), 'Country Haiku from Finland: Haiku Meditation Therapy for Self-healing', *Journal of Poetry Therapy* 18 (2): 85–96.

Ingold, T. (2010), 'Footprints through the Weather-world: Walking, Breathing, Knowing', *The Journal of the Royal Anthropological Institute* 160: 121–139.

Kempton, B. (2018), *Wabi Sabi: Japanese Wisdom for a Perfectly Imperfect Life*, London: Little, Brown Book Group.

Langdridge, D. (2007), *Phenomenological Psychology: Theory, Research and Methods*, Harlow, UK: Pearson Education.

Lave, J. and E. Wenger (1991), *Situated Learning: Legitimate Peripheral Participation*, Cambridge: Cambridge University Press.

Louis, R. (2017), 'Performing presence in the haiku moment', *Text and Performance Quarterly* 37 (1): 35–50.

Marshall, I. (2013), 'Stalking the Gaps: The Biopoetics of Haiku', *Mosaic* 46 (4): 91–107.

Marshall, I. and M. Simpson (2016), 'Deconstructing Haiku', *JUXTATWO* (Juxtapositions 2.1): 125–148.

Massey, M. S. (1998), 'Promoting Emotional Health through Haiku, a Form of Japanese Poetry', *Journal of School Health* 68 (2): 73–76.

Minagawa, N. (2017), '短詩型「俳句」の創作　鑑賞と21世紀の学びとの親和性' (Affinity between the Creation and Appreciation of Short Poetry Haiku and Learning in the 21st Century), 鳴門教育大学情報教育ジャーナル /*Journal of Information Education*, Naruto University of Education 14: 21–27.

Minagawa, N. and T. Yokoyama (2013), 'Examination of the Way of Learning Guidance Considering the Zone of Proximal Development of Children: Deepening Interest and Knowledge of Seasonal Words through Emotional and Empathic Experiences through Haiku' (子どもの発達の最近接領域を考慮した学習指導の在り方の検討－俳句をとおした感動　共感体験による季語への関心　知識の深まり), *Research Bulletin of Naruto University of Education* (鳴門教育大学授業実践研究) 12: 19–27.

Mori, T. (2021), 'Japanese Poet Itsuki Natsui Awarded for Dedicated Efforts to Broaden the Reach of Haiku' (https://mainichi.jp/english/articles/20211102/p2a/00m/0et/019000c). *The Mainichi*.

Murakami, K. (2021), 'Learning in Retirement: Developing Resilience and Becoming a Resourceful Practitioner of Life', *Learning, Culture and Social Interaction* 28: no. 100463.

Office of Aichi Prefecture (n.d.), 老後を支えあう（マニュアル（愛知県）A manual for supporting each other in old age.

Paz, O. (1981), Sendas de Oku (Translation of 奥の細道 Matsuo Basho), Barcelona, Editorial Seix Barral.

Pflaum, J. (2017), 'Haiku This Moment: Being Aware', *Skipping Stones* 29 (3): 32.

Pot, A., M. Keijzer and K. De Bot (2020), 'The Language Barrier in Migrant Aging', *International Journal of Bilingual Education and Bilingualism* 23 (9): 1139–1157.

Ranzijn, R. (2002), 'Towards a Positive Psychology of Ageing: Potentials and Barriers', *Australian Psychologist* 37 (2): 79–85.

Ross, B. (2002), *How to Haiku: A Writer's Guide to Haiku and Related Forms*, North Clarendon, VT: Tuttle Publishing.

Schmid, M. S. and M. Keijzer (2009), 'First Language Attrition and Reversion among Older Migrants', *International Journal of the Sociology of Language* 200: 83–101.

Seligman, M. E. P. and M. Csikszentmihalyi (2000), 'Positive Psychology: An Introduction', *The American Psychologist* 55 (1): 5–14.

Stephenson, K. and D. H. Rosen (2015), 'Haiku and Healing: An Empirical Study of Poetry Writing as Therapeutic and Creative Intervention', *Empirical Studies of the Arts* 33 (1): 36–60.

Stork, B. (2020), 'Haiku and Healing: Creating Connections', *The Permanente Journal* 24: 19.176.

Summers, A. (2018), 'Foraging for Haiku! – Ginko', *The Haiku Foundation Forums* (retrieved 1 December 2021, from https://www.thehaikufoundation.org/forum_sm/index.php?topic=10648.0 'Foraging for Haiku!'.

Sunaba. (2019, 24 Dec 2021), '俳句は難しくない！俳句づくりのコツを知って "心のシャッター" を気軽に切ろう (Tr: Haiku is not difficult! Let's feel free to release the 'shutter of the heart' by knowing the tips for making haiku) (19 November 2019)' (retrieved 15 December 2021, from https://www.chintai.net/news/2019/11/19/49211/#.

Thoreau, H. D. (1862), 'Walking, *The Atlantic Monthly IX* (Lvi): 657–674.

Veenhoven, R. (2003), 'Arts-of-living', *Journal of Happiness Studies* 4 (4): 373–384.

Welch, M. D. (2020), 'Haiku and the Art of Forest Bathing', *Modern Haiku 51.1 Winter-Spring 2020*: 27–41.

Wenger, E. (1998), *Communities of Practice: Learning, Meaning and Identity*, Cambridge: Cambridge University Press.

5

Poetry Lasts Forever: Case Study of a 100-year-old Brazilian Poet and His Daughter

Ana Cecília de Sousa Bastos

Except for brief, rare moments in Accident and Emergency, over his 100 years (celebrated in June 2022) my father has almost never been hospitalized. Last year, due to an unusually powerful series of seizures, he was admitted to the Intensive Care Unit of a large hospital and ended up staying for five days. He is, generally, very healthy, despite having suffered from epilepsy since young adulthood and, more recently, from Parkinson's disease. Fortunately, we, his children, insisted on staying, refusing to leave him at the hospital on his own, without really understanding what was going on. We succeeded in this, which meant that we were able to minimize the extent and impact of certain hospital procedures. For instance, protocol required that he be tied to his bed, to stop him pulling out the wires and tubes connecting him to machines and medication. He tried to break free of them and get out of bed but was not allowed. To avoid this oppressive regime, my sister and I took turns to stand by his side and hold his hands.

The hospital environment, alongside the strong sedatives and anti-seizure drugs he was taking, led to moments of mental confusion, when he did not understand where he was or why he was there. For a whole night and day, he called for my mother, the love of his life, who died eight years ago, soon after their 60th wedding anniversary. At times, he was very angry with his two daughters, because we would not take him home and, in his view, had agreed to keep him there, a prisoner stuck in a bed, tied down and with no clothes. 'Let me out! This is a crime!' he cried.

From time to time, he became delusional and wanted to get up and go and teach his classes. In his mind, he was 19 years old again and recently arrived in the big city from a little town in the countryside. Inadvertently, I told him he was no longer teaching and the school he wanted to go to no longer existed. He became desperate and asked: 'where am I going to sleep today?!' When he was 19, he was poor and lived at the school, exchanging Portuguese classes for rent. The feeling of helplessness that took hold of him in the hospital reminded him of his youth and showed us how he was feeling: losing his mind, in a way that had never happened before, was really distressing.

My father is lucid, in full possession of his faculties and able to make his own decisions. He is a professor and a poet and still organizes his daily routine, with readings and reflections, prayers and meditation, in his own idiosyncratic way. He watches the news and worries about the world and humankind, and is particularly concerned about the future of children and young people. He reads poetry every day. Some years ago, because of his neurological condition, he lost the ability to write, but he still has poetic thoughts that he brings to fruition. Sometimes, he creates poetically elaborated oral narratives and dictates verses to his children and grandchildren.

This chapter is based on my own narrative of my father's experience of poetry during his old age, in dialogue with both his and my writings, and his own reflections on the subject, following a recent interview I conducted with him. Methodologically, this is a scholarly, personal and autoethnographic work. The notion of poetic experience and how it changes over the life course is central both to my research – since I am trying to understand something about ageing and poetry – and to this narrative. Since I am a psychologist and poet myself, I will examine the frontier between human development and poetry, attempting to maintain a focus on poetry as human experience, rather than literary object (Lehmann et al. 2017). The notion of experiential wholeness (Abbey and Surgan 2012) is applied to this analysis, since it approaches the personal trajectory of a man who has struggled all his life to live sensitively and according to his ideals. Before presenting the poet, I will attempt to explain how I understand the two main concepts that constitute the background to this case study.

Poetic experience and experiential wholeness

Poetic art is born out of a sensitive experience of the world. When sensitivity combines with a particular writing technique, a poem becomes possible (Carvalho 1999). Rainer Maria Rilke (1910/2009), in *Os Cadernos de Malte Laurids Brigge [The Notebooks of Malte Laurids Brigge]* beautifully expresses this connection when he describes how long it takes to create a single verse: experiences, travels, encounters, farewells and memories are all required – memories that are forgotten to the point that they enter the poet's bloodstream and become indistinguishable from himself. These words show us how a poem depends on time. Poetic experience in itself, without taking account of the value of the poem, is ageless, and may become more beautiful as the poet ages, by incorporating time, wisdom and life experience into his writings.

Generally speaking, the poetic is part of every human experience (Lehmann 2015), anywhere and at any time, even when not linked to the writing of a poem or to a particular sensitivity. The origins of the word come from the Greek *poiesis*, the quality of something that is made or invented, implying the possibility of novelty (Bastos and Rabinovich 2009). In this sense, we speak of developmental poetics (Bastos and Rabinovich 2009), referring to the quality of transforming, and even expanding, our life horizons. Development entails change through poetic dynamics. This notion converges with the concept of poetic instants (Lehmann 2019), which are situations that arise out of everyday life, implying an interrelationship between the person and their immediate circumstances, one that changes their perception and enlightens everyday life, adding beauty and hope and, above all, expanding their sense of the present. When it involves novelty, ordinary experience therefore acquires a poetic quality. In this sense, poetry belongs to every human being. Many people are able to describe this experience in words; some, due to a heightened sensitivity and the need of expressing themselves, will write poems. Lehmann (2019) claims that 'the comprehension of poetic instants ... can lead to strategies to promote the perceived quality of life, and the consequent improvement of the quality of systems that persons coexist with' (62). Poetic instants may trigger turning points in people's lives. At any event, they have innovative potential, creating novelty and enhancing the future.

Strictly speaking, we may consider the poetic to be either the poet's own experience when creating a feeling or text (Freeman 2017), or the reader's experience when reading a poem (Vygotsky 1974). Poetry is the literary work as both process and result, and may be distinguished from other literary genres by its peculiar intensity, emotional burden, style, rhythm and music. Freeman (2017) integrates both approaches to the poetic when he says that:

> The first and most basic site of the poetic imagination is experience – specifically, how we relate to the world, both inner and outer. The second concerns the challenge, on the part of the experiencing person, of bringing experience to language. The third has to do with the process of writing, that is, the process by which the researcher/interpreter seeks to articulate in his or her own language the meaning and significance of what has been disclosed, whether by others or by oneself.
> (Freeman 2017: 139)

Moreover, poetry falls within an ancient oral tradition – if we think of the role of poetry in cultural realities such as Hinduism and ancient Persian, and in the Bible. The Brazilian poet Aleilton Fonseca (2021) argues that 'every poem is an epiphany, a game of divination with the meanings of words'. He notes that:

> Lyrical discourse goes beyond its own limits, since its effects are expanded by the polysemy of metaphors, a high degree of suggestion and the scope of language. The poet can say anything his imagination creates, because he works in harmony with everybody's perceptions. He accesses the collective unconscious and unveils what other people also feel without realizing.
> (Fonseca 2021: n.p.)

Similarly, Lehmann (2019) evokes Octavio Paz in connecting the word and silence with the poetic and spiritual lived experience: 'Poetic activity is born in the desperation of word's powerlessness, realizing the omnipotence of silence and thus, both poetic and religious lived-experiences change our nature of rupture (i.e., finitude), which could also mean a return to the original nature of totality' (58).

Poets may be highly sensitive people (Aron 1996/2013; Bastos and Rucker 2017) who long to be integrated to a totality, as Lehmann reminds us. Depending on particular constraints related to their interactions with personal, social, material and symbolic resources, highly sensitive people can poetically transform their lived experience. Sensitivity both opens up and closes down possibilities; these different directions should be analysed at the level of lived experience, organized within irreversible time and allow for 'experiential wholeness' (Abbey and Surgan 2012).

Human beings strive to adapt to an ever-changing and challenging world, while attempting to maintain a sense of continuity and stability, which represents the possibility of synthesis and restores a sense of order in time.

As Abbey and Surgan (2012) point out, experiential wholeness is closely connected to the human ability to approach the world through meaningful creations:

> We grasp the depths of our past, and [build] ways/strategies for moving toward an ever-uncertain future ... At the individual level, we actively build semiotic tools that mediate and regulate our relationships with the world, in order to face new situations as if they were part of larger totalities.
>
> (Abbey and Surgan 2012: 184)

The poet and professor

José Newton Alves de Sousa was born in Crato, Ceará, in the Northeast of Brazil, on June 5, 1922. His ancestors were of Brazilian indigenous and African origin. He married the great love of his life, Maria Ruth, and they lived together for 60 years, until her death in 2013. They had nine children and, to date, 17 grandchildren and seven great-grandchildren. His childhood memories focus on his mother's and grandmother's sweet and tender eyes and on the people who worked in his father's carpentry workshop, where the young José Newton sometimes built small cars and toys. He remembers the day he brought bricks to help his parents build their house. There were also games that he played, free as a bird, in his large back garden and out on the streets, as well as the deeply religious atmosphere that would remain with him throughout his life.

At the time, Crato had an intense and fertile cultural life. He had many opportunities to read and reflect. At the age of 19, he travelled to Salvador, the capital of the state of Bahia, to study medicine. He started teaching Portuguese to pay the bills and discovered his vocation as a teacher. As my brother Paulo said once, becoming *Professor José Newton* was a matter of time, love, natural talent, vocation and commitment.

Poetry has accompanied José Newton almost his entire life. In 1941, when he was still an adolescent, he printed a booklet of his first poems: *O Canto das Gerações Novas [The Song of New Generations]*. He maintained this format for the frequent editions he printed throughout his youth and adulthood; although in the last two decades his children have collected his poems and poetic writings for formal publication and national distribution. Prior to this, José Newton had been happy to print his poems himself and give them to family and friends. To justify these editions, he used to say: 'poetry doesn't cause any harm'.

He has published 33 poetry books over nine decades. His main themes are: his homeland, love, the sea and spirituality.[1] In his introduction to the recently published

---

[1] The following titles illustrate the poet's main themes: homeland (*Caririenses. Poemas e Postais [Cariri Land. Poems and Postcards]*, 1972, *Poeminhas de Era Uma Vez [Little Poems from Once Upon a Time]*, 1976); love (*Meu Cântico dos Cânticos [My Song of Songs]*, 1954, *José Newton e Maria Ruth, Uma História de Amor e Fé [José Newton and Maria Ruth, A Story of Love and Faith]*, 2017); the sea (*Poemar. Novos Poemas à Beira Mar [Poemar. New Poems by the Sea]*, 1982); and spirituality (*Sinfonia Interior [Inner Symphony]*, 1941, *Ramilhete para Telúricos e Transcendentais [A Bouquet for Telluric and Transcendentals]*, 1969).

Anthology to celebrate his upcoming 100th birthday – on June 5, 2022 – the poet Assis Lima says:

> His poetry is symphonic, due to its inner resonance, and polyphonic, due to the plurality of voices, whose foundations are formed by the sea, a loving spirit and a mystical pathway. Poetry strengthened by faith, lived in a state of grace and nourished by love.
> (Sousa 2022: 15)

Married and with four children, he returned to his hometown to become the Dean of a new Faculty of Philosophy, which later became a university, a project he headed for a long time. He and Maria Ruth also founded a school, which they ran together for eleven years. The poet was always present. In my mind I have an image of him coming home with a package of his recently printed poems, a little embarrassed at having spent money on this, instead of on household expenses. His teacher's salary was inadequate and sometimes uncertain; at the school they founded, our parents' hearts always spoke louder than any profit they could have made from it. Ours was a large family, its doors always open for others to come and live in our home. Although it spread love and education, this management by heart also led to the school's closure, a wound in the poet-teacher's heart, which was only eased by Maria Ruth's objectivity and practical good sense. 'The beans and the dream': this was how they often described themselves, Maria Ruth realistic, José Newton a dreamer. The latter often lived within an idealized world of dreams and beautiful projects, while Maria Ruth took care of the concrete, more mundane side of life. This image encapsulates certain important periods in our family life.

They decided to start afresh and moved back to Salvador, where José Newton continued working as a professor in two of the city's main universities. Everywhere he taught, he left an impression of competence, kindness, poise, integrity and elegance. The poet continuously reveals himself in his inexhaustible capacity for emotion, dreams, renewal and the enhancement of life. For his children and grandchildren, this capacity for wonder when faced with the world, with any natural or human scene, remains one of his strongest features.

In his introduction to the Brazilian edition of the *Noche Escura del Alma [The Dark Night of the Soul]* (the famous poem by Juan de la Cruz, the sixteenth-century Spanish poet and Christian mystic), the scholar Faustino Teixeira (2008) refers to this capacity for wonder, which is doubtless the raw material of poetry, as 'adhesion to cosmic beauty', when everything is absorbed into the soul: 'sung in its dignity, discovered in God and passionately loved in its greatness' (12).

On his 98th birthday, José Newton shared this reflection with me:

> I only have cause to acknowledge my happiness and to thank God for what I am. Within every human situation, I have been able to experience different possibilities, not limited to the self, but by maturing in communion with the other. I am grateful for the many occasions where I have been what I was, what I am and what I should be!

I myself recognize him in this poem he wrote in his thirties, which was included in the above-mentioned celebratory Anthology: 'The boat on the sea. / Cold, opaque afternoon. / Sad hills, absent singing. / Quests on the horizon, / and I, trapped in the Mystery, / pilgrim of the Infinite[2] (Sousa 2022: 52).

The last two verses of a poem I wrote some years ago describe my father in his old age:

>An old man crosses the street towards the bus stop.
>This street seems to be fixed inside me.
>The grimace in this man's mouth, the secret pain,
>twitches in my own face.
>Age, life and the umbrella heavy on his shoulders.
>There is my father who is sick.
>There he walks like an ancient being.
>Life is so fragile,
>being is so strong.
>
>(Bastos 2015: 42)

My father, his old age, and me

When I realized that my father was an old man, he was approaching his 90th birthday and dealing with the first symptoms of my mother's Alzheimer's disease. He was 92 years old when she died from cancer, and they were in love to the end. Very ill, she used to call him to her bedside just to say, 'I love you'. During her last years, he accompanied her to every activity, from meetings with family and friends to frequent medical appointments. After her death, when we, as his children, tried to distract him with suggestions of gentle activities, instead of trying to avoid it, he faced and even transcended, his pain, as we see in this poem:

><u>Beyond the extreme hour</u>
>Next to you, in the extreme hour, a bond of coexistence wrapped me
>in continuous time.
>Gradually, your movements ceased, until your soul,
>taking flight from your suffering body,
>was ready to receive the welcome embrace of God.
>I held back my emotions, letting our entire married life shine
>in that single moment.
>Your children, relatives and friends, the doctors and nurses were one reality,
>at that moment when you surrendered your soul to God.
>No dryness, no despair,
>for you were yourself to the end.

---

[2] This poem and the following poems and reflections were translated by the author.

> Now, however, we live in a new time, not without you,
> but with your memory,
> with your life and your being.
> Ruth yesterday, Ruth today, Ruth always.
> A blessed experience of love.
>
> (Sousa 2022: 191)

My father was quite healthy in himself, independent in his movements in both the home environment and outside. When he became a widower, we turned to him the attention that had, to a certain extent, been concentrated on my mother. We needed to manage his routines. Most of his children had busy working lives. One was unemployed and living in the house at the time, and the feeling that someone still depended on him was important. Later, this son changed direction, but kept the house as his symbolic home and came back to spend one or two nights there every week.

However, our symbolic farewell to my father began with his poetry, two decades ago. In 2002, on his 80th birthday, my mother and all of us, his children and grandchildren, wrote messages to honour him in a collected volume of most of his writings. I then had the occasion to read all his poetry books and select poems for inclusion in the book, called *A Life in Poems* (Sousa, 2002). I had read many of his poems – when I was a teenager, I used to type up his writings on a typewriter. But I had never before been faced with the full ensemble of his work.

Poetry came into my own life in its own way. To a large extent I share my father's sensitivity, even if the contents of my writing are quite different and interact with my own circumstances and worldview (See also Freeman in this volume). However, when I dived into his poetry, I was astonished to see the extent to which my own poems had acquired the – lyric or existential – imprinting of the poems he wrote when he was young. At certain times I even said to myself: I could have written this.

When he was 80, I did not view my father as an old man. He kept up his professional activities; he was still teaching and moving around the city of his own volition, attending to his multiple – cultural and religious – appointments. His family started undertaking a kind of review of his life and his presence in relation to us. His own personal life review, connected to ageing – he has always had a rich inner life – might have begun later. My personal message to him in the book *A Life in Poems* (2002) reflected this almost evaluative atmosphere and my own emotions:

> My father's poems have made his emotions untouchable throughout the years. In there, his gentle heart, his Poet's soul. In my father, the person and the poet are inseparable. He makes poetry simply by being the way he is. For him, making poetry is an act of generous, free giving, delicate and complete. (...)
>
>   My father is a safe haven in our lives, accepting that we are sometimes adrift, at the mercy of unpredictable tides.
>
> (Sousa 2002: 7)

Poetry is still the window through which I contemplate my father in his old age: both his self and his life. I have worked on other editions of his poems, always celebrating his birthdays: his 90th and his 97th. For his upcoming 100th birthday, I've been helping the poets Assis Lima and Everardo Norões organize an Anthology of José Newton's poetry, which is a collection of precious gems.

Of course, I am also very much engaged in caring for him: assisting him at medical appointments, supervising or directly managing his medication, supporting him in keeping up his cultural and social activities, for which he increasingly relies on his children's help. I am also in charge of handling his financial affairs. More than this, I am the oldest of his nine children and feel a great affinity with him, in terms of sensitivity and poetry, but also as a professor who has worked at the same universities.

Old age and the pandemic

The coronavirus pandemic opened up other windows through which I could view my father's old age. Here I will sketch certain scenes that stand out for me. For a while, life overtook my writing and reflections: I wasn't able to put this time into words, so powerful was it, so demanding in terms of everyday household tasks and caring for the family. Now, I've been taking advantage of a short holiday to reflect on the compelling experience we've been through over the last two years, when my father definitely became an old man, and I faced my own ageing particularly intensely. For both him and for me, editing books has been a powerful coping mechanism to get through these times.[3]

In the next section, I will organize my narrative around two situations that summarize my own perception of José Newton's life experience during the pandemic, as an old man and, always, as a poet. As a backdrop to these little sketches, I will revisit certain poems. Poetic experience is the switch that lights up the stage.

Situation 1. Living with his daughters and their families

When the unexpected and frightening shock of the pandemic arrived, my father (who was living by himself in his apartment, with regular, task-specific assistance from his children – especially his two daughters, my sister Beatriz and I, from domestic helpers) went to live with his daughters in their homes. For the first year, he lived with me and my husband in our apartment. Very often my daughter, who has two children (then a three-year-old girl and a baby boy of four months), joined us for several weeks at a time. During the second year, we all moved to my sister's and my beach house on the island of Itaparica, near Salvador. My daughter, her husband and children, and occasionally my son, his wife and two girls, joined us for weekly visits. For nine months, we therefore had the unusual experience of living as an extended family. This was both a blessing and a challenge.

For the first time in his life, outside of weekends and celebratory family meetings, José Newton was living with his daughters and their families. He was able to witness his great-grandchildren developing in a way he'd not been able to witness his grandchildren,

---

[3] My brother, Paulo de Tarso, himself a poet, and I edited José Newton's *Human Landscapes (Paisagens Humanas)*, a digital booklet containing writings made during his nineties, while I edited *The Impossible Transcription (A Impossível Transcrição)*, by Mondrongo Publishers.

or even his own children, who'd grown up when he worked three shifts a day, most days a week.

I am not talking about a holiday: but about living together for a year and a half. José Newton and Pedro, his youngest great-grandson (who was four months old in the beginning), became very attached to each other, something that enchanted me – and not only me, but my husband and his parents too. This relationship is filled with poetic experience, in its potential to move beyond the situation, adding joy and beauty to everyday life during those pandemic days.

During this time, I had many opportunities to witness, once again and in an everyday context, my father's way of poetically navigating life: he continued to see beauty in small details, to contemplate the life around him with renewed intensity and daily motivation, but also to suffer at news about the world and, particularly, about his country. Like the wise man he is, he is able to grasp minor and major life circumstances and turn them into true poetic instants – living with such a perceptive wonder that his immediate reality is expanded, both for himself and for the people with whom he relates (Lehmann 2015, 2019).

I am aware that these opportunities to create the space required to witness his process and keep him company were due to his specific style and to the way I was able to be present within the situation. Retired and entering old age myself, I feel I had a different perspective on my father's being. I was able to contemplate his ageing process in a way that was new to me, since I was experiencing a different relationship with time myself – with some stillness and some wisdom. His personal style reminded me to see the world through a stronger poetic lens.

By my father's side, I realized that, like all of us, he needed to adapt to this moment of confinement – which, in his case, involved leaving his own home, getting used to new places (away from his bedroom and, particularly, from his office at home) and dealing with different people from several generations, all with their own peculiar rhythms and styles. And he was an old man: 97 years old at the beginning of the pandemic. And that is exactly what he looks like: moving slowly, with continuous help from a stick; with increasing difficulty in articulating his speech; often choking when eating; and having lost the ability to write. His medical staff included a neurologist, a geriatrician, a general practitioner (who is his nephew), as well as a physical therapist, and a speech and language therapist. During the pandemic, all his appointments were held remotely, online.

Throughout the many changes he has experienced over the last two years, two things have remained strong for my father: poetry and faith. Secured by these two anchors, he remains a solid human being. This wholeness characterizes him and is felt by others in his family and in the educational and cultural contexts he still frequents – even participating in online meetings and live streaming events. He needs his children and grandchildren's support to handle the internet, experiences a feeling of wonder at these remote interactions and is always interested in understanding the mechanisms that enable these technologies. He elaborates on the meanings of 'on line', with a mixture of fear and fascination. Once he's in an online room, he follows the conversation and presentations, and speaks or asks us to write his messages in the chats, keeping the audience – many of them his former students – delighted and gratified by his presence and words, frequently expressing awe and respect. Of course, he is always the oldest person in the room.

My father has neurological problems (epilepsy, which has more recently developed into Parkinsonism). Three or four years ago he lost the capacity to write – to handwrite or type on his old machine. Suddenly, when he started living with us, he began to write again. This may be because of some new drills the speech and language therapist made him practice, or because he felt secure in this new family environment, constantly looked after by his two daughters. To some extent, he rediscovered the large family environment he lived in as a child and the family he raised with my mother. This is not a full recovery, because he cannot coordinate his ideas as clearly in writing as he can orally. He tried to write a short essay about a friend and a poem but was unable to finish them.

He has begun writing in very clear handwriting and enjoys the fact that his signature has been restored – he has, for instance, been able to sign dedications for friends in his books. Of course, there is still some way to go, with practice. I have tried to moderate both his and our expectations, in order to avoid more frustration later on.

Orally, however, he can express his ideas very clearly. Some themes are recurrent: worries about his country; his religion; some of his children, to whom he still provides some financial support. He makes recommendations about what should happen after his death, in a kind of testament in which he insists that we, his children, should not sell his apartment. He dreams of his children continuing to meet there. I wonder if this recurrent recommendation is a way of visualizing his children living in harmony after his death; a secure place, common to all, would guarantee this dream.

Reading; praying; contemplating nature and the family; making plans for the future: all this continues to constitute his routine. Around the family beach house, he dreams of a poetic garden to memorialize his loved ones for their descendants. A garden-memorial. It is not important whether these plans are feasible or whether his children will engage in making them happen: it is just something for him to dream about while he's alive. He is not stuck in the past, despite dearly missing his wife. He is very future-oriented. Undoubtedly, this capacity for dreaming protects him from the difficulties of our times, especially when the news upsets him. I can only really explain how his contemplation of life and world translates into poetry through a poem. I have chosen the poem 'Poetry travels alone', written in his thirties:

> The eyes became green,
> looking at the green sea.
> The eyes became deep,
> looking at the endless sky.
> (...)
> Poetry travels alone ...
> Who can see it?
> Who notices her?
> In the afternoon, which flutters,
> radiant, chaste, beautiful,
> the sky and the sea witness
> the solitude of Poetry,

> alone, among the passers-by,
> sipping in rays of light from the air,
> the eyes deep from the sky,
> the eyes green from the sea ...
>
> (Sousa 2022: 24)

When it comes to the garden, his persistent dreaming led my brother Roberto and his wife Maury to become involved and make it real: there are ornamental plants there now, representing each of José Newton's nine children.

Taking his life as a whole, from the present, I can see how his dreaming has had the power to inspire us to navigate hard times with hope. At least by not letting him lose heart along his long journey of teaching. His poetry has enabled us to maintain our own dreams as a family, despite eventually losing material and symbolic goods, such as the house where we once lived or the school that José Newton and Maria Ruth founded and ran for many years. That's why my mother used to say that he was the dream, and she was the bean, that is to say that she had to take care of the more concrete concerns. This is also a side of a poet's life course and is not always easy to deal with. Nevertheless, his dreaming has concretely expanded the family's life horizons. Many examples illustrating this impact come to mind. I have chosen one of these, which is particularly touching for me: his grandchildren have compared José Newton's capacity for wonder – more precisely, his capacity for cosmic adhesion (Teixeira 2008) – with the cynicism so prevalent in the contemporary semiosphere. As a result, they have gained a particular strength of persistence in their own personal projects. Of course, individual or collective family projects do not 'vaccinate' one against frustrations. But this a different reflection: what are the impacts of having a poet inspire the family? Let's believe that poetry brings benefits to everyone; although living poetically or relating to poets may not be that simple, poets and poetry let humanity be human.

To close this section, I'll include an entry from my journal, written on one of those pandemic days when we were living together (Bastos 2021). It is full of life. Mirroring my father's style, I look at his bruised feet and read condensed life stories in them, the substance of which poetry is also made. It is, in a way, contemplation with a poetic dimension. His bruised feet took me beyond the instant. They were no longer only his feet. Their literal meaning was transformed, through a dynamic that Abbey has called poetic motion (Abbey and Bastos 2014; Bastos 2017): in this situation, when I am able to contemplate, meanings move through words and change the everyday, opening windows onto life in its wholeness. In this sense, looking at my father's feet was a true poetic instant within my own experience:

> 'How beautiful upon the mountains are the feet of him who brings good news, who publishes peace' (Isaiah 52:7), as we sing at Mass.
> The stiffness of his feet contains entire narratives.
> Fear after falling so many times.
> Fear of falling.
> The rough surface.
> Chilblains.

Stains.
Nails so thick only pliers can cut them.
The residual that accumulates there.
The feet, the dents, the scars.
Fluids, odours, the anticipation of death.
All this is lived life, the body once young,
these feet that walked cities to bear us, his children.
To sustain dreams, so many, always.
Dreams that still sustain us.
Dreams dreamed for us and for all his offspring.
Tarsi scattered through the streets, as my brother Paulo would say.
Tired feet, in the absence of comfortable sneakers.
Sweaty clothes, jackets, heaviness.
Breastplates, disguises.
Smells ingrained in us, the smell of family, in colour and name.
In the smell of old age, life and death are condensed.

Situation 2: Recovering from hospitalization

My father experienced his five-day stay in the Intensive Care Unit as a kind of violence. Despite the excellent care and kindness of the medical staff, he reacted strongly to some of the treatments, and he experienced those days as if he were in a kind of prison, tied to a bed. He also suffered the side effects of the many medications he had to take to control the crisis. And everything was new and strange to him. He was indignant about being kept in bed; he couldn't understand what was going on; day and night, he had great difficulty sleeping. Even so, he tried to make sense of the strange situation. Was this a hotel room? Were we travelling somewhere? Who were these people, these doctors and nurses, what were their names, did they have children? He posed questions, but, probably because of the medication, he couldn't assimilate all the information he received. Fortunately, his doctors agreed to discharge him from hospital as quickly as possible, understanding that his behaviour was largely due to the strangeness of the hospital environment, as often happens with older people.

Indeed, my father felt much better at home. However, his unusual behaviour persisted: sometimes absent, at other times mentally confused and angry, which made simple tasks, like dressing or bathing, quite complicated. He was not in his usual frame of mind and did not engage in his usual activities; he didn't read, his conversation was vague and erratic. At certain moments, he seemed to be aware of his own strangeness. He once said to me: 'I'm kind of stunned. It seems like I'm going crazy'. After a few days, we found out that this behaviour was due to the increased doses of anti-seizure medication he was taking. The doctors made gradual changes – reducing the dosage and introducing a different medication, and his behaviour returned to normal. During the transition, which took a week, his struggle to make sense of the whole situation was even more evident. When he was better, he said: 'I'm back to my own self now'.

It was certainly a distressing experience for him. At home one day, still suffering from the effects of the medication, he woke up at 4 am, very anxious because he'd dreamt he had no name! Awake, he went to look for a pair of pyjamas with his name on; then he searched for his book, to see his name in print; finally, he sought out his identity card. He told his son: 'you cannot forget my name, you need to know that this is my name'. This struggle in search of his psychological integrity greatly moved us, his children. In this episode, his name became like a password to his self, in his search to restore a sense of experiential wholeness.

His personal progression was certainly supported by his affective bonds with the family. His younger child, Emanuel, who lives in another city, came to spend ten days with him, helping him with every detail, patiently waiting for him to come back to himself – as he would say. We stuck together to support him. Even little Pedro, to whom he is very attached, because they lived together during most of the pandemic, did his bit, as is evident from the episode narrated below.

The poetics of a reunion
José Newton, 99 years old.
Pedrinho, 1 year 10 months.
The pandemic gave them the gift of living together.
Father of nine children – a teacher working three shifts a day – grandfather of 17 grandchildren – with whom he mainly lived during the holidays – José Newton had never witnessed the everyday development of a baby this closely or intensely.
Living together for a year and a half created this immense novelty for both of them. The enchantment was mutual from the beginning. 'Tatá', 'Vovô Tatá [Grandpa Tatá]'. Pedro enjoyed the speech therapy exercises and from then on named his great-grandfather, who is resistant to nicknames, Tatá; and that was ok, because it came from his great-grandson.
The family experiences a return to normal life. Everyone returns to their respective homes.
Grandpa Tatá has health problems and is hospitalized for five days. He is at home, recovering well, but his convalescence is complex. One morning he is indisposed. He doesn't want to eat or even open his eyes. He can only speak with difficulty. Unexpectedly, Pedro arrives to visit and everything changes: his eyes are full of light now, he smiles, talks to his granddaughter, Pedrinho's mum. Grandpa Tatá holds Pedrinho. In their embrace, Pedrinho snuggles in Grandpa Tatá's lap. He stays there. They snuggle into each other. My daughter and I look at the scene in silence. No words, just emotion. Someone remembered to take pictures, which I later shared on social media. A friend of mine commented: 'If a grandmother is a mother with sugar, a great-grandfather is a grandmother inside a jar of jellybeans'.

The poet, old age and his poetry: An interview and recent writing

When asked in an interview conducted for this study how the feeling of poetry changes with age, José Newton reflects on old age and defines the feeling of poetry as something that does not need to be written down to exist or to organize experience of the world. 'I think old age is a second childhood. Fabricated poetry, with meter, is elaboration, not poetry. Feeling is something else. I tried to manufacture it once, but it didn't work out. In my experience, when I found the poetry of Cassiano Ricardo,[4] I saw that it was possible to be rational and sentimental [referring to writing free verses].' And does ageing change anything about this feeling? 'Ageing brings maturity! It doesn't change, on the contrary: you feel more vigorously, with greater awareness. I feel it.' Even when you are not able to write? , '*Poetry always comes*.'

Thus, poetry lasts forever. So does faith. This is José Newton's testimony. For him, intimacy with God and daily prayer overflow and become communicable and integrated through poetry. I can recall countless experiences in which poetic and religious experiences in José Newton are inseparable. The poem 'My soul on its knees", written in his later adulthood (also included in the 2022 Anthology) illustrates this connection well:

> My soul surrenders itself before God's face.
> In this very act of supreme annihilation,
> it becomes one with the Whole.
> Ah! Where, the uncertain vocatives,
> the shackles, the whips?
> Wings, in between light and infinity.'

The old poet faces physical limitations and experiences loneliness, especially after losing his wife, whom he loved dearly. During the interview, he describes his suffering as he thinks about a future that he views with so much uncertainty. He thinks about his country and the world, although he also has concerns about the future of his children. 'These times cry to heaven. Who will take care of the young?' At the same time, he evaluates his life and says: 'I am a happy man.' To finish, I have selected a text he dictated to one of his grandchildren three years ago, soon after he lost the ability to write. As he dictated, he was sitting in the hall of his building, watching people walking down the street. His neighbourhood is known for its many older residents. The text condenses a profound reflection, full of wisdom, including thoughts about his own finitude. Ageing and poetry come together in his words. I think of the concept of experiential wholeness as I attempt to create this synthesis of my father, a poet, at this moment in his life course.

> *Those who pass slowly but calmly, under the blessings of a heaven*
> Those who pass slowly but calmly, under the blessings of a heaven; I see them from afar, as if life has blessed them, letting them blossom calmly. What will be found in each tabernacle? In every prayerful heart of those who, with hesitant steps, await the last moment? In the white heads, in the minds that the days have nourished with life and hope?
> One by one, the steps continue. Tired, but revealing an inner life strengthened by the hope of a heaven that awaits them. This one, already bent by age, sees the sky when he looks at the ground, because life has demanded of him the hope of life

---

[4] Cassiano Ricardo is a Brazilian poet who founded the school of literary Modernism in Brazil.

without end. Others, without the balance of a laborious yesterday, show, in the mystery of existence, the hope of a tomorrow of blessings.

Some show how the calendar does not weaken, because the blessings of God take up residence in their depths. And those who barely see the life that holds them back hide, in the poverty of their body, the immortal light that emanates from the heart of God.

Do prayers shake this one, in the mystery of a self wounded by poverty but nourished by hope? They were all little children once, yesterday they were offered the milk that springs from every mother, amidst the pains of childbirth. They go through life with the mercy of God as their encouragement in pain, with faith in existence.

Every day I see them walking, already weakened by the calendar. In the existence of each one there will, of course, have been moments when every hour is hunger, sorrow, and sadness. Despite the fragility that so painfully builds our nights and our dawns, faith has always existed to illuminate our very interior.

In the meditation that the grace of God prescribes with hope and faith, it is up to me not to forget that I myself am called away from the rhythm of walking or life itself. I am awaited by the seven spans [the grave] contained in each moment. But there is hope that a blessed eternity will secure the calendar, without the marking of days and nights, but under the blessings of God who, in substance, is Love.

I feel, as a reality involving life itself, that a pulse of hope, emanating from an interior attentive to the goodness of the Creator, strengthens me, as I wait for the time that ends here and for tomorrows without a calendar.

The street where I live is an arena for a wide variety of yesterdays, which mark past times for the mystery of tomorrows. How do we stay between hope and negativity? How to live without merely existing?

The hours don't attempt to find out if it's night or if it's morning. Waiting for God's love is waiting without despair.

Everything comes together in this text: there is a synthesis of the poet's sensitivity, wisdom, faith and poetic experience. He expresses a profound empathy towards the old people who walk down the street, their steps opening up the whole horizon of their lives:

> Those who pass slowly but calmly, under the blessings of a heaven; I see them from afar, as if life has blessed them, letting them blossom calmly. What will be found in each tabernacle? In every prayerful heart of those who, with hesitant steps, await the last moment? In the white heads, in the minds that the days have nourished with life and hope?

He contemplates the various circumstances that surround ageing: solitude, poverty. Religious faith as a central axis. The poet goes on to ask about his own finitude, and his words reveal a quiet expectation of death: 'it is up to me not to forget that I am myself called away from the rhythm of walking or life itself'. Although any arbitrary moment can bring death, he trusts that 'there is hope that a blessed eternity will secure the calendar without the marking of days and nights, but under the blessings of God who, in substance, is Love'. This eternity is a 'tomorrow without calendars'. For himself and for the other old people with whom he has shared this text, his words poetically provide an affirmation of hope against the feelings of despair that can prevail in hard times.

Everyone experiences ageing differently, as José Newton understands and as the theories of developmental psychology maintain. Despite this uniqueness, people can search to integrate their lived experiences into personal life philosophies, guided by culture (Zittoun et al. 2013; See Lehmann and Brinkmann in this volume). No matter how diverse and unexpected life might be, this search for experiential wholeness provides the individual with constant recognition. In this sense, they are a living example of someone who has succeeded in achieving congruence with their life story and its ethical orientation, capable of finding meaning in every life circumstance, qualities that Lehmann and Brinkmann (2019) emphasize when they connect ageing with resilience.

José Newton, my father. Poet and professor. A man of faith and courage. A highly sensitive, sweet person. I concluded my introduction to his last book with these words:

> Seeing my father, about to turn a hundred, marked by age but so strengthened in spirit and by poetry, by the joy of this commemoration, I find possible synthesis by exclaiming: 'life is so fragile, / and being is so strong'.
>
> (Bastos 2021: 13)

Because, throughout all his life and in all his poetry, my father's being has spoken out loud.

Ethical considerations

José Newton closely followed the writing of this chapter. He enthusiastically agreed to include his personal information and writings in the text. My brothers and sister read the manuscript and gave explicit permission to share the details of our family history. The poet José Newton Alves de Sousa gave me explicit permission to include his poems and texts (both partial and complete) in this chapter. When I finished writing, I read the manuscript to my father, splitting the reading into two parts so as not to overburden him. Prior to this, he knew the general idea but had only heard certain fragments. He was really touched and grateful to recognize himself in my words. He said: yes, that is José Newton. He was silent and meditative for the rest of the day. He was contemplating what he had heard. Every now and then, he asked me about the publication: where would it be printed, who would the readers be, etc. For me, this is a sign of how lucid and attentive he is to every detail. I asked if he would like me to cut anything from the text, but he said no, he agreed with everything. I felt that the most sensitive parts were when I mentioned his body and the recent episode of mental confusion, especially because he was not aware of it. Feeling his discomfort, I reassured him about the temporary nature of the episode and how quickly it had passed. We commented on the general meaning and relevance of sharing our experiences as poets, which can help people live, especially through hard times. Together we concluded that individuals and societies need poetry. He also gave me some feedback – he could see how I had elaborated poetically on his life and writing. He shared his belief that I have a gift as a writer. I said that, if I do, it comes from him. In the experience of writing this chapter, the search for informed consent was truly a poetic instant.

Acknowledgements

I would like to thank Olga Lehmann and Oddgeir Synnes for their insightful comments about the manuscript. I would also like to thank the poet Olga Lehmann for her sensitive suggestions when revising my translation of José Newton's poems.

References

Abbey, E. and A. C. Bastos (2014), 'Creating Bridges to the Future: The Poetic Dimension Through Family Life', *Culture & Psychology* 20 (2): 232–243. https://doi.org/10.1177/1354067X14527840

Abbey, E. and S. Surgan (2012), 'Coming Closer to the Phenomenon: Better Understanding the Process of Human Meaning-Making', In E. Abbey and S. Surgan (eds), *Emerging Methods in Psychology*, 183–195. New Brunswick, CT: Transaction.

Aron, E. (1996/2013), *The Highly Sensitive Person*, New York: Kensington Publishing Corp.

Bastos, A. C. S. (2021), *A Impossível Transcrição (The Impossible Transcription)*, Itabuna, Bahia: Mondrongo.

Bastos, A. C. S. (2017), 'Shadow Trajectories: The Poetic Motion of Motherhood Meanings Through the Lens of Lived Temporality', *Culture & Psychology* 23 (3): 408–422. doi: 10.1177/1354067X16655458

Bastos, A. C. S. (2015), *Escritos Extraídos do Silêncio (Writings Extracted from the Silence)*, São Paulo: Scortecci.

Bastos, A. C. S. and E. P. Rabinovich (2009), 'Realities of Living: From Poverty to Poetry, and Beyond', in A. C. S. Bastos and E. P. Rabinovich (eds), *Living in Poverty: Developmental Poetics of Cultural Realities*, xiii–xxvi, Charlotte, NC: Information Age Publishing.

Bastos, A. C. S. and G. E. Rucker (2017), 'Living Against and Persistence of Being: Poetic Sharing of Being Sensitive Within Antagonistic Worlds', in O. Lehmann, N. Chaudhary, A. C. S. Bastos and E. Abbey (eds), *Poetry and Imagined Worlds*, 99–118, Cham, Switzerland: Palgrave.

Carvalho, F. (1999), 'Todas as Palavras Queimam' (All the Words Burn), in A. C. S. Bastos (ed.), *Uma Vaga Lembrança do Tempo (A Vague Remembrance of Time)*, iv. Salvador: Fundação Casa de Jorge Amado.

Fonseca, A. (2021), 'A poesia é a vacina da alma' (Poetry is the vaccine of the soul). Interview to Katia Borges. *Correio da Bahia 24h*, 20 February. Available online: https://www.correio24horas.com.br/noticia/nid/a-poesia-e-a-vacina-da-alma-diz-aleilton-fonseca-sobre-novo-livro/)

Freeman, M. (2017), 'Living in Verse', in. O. Lehmann, N. Chaudhary, A. C. S. Bastos and E. Abbey (eds), *Poetry and Imagined Worlds*, 139–154, Cham, Switzerland: Palgrave.

Lehmann, O. (2019), 'The Poetic Resonance of an Instant: Making Sense of Experience and Existence through the Emotional Value of Encounters', in G. Marsico and L. Tateo (eds), *Ordinary Things and Their Extraordinary Meanings*, 53–75, Charlotte, NC: Information Age Publishing.

Lehmann, O. (2015), 'Poetic Instants in Daily Life: Towards the Inclusion of Vertical Time in Cultural Psychology' in B. Wagoner, N. Chaudhary and P. Hviid (eds), *Integrating Experiences: Body and Mind Moving Between Contexts*, 165–177. Charlotte, NC: Information Age Publishing.

Lehmann, O. and Brinkmann, S. (2019), '"Humbled by Life": Poetic Representations of Existential Pathways and Personal Life Philosophies Among Older Adults in Norway', *Qualitative Inquiry* 27 (1): 102–113.

Lehmann, O., N. Chaudhary, A. C. S. Bastos and E. Abbey, eds (2017), *Poetry and Imagined Worlds*, Cham, Switzerland: Palgrave.

Rilke, R. M. (2009), *Os Cadernos de Malte Laurids Brigge (The notebooks of Malte Laurids Brigge)*, Rio de Janeiro: L&PM. (Original published 1910.)

Sousa, J. N. A. (2022), 'Poemas de Todas as Horas Antologia Comemorativa' (Poems from Every Hour. A Celebrative Anthology). Selection and organization by A. Lima, A. C. S. Bastos and E. Norões. Rio de Janeiro: Confraria do Vento.

Sousa, J. N. A. (2020), *Paisagens Humanas' (Human Landscapes)*, Salvador: Mimeo

Sousa, J. N. A. (2019), *Escritos Reunidos ao Entardecer (Writings Reunited at Sunset)*, São Paulo: Scortecci.

Sousa, J. N. A. (2017), *Uma História de Amor e Fé. José Newton e Maria Ruth (A Story of Love and Faith. José Newton and Maria Ruth)*, São Paulo: Scortecci.

Sousa, J. N. A. (2002), *Uma Vida em Poemas (A Life in Poems)*, Salvador: Mimeo

Teixeira, F. (2008), 'Introduction', in *São João da Cruz, Noite Escura (Dark Night of the Soul)*, 5–14, Petrópolis: Vozes.

Vygotsky, L. S. (1974), *The Psychology of Art*, Cambridge, MA: MIT Press.

Zittoun, T., J. Valsiner, D. Vedeler, J. Salgado, M. Gonçalves and D. Ferring (2013), *Human Development in the Life Course: Melodies of Living*, New York: Cambridge University Press.

6

'An Old Man Can Do Somewhat': Styles of Male Old Age in Shakespeare's *Henry IV, Part 2*

Arthur W. Frank

Little in Shakespeare is ever one way or the other. Whether Shakespeare explores love, tyranny, or old age, he focuses on tensions, and these are both nuanced and unresolvable. That impossibility of resolution is what makes Shakespeare a realist, albeit on stage he shows reality stretched to its extremes. I turn to Shakespeare because his writing refuses to take a single point of view; he never endorses any one perspective. On Shakespeare's stage, characters are as divided within themselves as they are between themselves, endings seem tentative, and the only reliable expectation is for continuing change, with the direction uncertain.

Those qualities – nuance, impossibility of resolution, multiple points of view or the uncertainty of any point of view – characterize poetic language, though they hardly define it. We neither turn to nor utilize poetic language to explain or conclude. Poetic language brings us up against the inexplicable yet recognizable. It is language pointing beyond language. Shakespeare's language is poetic not because the words are beautiful – although they are – but because whatever they say or describe, they seem to be about something more. That is one reason why Shakespeare's plays can be endlessly restaged in new variations of time and place, and why they lend themselves so well to adaptation. Those who hear or read Shakespeare's poetic language are left feeling there is more at stake than what the story is ostensibly about.

I read *Henry IV, Part 2* (written below as *2HenryIV*) as a play *for* old age: a play that can teach us how to be old, though more often it shows how not to be old.[1] On stage, characters refer to themselves being old, but they do not speak in generalities about old age. Instead, their speech embodies old age itself; old age *is* what they enact. Shakespeare depicts old age not as a condition with inherent qualities; rather, old age comprises multiple *enactments* that either the characters account for with reference to their age, or we, whether theatre audience or readers, attribute to age. Or we might decide that age has little to do with what a character does.

---

[1] This attitude of reading – *attitude* in a phenomenological sense of how consciousness relates to the givenness of what it encounters in the world – is what I have called *vulnerable reading*. See Frank (2019, 2022).

This chapter explores Shakespeare's two poetic languages of old age: the narrative and the lyrical. These receive unequal emphasis. Most of my attention will be to the poetics of dramatic narrative in which characters act within a plot structure: they respond to specific circumstances and to actions of other characters, and they pursue ends that are variously well defined. Dramatic narrative shows actions having consequences, although these consequences are seldom dichotomously good or bad. The story, like life, is ongoing, concluding with an Epilogue that announces the action will continue in the next play in the series. In dramatic narrative, characters make choices; they have time and space in which to change, albeit their possibilities become progressively narrower. What's poetic is the language in which characters express their situations; in this linguistic evocation, what is specific becomes more resonant, with expanding applicability to the human condition.

Embedded within the dramatic narrative, but then capable of standing by itself outside the narrative, is a poetic language that can be called lyrical. Lyrical lines seem to drop into the play from an unknown elsewhere; they disrupt context by transcending their occasion of being spoken. Lyrical language evokes feelings within us; it expresses what would otherwise evade expression. Thus, less can be said about these lines, because what is lyrical is already at a boundary of linguistic expression. Narrative language earns being called poetic by how it echoes in our memory; lyrical language seems already to be an echo. While the lyrical moments in *2HenryIV* are fewer, their weight in the effect of the whole is far greater than how much stage time is spent speaking to them.

I focus on *2HenryIV* because no other of Shakespeare's plays offers such detailed variations on ways to enact old age. Or at least ways that *men* enact old age. Among the worlds that Shakespeare creates, that of *2HenryIV* is especially male dominated, and a limitation of working with the play is that the women in it have comparatively peripheral roles. The play presents six men whom we understand as old because they either refer to themselves as being old or others call them old. None of the characters' specific ages is specified, as age-in-years is rarely specified in Shakespeare. In both *Romeo and Juliet* and *Hamlet*, a prolonged dialogue is required to work out how old a character is – suggesting that in Shakespeare's time, one's age was not necessarily available knowledge.[2] What people understood as being *old* was not measured in years.

Shakespeare marks age mostly in terms of generational positioning: to be *old* is to be of an older generation. For four of the old men, being old involves being a father or a father figure. Paternity, whether biological or as a choice of affinity, is the measure of age, and I want to show that paternity depends on different relations of responsibility. Fathers or would-be fathers are more or less responsible toward their sons, in different

---

[2] Within a voluminous literature on who is how old in Shakespeare, a recent comment is Rhodri Lewis, 'How Old is Hamlet?' (2017: 315–24). In Charney (2009), some of the characters he discusses could be in their late thirties, yet within the play, they are cast as *old*. Writing about age in the Sonnets, Charney observes: 'That a youth's beauty will be transformed at forty into a tattered garment of little value comes as a surprise to us, but forty is already well on the way to fifty, the conventional year for the onset of old age in Shakespeare's time' (4). How conventional that age threshold was is an issue beyond the scope of this chapter. What matters is that Shakespeare does not specify age in years.

ways. The one son, Prince Hal (also called Harry) – he who will succeed his father and at the end of the play become Henry V – must choose between two old men to whom he is close; but who will be the father on whom he models his kingship? For anyone who knows the least bit of history, whom Hal chooses as the father he follows is not very suspenseful; we wait to see how it will happen, rather than what will happen. For this chapter, it is worth adding that Hal's choice is consistent with his character and situation; it is *not* Shakespeare's own affirmation of how best to live old age. If Hal's choice is best in any sense, it is best for the kingdom. But again, Shakespeare rarely gives us any singular *best* of anything. Victories always include a measure of loss.

The choices made by the play's old men are more subtle than Hal's choice. Their choices plot different ways to live a life that is in decline, including ways to recognize that decline, or refuse to recognize it. How each lives his old age reflects inescapable habits of how life has been lived. In the language that expresses these choices, we hear lyrical expressions that might be openings to a different way of knowing old age, or more accurately, a different way that old age can know the world.

2HenryIV is one of Shakespeare's most loosely plotted plays, the middle play in a trilogy. In *Henry IV, Part I*, the king who has usurped his cousin, Richard II, faces a rebellion by the nobles who had once supported him. Their leader is Harry Percy, known as Hotspur. Henry IV's other problem is his rebellious son Hal, who spends his time drinking in taverns in a group clustered around Sir John Falstaff, the fat knight who prefers carousing to battle and lives by committing literal highway robbery, but with results more comic than predatory. Hal joins his father, saves his life in battle, and kills Hotspur when they meet in the climactic scene. The rebellion seems resolved, but as *2HenryIV* opens, it continues, until it is suppressed in Act IV. As the rebellion is being suppressed, Henry IV becomes progressively more ill, dying at the end of Act IV. In Act V, Hal becomes Henry V.

Amidst these events, Falstaff spins a couple of scams: first to pocket money paid to him by men whom he has been sent to recruit for the battle against the rebels. They bribe him to avoid enlistment. While Falstaff is on that mission, he meets his old schoolmate, Justice Shallow, and proceeds to con him out of a considerable sum. When Hal succeeds to the throne, Falstaff believes his fortune is made, but the climactic moment of *2HenryIV* is Henry V repudiating his former friend, definitively breaking with his own wild youth. *1HenryIV* made the character of Falstaff immensely popular, and in *2HenryIV*, Falstaff is the star role with 20 per cent of the lines, to 9 per cent each for Hal and Henry IV. In *Henry V*, Falstaff never appears. His dying is reported after happening off stage. *Henry V* is about he who is no longer Hal showing himself to be the great warrior king, defeating the French at Agincourt.

Northumberland: Irresponsible paternity

The Earl of Northumberland has only 3 per cent of the lines in *2HenryIV*, but I begin with him because the play does, and his actions present one extreme among the variations on old age as paternity. In *1HenryIV*, Northumberland played a key role in planning the rebellion against Henry IV. But when it came to the actual battle, he claimed illness prevented him from joining his co-conspirators. Thus, he left his son, Harry Percy/Hotspur, badly outnumbered without his father's soldiers. *2HenryIV* begins with Northumberland receiving news of his son's death in that battle. That news shocks him out of his illness, and he plans to join what remains of the rebellion. His wife and his daughter-in-law, Lady Percy, the widow of Hotspur, seek to dissuade him from joining the rebellion, advising him instead to escape to Scotland.

The kind of father who Northumberland has chosen to be is expressed in a speech by the widow Lady Percy, recalling what Northumberland's abandonment of his son, her husband, meant:

> He [Hotspur] was the mark and glass, copy and book,
> That fashion'd others. And him—O wondrous him!
> O miracle of men! —him did you leave,
> Second to none, unseconded by you,
> To look upon the hideous god of war
> In disadvantage, to abide a field
> Where nothing but the sound of Hotspur's name
> Did seem defensible: so you left him.
>
> (2.3.31-8)

Lady Percy's speech mixes the narrative and the lyrical. As narrative, it fills in the backstory of the battle past, and it advances the present story of the ongoing rebellion. Yet, at least for me, its lyrical elements overshadow its narrative function: The word play of 'Second to none, unseconded by you', the metaphorical force of 'To look upon the hideous god of war / In disadvantage,' the unexpected usage of 'to abide', and the finality of 'so you left him' all make the speech an expression of betrayal that exceeds its narrative context.

Northumberland readily takes their advice, and the scene ends with him departing for Scotland. It's his final appearance. I ask myself, why he is in the play at all? *2HenryIV* shows variations on the relationship between an older generation and a younger one, and that relationship is *moral* in the sense that it involves how to be responsible toward another to whom responsibility is owed. Northumberland is there, at the beginning of the play, to be a father who fails his son: 'him did you leave ... so you left him.' Lady Percy's words are devastating, calling out Northumberland for his failure to support his son whose actions he himself instigated, leaving him to probable defeat and death.

As brief as Northumberland's part is, he enacts old age as one side of a relation of intergenerational responsibility. In Lady Percy's speech, Northumberland's failure is not that Henry IV still rules; the failure is that he did not fight beside his son. We don't know how old Northumberland is; years hardly matter. What matters are responsibilities between generations, falling more on one than the other, at different times. Harry Percy was a better son in his responsibilities than Northumberland was a father. We now turn to other fathers who are given more to say and do, but Northumberland's two scenes of one father's failure have established old age as one side of a generational tension.

Henry IV: The last grasp

Throughout *2HenryIV* old age is haunted by the prospect of death, as when Falstaff warns 'do not speak like a death's-head' (2.4.231). When dying happens, it is haunted by past actions that remain fresh in memory.

Henry IV's protracted dying scenes lead toward the climactic moment of Henry V's repudiation of Falstaff; Henry's death is necessary to force his son's choice. The scenes of dying follow immediately after the resolution of the nobles' rebellion against Henry. During the first half of Act IV, Henry's second son, Prince John of Lancaster, meets with the rebel leaders, promises that their demands will be heard if they disband their army, and as soon as they do so, he orders their execution. Prince John's response to their charge that he acted in bad faith is a fine example of what the Elizabethans knew as equivocation: most basically, a use of language to deceive without lying, in the strictest sense.

> I promis'd to redress of these same grievances
> Whereof you did complain; which, by mine honour,
> I will perform with a most Christian care.
> But, for you rebels, look to taste the due
> Meet for rebellion and such acts as yours.
>
> (4.2.113–17)[3]

This anti-climactic end of the rebellion prepares for Henry's death by finishing what was unfinished business. But as I reflect on the sequence of events, Prince John's actions perpetuate what has always been the questionable legitimacy of Henry IV's reign, its dark side. In *Richard II*, whether Henry consciously sets out to gain the throne, or if he sought only to reclaim his patrimony that Richard had seized and then one thing led to another, is left ambiguous. Richard had been an irresponsible ruler, but to displace God's anointed sovereign is always ominous.[4] Henry's dying is pervaded by his past catching up with him: his dying mixes guilt for the past with apprehension for how his son will rule, but above all, his dying shows his grasping desire to hold on, literally, to a crown he never held securely.

In Henry's dying scenes, the crown itself becomes another actor, spoken to as if it has independent agency—and Shakespeare's view may be that it does. The death is operatic: Henry gives a farewell speech, seems to be dead, then Hal puts on the crown and goes into another room. Henry revives, frantic over where the crown is. Hal returns, makes amends in a speech that reconciles father and son, and Henry dies, this time for good. Throughout all this, the crown acts: it both oppresses Henry, and it is that which he refuses to let go of, setting him against his son. The drama of Henry's dying, and his variation on old age, hinge on his refusal to give up the crown.

---

[3] On equivocation in the politics of Shakespeare's time, see Shapiro (2015). I regret Shapiro does not discuss Prince John's treatment of the rebels.
[4] Or, almost always, because Shakespeare's political survival requires that the Tudor succession is the exception. When Henry Tudor defeats Richard III at the end of that play, that succession could not be a usurpation while Henry's granddaughter was on the throne.

Henry is a far more responsible father than Northumberland, but he represents an older generation that is unwilling to cede its position to the younger. The tensions of Henry's kingship, and what makes him old, are first expressed in Act III, when Henry gives a long soliloquy complaining about his insomnia:

> How many thousand of my poorest subjects
> Are at this hour asleep! O sleep, O gentle sleep,
> Nature's soft nurse, how have I frighted thee,
> That thou no more wilt weigh my eyelids down,
> And steep my senses in forgetfulness?
>
> (3.1.4–8)

Henry may mean 'how have I frighted thee' as a rhetorical question, but it has a specific answer: he has frightened away sleep by his usurpation of Richard; his wakefulness reflects his guilt. Henry prefers to attribute it to the stress of ruling. The speech ends with one of the play's most widely quoted lines, 'Uneasy lies the head that wears a crown' (3.1.31), which as Henry says it about himself is both true and self-serving. That combination is who Henry is. Prince John, after sending the nobles to their execution, probably doesn't lose any sleep. Henry, having dispatched a king, never again sleeps soundly.

The psychology being played out is summarized by the Earl of Warwick, one of the nobles attending Henry. Warwick expresses the inevitability of how old age recapitulates the life that has preceded it.

> There is a history in all men's lives
> Figuring the nature of the times deceas'd;
> The which observ'd, a man may prophesy,
> With a near aim, of the main chance of things
> As yet not come to life, who in their seeds
> And weak beginnings lie intreasured.
>
> (3.1.80–5)

Henry's dying is what those seeds look like when they have fully come to life and now are passing into death. Prince John's equivocation shows one way those seeds develop in the next generation; the career of Henry V shows another.

How the cares of office have worn down Henry is repeated by those around him as he dies. In an anticipatory eulogy, perhaps even an apology for how Henry has lived, his youngest son, Thomas, Duke of Clarence, speaks of 'Th'incessant care and labour of his mind' (4.4.118). But the longest speech is Hal's, as he sits beside his sleeping father. He picks up from his father's earlier speech about sleep, but now displaces the trouble onto the crown, which he personifies or anthropomorphizes:

> Why doth the crown lie there upon his pillow,
> Being so troublesome a bedfellow?
> O polish'd purturbation! golden care!

> That keep'st the ports of slumber open wide
> To many a watchful night!
>
> (4.5.20–4)

Hal eventually puts on the crown; his motives, like those of his father long before, are mixed. He expresses feelings of having waited long enough for his inheritance, but also he is relieving his father of a burden that has oppressed him. Taking the crown seems both appropriation and generosity, in a relation we cannot parcel out. It is also unclear whether Hal believes his father to be already dead.

> ... My gracious lord! My father!
> This sleep is sound indeed; this is a sleep
> That from this golden rigol hath divorc'd
> So many English kings. Thy due from me
> Is tears and heavy sorrows of the blood,
> Which nature, love, and filial tenderness
> Shall, O dear father, pay thee plenteously.
> My due from thee is this imperial crown,
> Which, as immediately from thy place and blood,
> Derives itself to me. (*Putting it on his head.*)
>
> (4.5.33–42)

I note how this speech balances 'Thy due from me' with 'My due from thee'. Then Hal leaves the room. Henry's sleep was less sound than it appeared. He awakens, demanding of his attendants both where Harry is and where the crown has gone. Henry's rage shows old age at its most grasping:

> The Prince hath ta'en it hence. Go seek him out.
> Is he so hasty that he doth suppose
> My sleep my death?
> Find him, my Lord of Warwick, chide him hither.
> This part of his conjoins with my disease,
> And helps to end me. See, sons, what things you are,
> How quickly nature falls into revolt
> When gold becomes her object!
>
> (4.5.59–66)

Henry's speech continues, elaborating all the work that fathers do for their sons, only to be 'murder'd for our pains' (4.5.78).

Warwick returns and tells Henry that his son was in the next room, 'in great sorrow' for his father (4.5.84). 'But wherefore did he take away the crown?' Henry replies (4.5.88). He then berates Harry, who has returned:

> I stay too long by thee, I weary thee.
> Doth thou so hunger for mine empty chair

> That thou wilt needs invest thee with my honours
> Before thy hour be ripe? O foolish youth!
> Thou seek'st the greatness that will overwhelm thee.
>
> (4.5.93–7)

Multiple fears define Henry's age and his dying. As ironic as Henry may be saying 'I stay too long', those in old age do fear becoming tiresome; old age is afraid that the younger generation wishes only to seize what the old have built up. Finally, old age expresses the resentful prophecy, which might be half a wish, that the younger generation will never be what the older has been: they will be overwhelmed when they actually have to do what the elder has done. Henry's speech is long, continuing for 46 lines.

Hal replies with an almost equally long speech. He again addresses the crown directly, 'upbraiding it': 'But thou ... Hast eat thy bearer up' (4.5.158, 164). Henry accepts this most eloquent of apologies and gives another long speech in which he acknowledges his own questionable past:

> ... God knows, my son,
> By what by-paths and indirect crook'd ways
> I met this crown....
> How I came by the crown, O God forgive,
> And grant it may with thee in true peace live!
>
> (4.5.183–5, 218–19)

Henry's sons and attendant lords return, and he dies surrounded by those who honour him. But the effects of his 'indirect crook'd ways' remain. In the next play in the sequence, when Henry V faces the overwhelming French forces at Agincourt, he tries to keep up at least his own morale by telling an attendant lord to 'think not upon the fault / My father made in compassing the crown' (*Henry V*, 4.1.249–50). He specifies the amount he pays priests to pray for Richard's soul but concludes: 'Though all that I can do is nothing worth, / Since that my penitence comes after all' (*Henry V*, 4.1.259–60). As Henry once came back to life when Hal thought his sleep was death itself, so he remains a presence demanding his son's continuing penitence, which, however, will always be 'nothing worth'. Thus the presence of the dying and the life they lived reverberate after death.[5]

Henry's dying, both haunted and honoured in equal measure, deconstructs the ideal of a good death. Shakespeare, I think, would smile at such a notion. A death is rarely unambivalently good nor bad, but some mixture of both, as the life preceding it has been. Nor is one person's death ever theirs alone. Henry dies amid ongoing, troubled dialogue with his son, attended by his nobles, but most of all, he dies tied to his crown that has both acted to specific effects – it has frightened away sleep – and is a potent symbol of intergenerational inheritance, as that is both desired and resisted by

---

[5] On ghostly presences in Shakespeare, see Garber (2010).

father and son, each in his own way. As long as Henry has any life, he will not give up the crown.

The Chief Justice: Responsibility as law

Soon after we first meet Falstaff, he is accosted by the Lord Chief Justice who pursues him for failure to appear in court on robbery charges. Falstaff is tentatively protected by being called for military service to repress the rebellion. Their encounter becomes a verbal duel in which the Chief Justice and Falstaff each castigates the other for how he lives his old age. Thus, the play first refers explicitly to old age by making it a cause for insult.

Falstaff deflects the legal charges against him with banter about the Chief Justice's age:

> I am glad to see your lordship abroad, I heard say your lordship was sick. I hope your lordship goes abroad by advice; your lordship, though not clean past your youth, have yet some smack of age in you, some relish of the saltness of time; and I most humbly beseech your lordship to have a reverend care of your health.
> (1.2.93–9)

The Chief Justice is not wholly distracted from his duty at hand, but he is drawn into the game of mutual insults, replying to Falstaff:

> You are as a candle, the better part burnt out.
> ....
> There is not a white hair in your face but should have his effect of gravity.
> (1.2.155–6, 159–60)

Again, they play a verbal game; the point is not to parse the exact meaning of each insult, but to feel the flow of the competition. Insults escalate as Falstaff positions himself as younger and oppressed by resentful elders: 'You that are old consider not the capacities of us that are young; you do not measure the heat of our livers with the bitterness of your galls' (1.2.172–5). The Chief Justice replies by describing Falstaff with a sequence of stereotypes of old age:

> Do you set down your name in the scroll of youth, that are written down old with all the characteristics of age? Have you not a moist eye, a dry hand, a yellow cheek, a white beard, a decreasing leg, an increasing belly? Is not your voice broken, your wind short, your chin double, your wit single, and every part of you blasted with antiquity? And will you yet call yourself young?
> (1.2.177–84).

Falstaff seems to get the last word: 'the truth is, I am only old in judgment and understanding' (1.2.190–1). That is a good line, although it is anything but the truth as Falstaff himself occasionally acknowledges. The Chief Justice exits, admonishing

Falstaff to go about his military duties. Left alone, Falstaff expresses greater honesty about his intentions: 'A man can no more separate age and covetousness than [he] can part young limbs and lechery' (1.2.229–31). That may be the biggest insult to old age, and it foreshadows Henry's dying grasp of his crown.

What should be made of this dialogue of insults about who shows the greater effects of age? Shakespeare may only be using the trope of old age for a quick laugh, but he usually jokes to some purpose. This scene occurs near the beginning of the play, and the characters will subsequently show us old age in a detail that reveals truths behind the clichés that the insult game trades in.

The Lord Chief Justice is one of Shakespeare's characters who is less a person than a representation; known only by his title, he represents the Law as a demand upon the old and the young alike. Hal, upon becoming king, must finally choose between Falstaff, the friend of his wild youth who represents misrule, and the Chief Justice, for whom majesty itself remains legally accountable.[6] From the perspective of the young, old age shows choices the young are vaguely aware of already making, as they approach a threshold of their own ageing. What choice does the Chief Justice represent?

I understand the Chief Justice as a model for Sigmund Freud's understanding of the super-ego (*über-ich*). Freud (1989a: 637–45); 1989b: 769–71) conceived the super-ego as the son's internalization of the power of the father. The son manages the threat posed by the father by turning it into his own internal commitment, even compulsion, to follow the Law prescribed by the father. The super-ego is the demanding voice of that Law, calling the ego – which in Freud's original German non-Latin usage is simply the *I* – to account for its actions. Hal's problem, at least one problem, is that his father is an imperfect representation of the Law: his usurpation of Richard violated a fundamental law. The Chief Justice represents the perfection of Law, and that is why we need to know as little about him as possible: his human flaws would render imperfect what he is in the play to idealize.

The speech in which the newly crowned Henry V declares his chosen paternity, addressing the Chief Justice, is a gloss on the work of the super-ego:

> You shall be as a father to my youth,
> My voice shall sound as you do prompt mine ear,
> And I will stoop and humble my intents
> To your well-practis'd wise directions.
> And Princes all, believe me, I beseech you,
> My father is gone wild into his grave,
> For in his tomb lie my affections . . .
>
> (5.2.118–24)

---

[6] The Lord of Misrule was a stock figure performed in Elizabethan country festivals that marked changes of season; he presided over drinking and dancing and depending on the season, he enacted 'the roughest pleasures of defiance and mockery' (Barber 1959: 24). Opposed to the Lord of Misrule was the figure of the killjoy, thus representing 'movement between poles of restraint and release in everybody's experience' (8). In *2HenryIV* Falstaff and the Chief Justice may be readily recognizable to audiences as the Lord of Misrule and the killjoy, respectively, but Shakespeare's art is how much more he makes of each, especially Falstaff.

In Henry's tomb lie Hal's affections, yet because Henry is 'gone wild' to that tomb – the effects of his usurpation still upon him – the Chief Justice must be the father who guides the future king. His voice becomes the super-ego, heard in the ear of the ego, prompting to right action, or action that is right because the super-ego prompts it.

Although Hal, now Henry V, praises the Chief Justice's 'well-practis'd wise directions', I cannot understand the Chief Justice representing what is often called the wisdom of old age. The Chief Justice describes himself as acting on behalf of the king, who is himself a representation of the law:

> I then did use the person of your father;
> The image of his power lay then in me;
> And in th'administration of his law,
> Whiles I was busy for the commonwealth ...
>
> (5.2.73–6)

It is law, the Chief Justice reminds the new king, 'That guards the peace and safety of your person' (5.2.88), and thus kings should willingly make themselves subject to the law. The Chief Justice's authority is *not* the wisdom of one man's accumulated years of experience. Rather, his authority depends on his office, and holding office requires the subordination of self to impartial law. Hal learns that lesson well.

I pause to note that among the variations of old age that Shakespeare shows us, none represents wisdom in the sense of accumulated personal experience. Subordination of self to office, not experience, is what 'well-practis'd wise directions' derive from. The idea that old age confers wisdom is not wholly absent in Shakespeare's plays, but I find it only momentarily in secondary characters, and these characters are less effective in asserting as much wisdom as they may have. My choices for Shakespeare's best representations of wise old age are Paulina in *The Winter's Tale* and Gonzalo in *The Tempest*. Paulina speaks truth to power, consistently telling the tyrannical king that his jealousy of his wife is groundless and cruel, and Gonzalo saves the life of the deposed Duke Prospero. But neither's wisdom by itself effects change. Both have to wait for events to set things right. Paulina plays a more active role, manipulating events to bring about the climactic moment, but she needs events she has not caused. The ability of wisdom to set things right seems contingent in its dependence on other factors.

Justice Shallow: Nostalgic old age

Justice Shallow first appears as a local magistrate whose duty is to assemble the men from whom Falstaff will choose recruits for the king's army against the rebels. Falstaff senses further opportunity and returns to visit Shallow after the rebels have been dispersed. He now seeks to borrow – with no intention of repaying – the immense sum of one thousand pounds, his collateral being his friendship with Prince Hal and the preferment he can offer Shallow once Hal succeeds to the throne. Shallow hosts an elaborate dinner for Falstaff, including his friend and neighbour Justice Silence. The old men talk into the night until interrupted by Falstaff's confederate Pistol, who brings news that the old king is dead, and then they all go to London where they expect to be welcomed by the newly crowned Henry V. Falstaff is conning Shallow, but he is also deluding himself about his place in Hal's affections and plans. Shallow enters as the mark, or gull, of Falstaff's con game, but at the end he becomes a sort of chorus that witnesses Falstaff's repudiation. Throughout, Shallow shows another way to live old age.

Shallow defines himself by his reminiscences of student days that he and Falstaff shared. As elsewhere, close behind reminiscence is death:

> The same Sir John, the very same. I see him break Scoggin's head at the court gate, when [he] was a crack, not thus high; and the very same day did I fight with one Samson Stockfish a fruiterer, behind Gray's Inn. Jesu, Jesu, the mad days that I have spent! And to see how many of my old acquaintance are dead!
>
> (3.2.28–34)

Shallow's nostalgic version of the past is affirmed by his friend Silence: 'You were called "lusty Shallow" then, cousin' (3.2.15).

Falstaff plays along with Shallow's nostalgia, although he injects a note of realism when he says that a woman Shallow recalls is now 'Old, old' (3.2.201). Falstaff's capstone to Shallow's nostalgia may be the most lyrical line in the play: 'We have heard the chimes at midnight, Master Shallow' (3.2.209–10). Orson Wells chose that phrase – the chimes at midnight – as the title for his 1965 film adaptation conflating both parts of *Henry IV*. It exemplifies a line that detaches from the context. The words said by themselves can suspend time, casting the past in moonlight. In context, Falstaff uses the words to ingratiate himself, not sharing their sentiment.

Once Falstaff has departed to the anticipated battle, he speaks a soliloquy that deprecates Shallow's style of old age. Shallow does not simply remember through a gauze of nostalgia; on Falstaff's account, he lies:

> As I return, I will fetch off these justices. I do see the bottom of Justice Shallow. Lord, Lord, how subject we old men are to this vice of lying! This same starved justice hath done nothing but prate to me of the wildness of his youth, and the feats he hath done about Turnbull Street, and every third word a lie. . . . I do remember him at Clement's Inn, like a man made after supper of a cheese-pairing. When [he] was naked, he was for all the world like a forked radish, with a head fantastically carved upon it with a knife.
>
> (3.2.295–306)

The soliloquy continues for some time, making fun of Shallow's nostalgia while demonstrating Falstaff's virtuosic command of language and his capacity for stringing people along as his self-interest requires.

How subject we old men are to this vice of lying shows Falstaff's considerable capacity for self-reflection – he does say *we*. Falstaff knows what game he plays, yet he also believes he lives only so long as he continues playing. His old age depends on his games, no less than Shallow's depends on nostalgia.

Falstaff: Rebellious old age

In the structure of *2HenryIV*, Falstaff opposes the Chief Justice, but the matching is unequal. Falstaff, as his character develops over both parts of *Henry IV*, is as multi-dimensional as anyone in Shakespeare's gallery. The Chief Justice may reduce to the Freudian super-ego, but Falstaff's wit and powers of observation make him much more than Id or unrestrained Ego, although these qualities seem more readily observed in *1HenryIV* than in *Part 2*. Falstaff is vitality itself, and for me, the deepest question posed by *2HenryIV* is at what point this force-of-nature needs to accommodate itself to the demands of responsibility that are necessary to civil society. When Hal, having become Henry V, claims he will now speak in the voice of the Chief Justice, and does so, he's not much fun anymore, but he is being a king. For me, the play leaves us wondering about that balance in our own lives with our own responsibilities. We wish there could be a middle way beyond Falstaff but not banishing him.

For all that Falstaff plays the part of being young in his game of insults with the Chief Justice, he is capable of expressing the truth of his time of life. The reality of his age may be most poignant in his dialogue with the tavern prostitute, Doll Tearsheet:

> FALSTAFF
> Thou dost give me flattering busses.
> DOLL
> By my troth, I kiss thee with a most constant heart.
> FALSTAFF
> I am old, I am old.
> DOLL
> I love thee better than I love e'er a scurvy young boy of them all.
> FALSTAFF
> What stuff wilt have a kirtle of? I shall receive money a-Thursday, shalt have a cap tomorrow. A merry song! Come, it grows late, we'll to bed. Thou't forget me when I am gone.
>
> (2.4.266–74)

Each of Falstaff's sentences veers in a different direction, his ambivalence toward old age reflecting his own self-dividedness. *I am old, I am old* is another line that, well delivered, can suspend time. But opposite to the chimes at midnight, here Falstaff is sincere as he anticipates decline and death. Then having conceded old age, Falstaff gathers strength, anticipates making money, and calls for song. But the speech ends in a different anticipation that seems less bitter than simply realistic; *gone* may mean gone to war or gone as dead. So many dialogues end in references to death.

Falstaff is too intelligent not to have moments of self-reflection, but he has long chosen not to let the past catch up with him: he needs to deprecate Shallow for being mired in the past. Falstaff is all forward movement, denying age except when he acknowledges it. Falstaff moves specifically toward the moment of Hal's ascension, and some of the play's saddest lines express his anticipation:

> I will devise matter enough out of this Shallow to keep Prince Harry in continual laughter the wearing out of six fashions …
> O, you shall see him laugh till his face be like a wet cloak ill laid up!
>
> (5.1.75–7, 81–2)

> I know the young King is sick for me. Let us take any man's horses—the laws of England are at my commandment.
>
> (5.3.131–3)

And then his fantasy crashes. When Falstaff calls out to Henry V from the crowd, he receives this reply:

FALSTAFF
  God save thee, my sweet boy!
KING
  My Lord Chief Justice, speak to that vain man.
CHIEF JUSTICE
  Have you your wits? Know you what 'tis you speak?
FALSTAFF
  My King! My Jove! I speak to thee, my heart!
KING
  I know thee not, old man. Fall to thy prayers.
  How ill white hairs becomes a fool and jester!
  I have long dreamt of such a kind of man,
  So surfeit-swell'd, so old, and so profane;
  But being awak'd I do despise my dream.

(5.5.42–51)

How ill white hairs becomes a fool and jester complements Henry IV's 'I stay too long by thee, I weary thee' (4.5.93), but what the king says ironically of himself, Falstaff needs to be told.

Falstaff elicits our sympathies while he lives his rebellion against old age, but we know it can't last; thus the drama depends on poignancy rather than suspense. The hard reality is that rebellion will someday deteriorate into denial, and denial is a losing game. The newly crowned Henry V, when duty calls, will no longer play two loyalties against each other. Is his call to kingship also Falstaff's death? Not quite.

Shakespeare adds an Epilogue, which in performance was probably spoken by the author. He promises a next play 'with Sir John in it … unless already [he] be killed with your hard opinions' (Epilogue, 28, 30–1). Thus the sadness – is it tragedy? – of Falstaff's repudiation is muted by the promise of his return, but do we believe it? When the play *Henry V* arrives, Falstaff does not appear. His offstage death is reported by Mistress Quickly, who has been both his friend and his adversary in *2HenryIV*. What happens to Falstaff between the two plays, we can imagine, but I prefer not to. What the Epilogue promised could never be delivered.

Justice Silence: Lyrical old age

If Shakespeare offers language that shows old age having distinctive access to a poetic view of life, I find that language in the minor character of Justice Silence, Shallow's close friend and appendage to his household. Falstaff's 'chimes at midnight' line might be such poetic language of old age, except that in its narrative context the line is self-serving collusion in Shallow's nostalgic delusion. The line's lyricism is a facade behind which one lie is responding to another. *How subject we old men are to this vice of lying!* Falstaff says about Shallow, and he proves his own point as we realize that Falstaff has been lying to himself about his relationship to Hal. The chimes at midnight ring off key, although we are still free to make the line our own out of context – Shakespeare's language invites that quotability. But in the ramblings of Justice Silence, lyrical old age can be heard.

Silence says most in the garden scene, during which, time becomes suspended before the news arrives that Hal is king. Most of Silence's lines are not spoken but sung. Silence breaks into song six times during the 80 lines before Pistol enters with the news of Hal's succession to the throne, and possibly once after. The songs seem to be traditional rather than Shakespeare's own verses, but for most of these fragments, the originals are not known. Silence's songs thus come out of a time past that is remembered but without anyone – characters in the play or audience of it – knowing quite where the words came from. Lyrical language has that quality of being from anywhere, or nowhere.

Silence quietly sings drinking songs, calling for merriment: 'Do nothing but eat, and make good cheer' starts the first (5.3.17), although the words matter less than the effect. His singing surprises Falstaff: 'I did not think Master Silence had been a man of this mettle', he says (5.3.36–7). Silence's reply is my candidate for the truest poetic language of old age: 'Who, I? I have been merry twice and once ere now' (5.3.38). Editors note that the inversion of once-or-twice is comic; I find the inversion contributes to the archaic charm of the words. Archaic is not the same as nostalgic. Silence does not participate in Shadow's nostalgia by recalling, or misrecalling, any specific past events. But a mood can for a moment be revived in song. Silence has two later lines that rival *I have been merry*. First: 'And we shall be merry, now comes in the sweet o'th' night' (5.3.48–9); and then, most provocatively to me, 'Why then, say an old man can do somewhat' (5.3.77).

Somewhat is the question of old age posed throughout the play: what are the boundaries of *somewhat*? When does old age not do enough – Northumberland's failure to appear in battle – and when does it venture too much, as when Falstaff imposes himself on the new king. An old man can do somewhat, but the parameters of that can only be shown by multiple examples, not stated abstractly. We can only perceive *somewhat* as we see actions evolving into consequences.

In the plot of *2HenryIV*, Justice Silence is dispensable. But in the balancing of the characters who, as an ensemble of possibilities, enact old age, he seems crucial. The other old men are noisy; Silence's words point toward what his name makes present.

When old age usurps

In *King Lear*, upon Lear's death, his faithful lord Kent proclaims: 'He but usurped his life' (*King Lear* 5.3.338). The choice of verb, *usurp*, is provocative: to usurp is to take wrongfully; Richard III and Macbeth both clearly usurp the crown by causing the deaths of those who are in their way. Henry IV has usurped Richard II for defensible reasons, but both parts of *Henry IV* question the extent to which any usurpation can ever be legitimate, and as quoted earlier, that question continues into *Henry V*. With political usurpation in the background of Kent's choice of words, what can it mean to usurp one's *own* life? When Falstaff says and seems actually to believe 'the laws of England are at my commandment' (5.3.132-3), I see him as usurping his life, and in that usurpation, he who has been Hal's sometimes chosen surrogate father eventually mirrors the darkest side of Hal's kingly father. If we dare simplify Shakespeare so far as to refer to the-problem-of-old-age, that problem seems to be when – at what moment – a person lives in a way that usurps her or his own life.

An issue around which any society necessarily organizes itself is whose participation in which activities is required, invited, or tolerated, and from which activities are some persons unwelcome or legally excluded. Those activities include military service, forms of economic activity (for example, lending money), holy communion, attendance at court, and in modern societies, voting. To usurp was and still is to claim a participation that is beyond one's place and capacities. Falstaff usurps when he *fails to see limits* that he ought to recognize. Is it dramatic necessity or realism that leads Shakespeare to break the Epilogue's promise and keep Falstaff off stage in *Henry V*? By the end of *2HenryIV*, Falstaff has already usurped his life.

To find Shakespeare's clearest example of an old age that is furthest from usurping itself and earns its continuing participation, I look to the old servant appropriately named Adam in *As You Like It*. In that play the older brother, Oliver, fails to honour the responsibilities entrusted to him by their father for the care and education of his younger brother, Orlando. In that failure, Oliver usurps a parental authority and uses it badly. Orlando becomes increasingly threatened, and Adam makes his escape possible offering Orlando all the money he has saved to 'Be comfort to my age.' 'Here is the gold,' Adam tells Orlando; 'All this I give you. Let me be your servant' (*As You Like It*, 2.3.46-7). They flee into the Forest of Arden, and when Adam can go no further, he tells Orlando to abandon him. The younger man refuses and eventually saves them both. That stands out in Shakespeare's works as a moment when those who are older *earn their participation* through generosity that later becomes reciprocal. In most of Shakespeare's plays, however, the older generation causes the problems that the younger must suffer: *Romeo and Juliet* is the most obvious example, but the same generational tension is seen in *Hamlet*, *King Lear*, and *The Winter's Tale*. In *The Tempest*, Prospero will yield to the generational succession that he prepares for, but in those preparations, he establishes that succession to be as he has willed it to be.

Where all this leaves us – we who live old age now or who face it eventually – is open but not quite as you like it. Almost all the characters act badly at some point in *2HenryIV*, but no firm line separates good and bad. Action is compelled to respond to multiple claims, and plans are constantly interrupted by unanticipated contingencies.

Mistakes, at least most of them, are only retrospectively visible as mistakes. Henry IV is haunted by what might have been the mistake of usurpation, yet he clings to the crown as what he has earned by right of his more responsible kingship. Falstaff's games keep wit alive in the world, until he takes his pretensions seriously. The old men in *2HenryIV* do not make, nor seem headed toward, an entirely good end, as Ophelia in *Hamlet* hopes for her father. As to what a good end might be, dramatic narrative does not assert conclusions that can be summarized and generalized.

This severe but not unforgiving narrative perspective is complemented by lyrical moments that offer not recompense, but at least the solace of life momentarily in suspension, its beauty shining through. Narrative casts a harsh light on what people do to each other and to themselves. The lyrical elevates living; within its moonlit moments, what is and what could be merge and life is perfected.

An old man can do somewhat, says Justice Silence. For Falstaff, and also for Henry, the *somewhat* he did outlives the somewhat he usurped. Here is what Falstaff did, as only he himself can offer a summation of himself. When we first see Falstaff in this play, he introduces himself with a self-appraisal that is as inflated as it is true:

> The brain of this foolish-compounded clay, man, is not able to invent anything that intends to laughter more than I invent, or is invented on me; I am not only witty in myself, but the cause that wit is in other men.
>
> (1.2.5–9)

That should be not only Falstaff's epitaph, but a fine ideal for old age: To have your best qualities be the cause of such qualities in others.

References

Barber, C. L. (1959), *Shakespeare's Festive Comedy: A Study of Dramatic Form and Its Relation to Social Custom*, Princeton, NJ: Princeton University Press.

Maurice Charney, M. (2009), *Wrinkled Deep in Time: Aging in Shakespeare*, New York: Columbia University Press.

Frank, A. W. (2019), '"Who's There?": A Vulnerable Reading of *Hamlet*', *Literature and Medicine* 37 (2): 396–419.

Frank, A. W. (2022), *King Lear: Shakespeare's Dark Consolations*, London: Oxford University Press.

Freud, S. (1989a/1923), *The Ego and the Id*, in P. Gay (ed.), *The Freud Reader*, 628–658, New York: Norton.

Freud, S. (1989b/1930), *Civilization and Its Discontents,* in P. Gay (ed.), *The Freud Reader*, 722–772, New York: Norton.

Garber, M. (2010), *Shakespeare's Ghost Writers*, New York: Routledge.

Lewis, R. (2017), *Hamlet and the Vision of Darkness*, Princeton, NJ: Princeton University Press.

Shakespeare, W. (1967/1599), *King Henry IV, Part 2*, The Arden Shakespeare, Second Series, A. R. Humphreys (ed.), London: Routledge.

Shakespeare, W. (2007), *As You Like It*. In *William Shakespeare: The Complete Work*, Royal Shakespeare Company, J. Bate and E. Rassmussen (eds), London: Macmillan.

Shakespeare, W. (2007), *Henry V*. In *William Shakespeare: The Complete Works*, Royal Shakespeare Company, J. Bate and E. Rassmussen (eds), London: Macmillan.
Shakespeare, W. (2007), *King Lear*. In *William Shakespeare: The Complete Works*, Royal Shakespeare Company, J. Bate and E. Rassmussen (eds), London: Macmillan.
Shapiro, J. (2015), *The Year of Lear: Shakespeare in 1606*, New York: Simon & Schuster.

7

Virtuous Ageing as a Poetic Endeavour: Motivations to Write and Effects of Writing among Older Adults in Norway

Olga V. Lehmann* and Svend Brinkmann

What makes writing important for human living? Why do we keep diaries, write letters or tweet? Writing is motivated by various psychological, historical, social, and political circumstances. For example, writing can take the form of communication, a source of artistic or personal expression or an act of philosophical enquiry or reflection. It can also reflect a person's intention to leave a legacy – an effort to claim permanence within the ephemeralness of life. In psychology, there is growing evidence of the therapeutic effects of writing, such as expressive writing (e.g., Pennebaker 1999) and, in some cases, creative writing (e.g., Niemeyer 2016). What both forms of writing have in common is that when used alongside therapeutic goals, those who practice them can more easily pay attention to the emotional tonalities that shape their memories and notice the transformational power of crafting storylines to maintain or restore their sense of dignity and identity. When writing has therapeutic effects, it fosters meaning-making and affective processing, transcending the mere description of events that other forms of writing can have. In other words, storytelling can become a way of preserving our narrative identity with dignity when it fosters acceptance and compassion towards our past and its integration with who we are in the present, especially the parts of our everyday lives in which we function or thrive despite our physical or mental constraints (Synnes 2016).

In this chapter, we explore what motivated a group of older adults in Norway to enrol in an autobiographical writing course as well as the imagined and experienced functions of writing, especially in a poetic style. We also theorize our findings further in light of 'virtuous ageing' (Laceulle 2017) and 'existential pathways' (Lehmann and Brinkmann 2019a). The notion of virtuous ageing entails an effort to make discourses on health and ageing more faithful to the human condition and more ethical in reassuring the dignity of those who age (Laceulle 2017). This quest to reconcile psychology with ethics has also been at the core of some of our previous work (e.g.,

---

* This chapter is part of the work Olga Lehmann did during her postdoctoral fellow at the Department of Mental Health at NTNU – Norwegian University of Science and Technology.

Brinkmann 2011; Lehmann and Klempe 2015; Lehmann 2018a). For example, we developed the concept of existential pathways to highlight the fact that people can move through life from different positionings – modes or perspectives of being-in-the-world and being-with-the-world – that shape our attitudes and decisions to cope with uncertainty, freedom, finitude and other existential givens (Lehmann and Brinkmann 2019a). The notion of existential pathways, therefore, is closely related to that of 'personal life philosophies'. A personal life philosophy synthesizes some of the attitudes or preferences that are integrated into our biographies as short sayings or maxims that guide the meaning-making process for our past experiences and imagined futures (Zittoun 2017a). This is exemplified by the following statements made by some of our study participants prior to enrolling in the course: 'Life does something to us; indeed, it humbles us'; 'One cannot be eighteen years old and have sixty years of life experience'; 'It will all work out, yes … one way or another … it will all work out' (Lehmann and Brinkmann 2019a: 5).

As discussed elsewhere (Lehmann and Brinkmann 2019a), people do not necessarily integrate their existential pathways into personal life philosophies. At times, many of us are not even aware of the existential pathways we are taking. We can assume that this is just the way life is, for us specifically or for human beings in general. Many people may avoid returning to difficult memories or finding meaning in our suffering. They can also simply accept their lives contain contradictions and open-ended questions and carry on better integrating other aspects of their lives into a personal life philosophy while leaving other dimensions of their biographies aside. Adopting the assumption that autobiographical writing, especially writing that cultivates a poetic style, is a tool that people can use to get in touch with their emotional worlds, in this chapter, we qualitatively explore the following questions: a) How did the participants experience and imagine the functions that writing had in their lives? b) What motivated the participants to write?

The writing course

During the spring of 2019, the first author of this chapter coordinated a seven-week writing course for older adults (2 hours per session), hiring the Norwegian poet Marte Huke as the main teacher and the up-and-coming Norwegian novelist Cecilie Wold Andersen as her assistant. We also collaborated with the Literature House and the Public Library of Trondheim, which helped us with marketing and finding a location for the course. After conducting screening interviews, 16 participants were selected to enrol in the course, of which 13 attended all the sessions. The criteria for enrolment included being at least 62 years old, not having any active symptoms of suicidality or psychosis, and being able to attend classes according to our schedules. Fourteen of the 16 participants were retired by the time they enrolled in the course, and the other two were set to retire in a few months. Some of them went into early retirement due to illness, while others retired because of their age. Most of our participants had an academic background and had been university teachers, schoolteachers, or instructors in diverse areas.

Each class started with five minutes of free writing, during which most participants wrote descriptions of their current day or memories of their past. This exercise was followed by a short theoretical introduction to writing styles, especially poetic ones, drawing on the background of Marte Huke, the main teacher. Then, our study participants had individual time to write after having been given a prompt (e.g., the word 'drop', or the incomplete sentence 'everyone says that ... but in reality ...'). Immediately after, each participant was invited to read their texts aloud and receive feedback from the teachers and their classmates.

Methodological remarks

Inspired by approaches of phenomenological research in existential psychology and anthropology (Churchill 2022; Giorgi 2012; Jackson and Piette 2015; Osborne 1990), we explored the lifeworlds of our study participants, collecting data in different forms. Before the writing course started, the first author of the chapter, hereafter referred to as Olga, conducted in-depth interviews with the participants, 14 of which were included in the study and analysed. She documented her participant observations during the seven weekly encounters; although she helped plan the structure and content of the course, she seldom interfered during the sessions themselves unless the study participants asked her to share specific feedback. At the end of the course, the participants also completed an open-ended questionnaire about how they experienced the writing course. Both in-person conversations and electronic communications (i.e., e-mail exchanges and text messages) were also included as data.

Data-driven themes were created to address the research questions. All the information was in Norwegian, and Olga has translated into English the excerpts shared within this chapter. For the first question, we created three sub-themes: a) contact with the poetic, given that the advertisement for the course disclosed that it would cover, among other things, poetic techniques and poetic styles; b) therapeutic effects that respondents experienced or wanted to experience through writing; and c) writing as a form of legacy. For the second research question, we created sub-themes that addressed respondents' core motivations to be part of the writing course: learning, improving their cognitive skills and navigating the transition to life after retirement. Other relevant aspects of the interviews in relation to moral values, virtues, spirituality and their reflections upon life and society have been narratively analysed elsewhere (Lehmann and Brinkmann 2019a).

Ethical considerations

This project has been reported to and received approval from the Data Protection Official for Research at the Norwegian Social Science Data Services (NSD). Participants signed a consent form, and their information was encrypted and anonymized. Pseudonyms are used throughout this book chapter to respect participants' confidentiality. In addition, the Regional Committee for Medical and Health Research Ethics (REK) did not consider their approval necessary, as the project did not pose any potential risks to the participants' health.

Results and analysis

Perspectives on the functions of writing

Contact with poetry and poiesis

Most of the participants had read or written poetry, especially in childhood and early adulthood. Participants frequently described poems as shortcuts to their emotional worlds, whether in terms of finding their innermost longings or treasured experiences conveyed in a piece already created by someone else or daring to create it themselves. Maria said that 'It [poetry] says a bit without saying it all, maybe? It gives shape to feelings.' Stina also shared the following: 'The transparency of existence fascinates me. So, to be precise with few words, I think, is very much so … finding that which is unsaid – that which lays there. So, I find these things very exciting.' Maria and Stina describe a very human quest to master the craft of language in ways that are not only accurate and accessible, but also evocative and concise. One of the fascinating mysteries of poetry is that in it, we can find words that shape what otherwise we would have only felt and would have remained unsaid; indeed, it can also be about what is unsaid. Although the participants seldom wrote haikus in the writing course, this form of Japanese poetry (see Murakami in this volume) exemplifies the importance of not necessarily what is said but what is not; what remains in us as a question or reminiscence.

At first, this process of attending to words and aiming to make them faithful and concise was not easy for most participants. Poets often devote their lives to the art of finding words that masterfully portray the emotional tonalities of life events; poets invite us to touch and breathe in the beauty inherent in the fragility of life (Lehmann and Brinkmann 2019b). For our study participants, what appeared to motivate them most to explore poetic language was that Marte Huke, the main teacher, presented it to them in many forms. This was experienced as both inspiring and challenging because poetry is such a complex way of shaping felt images through language, which elicited resistance among various study participants. For instance, in the evaluation survey, Kristine shared how writing 'poems is the biggest challenge. It takes longer to express oneself briefly. Instead of expressing oneself as a blend between noble metals, one can find the grains of gold.' Although most of the study participants described the process of writing poetry as challenging, in the evaluating surveys, many of them wrote that they would have loved to learn more about it and finished the course with a willingness to explore it further.

Our study participants described their experienced and imagined contact not only with poetry but being part of a writing course; and then forming their own writing group after the course had ended also gave them contact with the empowering possibilities of *poiesis*. In Greek, the word *poiesis* refers to the act of creating something, such as a poem (Argüello Manresa and Glăveanu 2017). Poetic experiences can be transformed into artistic pieces that can be seen to 'share or to magnify a specific emotional experience' (Zittoun 2017b: 87). For the participants, the subjects of their emotional experiences were apparently secondary. What became more salient in the evaluation surveys was that these experiences were both unique in some ways and shared in some others – that the very act of creating and learning about poetry occurred in the context of the group they had consolidated. In the words of Alex: 'I cannot choose only one highlight of the course. One of them was that I could create texts of my own. Another was the inspiration and joy I felt when I could listen to the others as they read their own texts.' Ole noted: 'I was surprised by how easy it was to make eight new texts during six weekly encounters. I had some of my old poems, but I did not need them. New ideas emerged all the time.'

We identified a need amongst the participants that is perhaps familiar to any artist in the making, namely the need to find a voice and a style that felt genuine. During this search, learning about the different shades of a poetic style of writing became even more significant. This helped one of our participants, Nina, mitigate some of her resistance to poetry:

> I haven't read poetry in ... I have a lot of poetry; I read a lot some years ago. I am a bit more impatient. But I heard a programme on slam poetry on the radio not so long ago. Then I figured out, oh, that's something for me. I think it is great. I don't need to learn so much or experience so much every time I read.

Nina's reflection shows that how much poetry one wants to experience or how deep one is willing to go when reading or writing can vary. Beyond fancy or difficult words, the poetic can also be straightforward, raw, or ironic. Rediscovering themselves and their life stories through a variety of tonalities helped our study participants connect with a virtue that Scandinavians are proud of defending: freedom. Participants were more motivated by the freedom to investigate different shades of meaning and forms in their writing, as well as the opportunity to shift between narrative and poetic forms of writing instead of feeling forced to become poets. That is, many of them struggled to identify as poets, but all of them agreed that poetic language was a bridge between the felt intensity of their memories and the ways in which they aspired to be remembered. However, the recognition of *poiesis* as an opportunity to connect with freedom as a virtue did not end there. This sense of freedom was essentially linked with the feeling that participants could maintain their sense of dignity, not as older adults but as human beings. For example, Kristine shared the following with us: 'I was really impressed with the many stories that were read. Seen from the outside, we are a group of retired people, but from the inside, we are a potpourri of thoughts and experiences.' Writing served as the consolidation of a live library of experiences that speak of the many existential pathways that form the human condition.

The therapeutic effects of writing

Although this course was neither advertised nor conducted as a therapeutic writing course, many participants portrayed the art of writing as having a therapeutic function. For example, Sue pointed out: 'I have written ... during difficult periods. ... Now ... I write about my own memories, often on specific themes such as my train travels.' Writing is an opportunity to meet with one's life and choose not only what to say about it, but how to say it. What is common then, between 'difficult periods' and 'train travels' is the motivation to capture these memories as though they are transformed through a creative act, through the process of *poiesis*. In the opening of his novel *Living to Tell the Tale*, Nobel laureate García Marquez (2002) writes that life is not necessarily about what has really happened to us but more about the life we remember and the way in which we narrate it. Writing can then become a platform for meaning-making and emotional processing, which was reflected in our study participants' need to retain and enhance their sense of freedom while they attended the writing course. For example, Stina mentioned the following during an interview: 'So, I wrote about things I have experienced, obviously. Some were of a traumatic character – things that I experienced that were a bit special.'

In the specific case of our study, the *poiesis* was not just about writing, but also about sharing and listening to one another, conveying a meaning beyond that which was created. Therapeutic writing itself can be a form of inner dialogue with different parts of the self and a form of dialogue with others (e.g., Lehmann et al. 2022). Such a dialogical function of writing gives us perspective as we navigate through a variety of emotional tonalities (Lehmann and Brinkmann 2019c; Lehmann et al. 2022). Some of our participants had confirmed this in formal therapeutic settings, such as Maria, who told us: 'I have written for myself [laughter] and for my psychologist.... That poetry was helpful for putting feelings into words.' However, one does not need to have a formal addressee, such as in Maria's case, for one's writing to be a dialogue. What motivated our study participants to write during difficult periods of their lives? What is it that occurs as part of the process of *poiesis*, and as part of the participant's process of finding a poetic style for their autobiographical texts?

On 6 February 2021, exactly two years after the writing course's first session, Ivar emailed Olga. He wanted to thank her again for having arranged the writing encounters, and he shared two short stories he had written since. One of them was about a colleague who was recently diagnosed with Huntington's disease. Like most of his stories, this one also interweaves the lyrics of his favourite music with his reflections about the paradoxes of the passing of time. What follows in an excerpt from the end of the story:

> I remember that party night. We sat side by side. There was about a centimetre between our arms, but there was a long distance between his head where that illness had already appeared, and my head, which struggled to perceive what was about to happen to him. Each time I listen to 'Song to Woody', I think right back on him, who had to head down the 'Huntington Road'.

Given that Bob Dylan wrote 'Song to Woody' (1962) for his friend Woody Guthrie, who was also diagnosed with Huntington's disease, this ending is an opening into the fragility of being, portraying the challenges that those close to the diagnosed person must go through. Ivar's words meet those of Dylan in the shared humanity they convey. In Scandinavian languages, a sense of shared humanity is often referred to as *menneskeheten*, which was used frequently by the study participants during the in-depth interviews and throughout the writing course itself. Ivar did not refer to his writings as therapeutic. His words, however, exemplify the ways in which both poetic and narrative nuances can enhance meaning-making and affective processing. It is the aesthetic quality of the image that Ivar portrays that makes us bear, as readers of the story, the fragility of life as a treasure. When we finished the second draft of this chapter and emailed Ivar to ask for some feedback, he sent us a letter in which he said the following:

> Therapeutic effect? Yes! For most of us, the 14 hours during which the course took place, as well as the encounters that followed it, have been a 'free space' in which we have been able to put our sadness into words – due to illnesses such as respiratory issues, cancer – writing about our own illnesses or those of our partners.

In the context of writing groups, texts from older adults can express powerful emotions that must be treated carefully because they can bring up emotional injuries and traumas (Bendien 2016), even if they can also contribute to an expanded understanding of ageing. Such emotional injuries or traumas cannot always be 'healed' or 'treated', nor is that always the intention. It is said that by connecting our lived experiences with virtues or attitudes that help us turn tragedies into heroic journeys, we can better endure suffering, even if we are not always able to make such suffering dissolve (Frankl 1994). At times, human beings simply aim to accept their experiences as they are and to feel that their sense of humanity is cherished despite these experiences being inconclusive, ambivalent, or dark. The participants sometimes discussed difficult experiences in the group without any explicit intention other than to share. It was important for them to feel they preserved their sense of freedom. It was often comforting for participants to have the autonomy to choose whether to change the course of their existential pathways. This made them feel that they could preserve their freedom. Whereas sometimes they directly addressed these pathways in the form of maxims that represented their personal life philosophies, at other times, they simply told stories that they wanted to narrate or depicted an image of an instant that they wanted to immortalize in stanzas. It was comforting for them to affirm that it is up to each person to decide whether to change course on their existential pathways, let them be roads of possibilities in the making.

Our participants revealed that writing can have therapeutic effects, even if the writing was not done in a formal therapeutic setting (Lehmann and Brinkmann 2019c; Lehmann et al. 2022). Furthermore, even today, three years after the writing course ended, nine of our study participants continue to meet and write together, which to us explicitly acknowledges that it is belonging to a writing community and not just the act of writing that may yield a perceived therapeutic effect. Many of them continue to contact Olga Lehmann on social media and by email to share their gratitude for establishing a network of human connections and an opportunity to leave a legacy.

Writing as a legacy

Among the participants, writing often functioned as a way to leave a legacy. Lisbeth mentioned the following: 'I wanted to write a book, just for private use, so that in the years to come, the younger people in my family can get to know who I was, who I have been – especially because I have lived a life which is quite different from the usual life of people here in Norway'. For Lisbeth, the motivation to leave a legacy through her writing also followed reflections about commonalities and differences between generations: 'When you reach an age at which you look back on your life, it looks like my life has so much in common with that of the younger generations, but it is also very different'. This is also not only about leaving a legacy for others, but in part also for themselves. That is, they also found meaning in looking back to the lives they have lived; a process of self-exploration, which has also been reported as an important experience in other writing courses for older adults in Norway (Lehmann and Brinkmann 2019b). In the words of the American gerontologist Karl Pillemer, who has written about the legacy of older generations in the USA:

> We are on the verge of losing an irreplaceable natural resource. The inexorable process of human aging is depriving us of one of the most extraordinary groups of human beings that has ever lived. . . . When this generation has passed, where will we go to recover the lessons they learnt about life and the wisdom they can offer us about surviving and thriving in a difficult world?
>
> (Pillemer 2012: 7)

Pillemer suggests that there is a source of wisdom in the lived experiences of older generations that we need to preserve. In Colombia, there is a saying that goes: '*Más sabe el diablo por viejo, que por diablo*', which roughly translates to 'The devil knows more because he is old than because he is the devil', which resonates with the notion of the importance of life experience. This is very similar to the saying Peter shared during the in-depth interviews and that we mentioned in the introduction to this chapter: 'One cannot be eighteen years old and have sixty years of life experience' (Lehmann and Brinkmann 2019a: 5). Clearly, we cannot affirm and guarantee that all the perspectives of our study participants are the 'wisest' available. What we can do is argue that their efforts to find meaning in their life stories are worthy of listening to and considering. As part of a former study that we conducted with this group of people, we created poetic representations based on the transcripts from the in-depth interviews that we conducted with them before they enrolled in the writing course. These poetic representations were an attempt to condense the emotional intensity and depth of meaning that the study participants shared with the researchers into poems. They are reorganizations of the exact words of one or several participants in stanzas that represent their humanity as faithfully as possible (Faulkner 2005, 2009). What follows is an excerpt of one of these poetic representations:

> Throughout a long life
> you ought to be prepared
> to change, at times,
> your image of the future,
> with no notice at all.
> Not everything goes as you want (laughter).
> [...]
> Life does something to us,
> indeed, it humbles us
>
> (Lehmann and Brinkmann 2019a: 5)

The aim of writing to leave a legacy is not limited solely to inspiring or teaching others. It can also be done with a view to leaving a trace of one's existence, to avoid being forgotten or to represent oneself and one's life as it unfolds. This does not always come with ready-made learnings and meanings, but also with insights and perspectives on the making. For the participants, recognizing that their lives were unfinished became a motivation to acknowledge themselves as authors who could restore the dignity of their identities through narrative and poetic means. One example of the impact of such motivation is the consolidation of a formal writing community after the research project ended, where participants continue to write today, and some of them even publish their texts in newspapers and elsewhere.

Motivation (needs and wants) in relation to writing

Learning and cognitive functioning

This theme included aspects such as the desire that our study participants had to challenge themselves to learn something new, a desire to maintain their cognitive capacities and being part of a learning community. For example, Bente said the following: 'One reason is to have a challenge or experience something interesting while I challenge myself. The possibility of meeting others who have the same interests is also very motivating [and] to learn something new'. For Lisbeth, it was not only about the challenge of learning something, but also about improving her writing skills: 'Yes, I have done this for a hundred years. Writing everywhere. But it would have been more fun to challenge oneself ... and then it is about learning other techniques, right? – to be able to describe something with fewer words'. In a similar vein, Peter's motivation was to prevent the memory and attention pitfalls that come with ageing:

> When one becomes older ... it is maybe an age thing that one remembers badly. I mean that I had it, and some years ago I went to see my family doctor and he said I would still have more memory problems and concentration problems over time. I had problems focusing then. And I think I have been losing my skills to communicate well.

Studies like ours have also found that older adults experience participation in writing workshops as an opportunity to challenge themselves intellectually and prevent dementia (Saunders 2006; Alex 2010). Much of the literature on writing workshops for older adults concerns people who have already been diagnosed with dementia or have dementia symptoms (e.g., Synnes et al. 2021; Swinnen 2016; Swinnen and de Medeiros 2018). However, there is growing interest in developing writing courses for older adults before they receive such diagnoses (e.g., Aadlandsvik 2007; de Medeiros 2007).

Given that losing one's capacities and feeling closer to death are common but still difficult experiences among adults (Ruddick 1999), our study participants shed some light on an important existential need: that of crafting more availability in society for older adults to participate more actively in an ageing process that feels dignified. For example, during a talk that Olga gave at the public library after the course ended, she mentioned that she had been doing research on a writing course for older adults, to which one of the study participants shouted out loud, laughing: 'Olga, why is there always an emphasis on older adults and not just on adults?' Most of the participants expressed that what they valued the most about these encounters was having an intellectual challenge that made them feel mastery or confirmed that they had not lost intellectual skills after retirement, as well as having a shared activity that allowed them to connect through the vulnerability they shared in their life stories, not just as old people, but as people. The participants' experiences give an account of how unique the ageing processes and motivations for learning are. They also shed light on the existential concerns of older adults, such as their need to still feel capable of learning something and belonging to learning communities while being involved in activities that help them improve their cognitive capacities.

Minding the transition: Life after retirement

Although throughout the writing course, participants were mostly invited to write about their past and present, the participants often shared their concerns, desires and wishes regarding the future. Most of this sharing related to adapting to their lives after retirement. For example, Maria said:

> I need to take care not to start filling up the empty slots of the calendar of life with housework or with things that are not meaningful. I need to do things that are good for me, as well. I also think it is good to go out and meet people because it is a lonely existence to be on the outside, outside of society, in a way.

In addition, Stina said: 'The first three years after I turned 67 years old, I continued to work part time.... I liked my job so much. It was very sad to stop working'. Both of their comments suggest a change in their sense of identity, which might also lead to the awareness of a transition into the last stage of life. Iselin approached Olga once at the elevator in the library, as both were on their way to the writing classroom, and said 'Why don't you, as a psychologist, develop activities like this writing course so that geriatric centres become more interesting places to be in? Influence the system, so that we feel motivated in this transition'. Later that day, Iselin shared with the group what she had told Olga at the elevator, which led to a discussion about the common worries about becoming old. For example, they shared their curiosity about how to adapt to being retired as well as possible, such as keeping themselves active and busy and their desire to enjoy the 'here and now' while also feeling an urge to plan the rest of their lives, which can be very difficult. Enrolling in our writing course confirmed to them that the process of *poiesis* could prevail in them while challenging themselves intellectually and emotionally to create. It was as if they had lost hope that there would be enough community space available for them to feel active and creative human beings and not just passive and withheld 'old beings' – as if they feared activities for older adults would rob them of their dignity. During an email correspondence, Ivar shared a similar perspective on this topic:

In the little black notebook that we got that 6th of February, I see that Marte Huke wrote about 'training our writing muscle'. When I google 'retired people and physical training', I get 193,000 results. But 'retired people and writing group' has only 2,450 results! It would be fun to include Marte's use of training and writing in the article ... and the suggestion of having more writing courses available – and not only training at a gym – I fully support that!

In Norway, few studies have been conducted on the strategies that organizations must use to prepare their employees for active ageing and to prevent early retirement (Midtsundstad and Bogen 2014). Moreover, these reports are lacking when it comes to ways in which older adults experience the transition into retirement or how to promote their mental health. According to the American Psychological Association, 'too few people consider the psychological adjustments that accompany this life stage, which can include coping with the loss of your career identity, replacing support networks you had through work' (Chamberlin 2014: 6).

In most European countries, the transition out of an active working life is strongly associated with the notion of ageing – a transition that also affects the sense of identity of older adults and involves learning processes seldom acknowledged (Zittoun et al. 2013). In Norwegian culture, being part of larger social groups and having harmonious relationships are core values for older adults, even though self-sufficiency and freedom are also part of their cultural identity (Low, Molzahn and Kalfoss 2014). Education programmes for older adults support their quest to find meaning in their lives and contribute to their development and the maintenance of their social skills (Bendien 2016). This is perhaps one of the greatest impacts that the writing course had on the well-being of the participants, given that nine out of the 16 older adults who enrolled in the course continue to meet monthly, three years after the project's conclusion. They even maintained their writing club meetings during the COVID-19 pandemic. These findings are in line with Scandinavian values that speak of the responsibility that older adults have for promoting one's wellbeing and sense of community as they age (Bahl et al. 2017). Some of them continue to reach out to Olga regularly, expressing their gratitude; for example, one of them said once that 'I never imagined I could make so many good friends being so old'. This has previously been reported in other writing courses for older adults in Norway – the shared reciprocity and the human condition that they promote being at the core of what makes these courses effective as community interventions (Lehmann and Brinkmann 2019c). That is, the contact with the poetic and with writing as an intellectual activity was valuable for our study participants, but it was the sense of community and belonging as a result of their interest in writing for which they were most grateful.

Discussion

Our study participants experienced the act of creating – and that of creating in a community – as a confirmation of the dignity of their identities and a motivation to keep pursuing virtuous living. There were, of course, other needs and motivations that coexisted in this quest. For example, they referred to their need to feel that they were actively contributing to taking care of their mental health and well-being and not only expecting to receive care from others. Enrolling in this writing course was, after all, important to many of them because it was an opportunity to train their cognitive skills and to better adapt to their transition into retirement. When theorizing about *virtuous ageing*, Laceulle (2017) begins by recognizing our existential vulnerability. She reminds us that there is a realm of human vulnerability and fragility that is not a problem to be solved or a target to be avoided as we age. Our participants appealed to a need to not just be recognized as 'old' or 'retired', but also as active human beings who still have the capacity and the need to belong to learning communities. Recognizing the shared vulnerability of our human condition can enable self-exploration and a deeper feeling of otherness and togetherness among participants in writing courses (Lehmann and Brinkmann 2019c). Such reciprocity is crucial for health and community interventions for older adults because it not only entails receiving care, but also encourages them to honour what they can contribute, such as their writings. Learning communities not only can help prevent dementia (e.g., Lehmann and Brinkmann 2019c), but the literature has widely shown that they also serve as part of the treatment of dementia when symptoms appear (e.g., Synnes et al. 2021; Swinnen 2016; Swinnen and de Medeiros 2018).

It is said that for Aristotle, *poiesis* – creation – was an end in itself and would not necessarily lead to virtuous actions in praxis (Argüello Manresa and Glăveanu 2017). Laceulle (2018) resolved the dilemma of whether *poiesis* can lead to virtuous actions in praxis by highlighting the need to include authenticity discourses as part of the new cultural narratives of ageing. Among the features of this quest for better integrating authenticity into our narratives of ageing, the author highlights the recognition that older adults have the potential to actualize, and that they can embrace their vulnerability with courage or openness, in contrast to stereotypes of decline. The notion of old age involves ambivalent associations, such as wisdom, freedom and mature relationships on the one hand, and loneliness, economic challenges, illness and death on the other (Längle and Probst 2000). To transform the notion of ageing and convey its dignity faithfully, we need to reconstruct it on individual and collective levels, giving account of the challenges and transitions that many older adults undergo (Zittoun et al. 2013).

The participants experienced this sense of authenticity as *poiesis*; feeling human without further labels and, therefore, being able to create. That is, 'poetic acts, "poiesis" as making, as bringing into existence, have a reflexive potential for engaging people in political collective actions (that might be defined as praxis) that are socially creative' (Argüello Manresa and Glăveanu 2017: 48). It is also our interpretation that *poiesis*, both as a process and as an artistic outcome, has a connection with the praxis of virtuous actions. Here, we suggest a crossroad between psychology as a developmental lens to investigate ageing, and ethics. This approach can also shape more effective ways in which we can approach the promotion of mental health and well-being. In doing so, we hope to contribute to the trend in cultural psychology that is set to provide deeper theoretical and empirical explorations of ageing, which have practical implications for the transformation of policies and institutions that affect older adults (Zittoun and Baucal 2021).

The experienced and imagined effects and motivations to write that the participants gained illustrate the process of *poiesis*: the challenges of finding a writing style, and poetry becoming at times a daunting bridge between their memories and emotions. Our attention to poetic instants in our everyday lives does not itself release us from the tensions and challenges of virtuous living, but it can help us bear and endure unavoidable suffering (Lehmann 2018b; Frankl 1994). If there were a personal life philosophy that evoked this, it would certainly be the one that William Randall shared with us when reading through an earlier draft of this chapter: 'making a virtue out of necessity', a popular saying in the English language. We can experience and create beauty through our own fragility and appreciation of the fragility of the world in which we live, which is something of which the arts remind us (Lehmann and Brinkmann 2019b). However, this is not an easy task; it is a quest to find meaning in our everyday life experiences. We cannot say whether the feelings and emotions about which our participants wrote, as well as the meanings associated with them, were the healthiest or the wisest they could be because it was not the aim of our research project to judge the quality of their writings. The stories, images and questions that arose in their texts, that were vocalized in class and discussed in the in-depth interviews, revealed the wide realm of existential pathways on which we as human beings can embark.

Octavio Paz (1956/1999) reminds us that all of us can experience the poetic and embrace poetic instants, but just a few people devote their lives to the craft of words and become poets. As much as this chapter is part of a book about 'the poetic language of ageing', it is important to be precise and say that many of our study participants would not call themselves poets. For the group of older adults who participated in this project, aspiring to find a poetic style that made them feel authentic was a process in itself; what they wanted was to express themselves, to create, and not necessarily to do it professionally. Writing poetically is not only about insights that are 'ready to go' but about insights into the making. Our study participants, by making sense of their own histories, have continued to craft stories of being and becoming human instead of merely being 'humans who have been' and whose insights and wisdom are complete and ready to be delivered. This process consists of both narrative efforts to bring congruence and sequential logic into our life stories, and poetic turns where the tensions, ambiguities and open-ended aspects of our experiences and the ways in which we remember and want to remember them coexist and are reconciled (Lehmann and Brinkmann 2019a). As Ivar shared, the nine study participants who continue meeting today would often hold space for each other's suffering, whether due to an illness or being the caregiver for an ill spouse. This was not, of course, the only theme of their conversations or writings, but it highlights the fact that vulnerability is inescapable and that it is reassuring to have a group with whom to share thoughts about it. When exchanging ideas about the foreword of the book, Gregory Orr shared a note and poem that synthesized this well:

> I love what you are doing.... Here's another poem of mine about Whitman (one of my heroes along with his sister Emily Dickinson). Whitman, as an old man, used to be dropped off in the woods near his home to do the things I mention here (he loved to make lists of things around him). I don't know if the pun on 'pupil'

comes across, but a pupil is both part of an eye and a student (in the school of being, I suppose). And 'the Book' is a giant anthology I imagine that contains all the lyric poems and songs ever written – it exists as testimony of what it is to be human, and we go to it (or small versions of it) seeking the poems and songs that will illuminate our lives and make sense of our joy/suffering....

(G. Orr, 9 January 2022, personal communication)

<u>Whitman's list of the things he could see</u>
As he sat, half-paralyzed,
An old man by a woodland pond.

The names of the different trees.
The birds he glimpsed or only heard
Yet recognized by their songs.

The bushes and grasses that grew there.

How happy those lists made him:
Red oak, hickory, poplar, larch . . .

Gazing from where he loafed
On the bank or from the pond itself
Where he floated naked
In the round pool of it:

As if he were the pupil
In a wide-open eye.

And the trees around it
Delicate and strong as lashes.

Oh, the world, the world,
What eye is wide enough?
What pupil sufficiently diligent?

Let's put our poems in the Book.

(Orr 2022: 286)

In line with Orr's words and his touching reconstruction of Whitman's old age, the writings of our study participants also become testimonies of the human condition and have the potential to be available to others – their family members, their fellow group members or other potential readers – as torches that help make sense of life in its peaks and valleys and perhaps even integrating them with specific virtues. Another example comes from the second author's recent book on the life of an elderly woman, Lili, who is now 93 (Brinkmann 2021). Lili contacted the second author in 2018 because she had read some of his books, and they began to exchange letters and have since then met in Lili's apartment. Brinkmann recorded their conversations, and Lili also gave him her collection of poems and novels, which she had written over the course of many decades. Lili's life story is now told in a book, and it is about a young woman who fell in love with German soldiers during the Nazi occupation of Denmark and spent 33 years in psychoanalysis to strive for what she called human dignity. An important factor in her life story concerns the way she used literature, music and film as symbolic resources (Zittoun 2006) to understand life better, and she began to write herself in the later decades of her life, which has contributed greatly to her development as a human being. Lili has no children; her husband has been dead for a couple of years, but she finds consolation in writing stories and sharing her experiences with the second author. Lili has not attended a writing course but has found a way to integrate writing into her daily life practice, which diminishes her loneliness and reconciles her with her past.

Human beings do not necessarily integrate their existential pathways with specific virtues, such as attitudes towards love and marriage, but explicitly conferring meaning onto their experiences in terms of virtues such as freedom or authenticity can improve mental health and well-being (Lehmann and Brinkmann 2019a). Whether it is suffering or other existential givens (such as freedom of will), our quest for meaning, the responsibility to make choices, the impending finitude of life and loneliness belong to the human condition and are not exclusively experiences of the 'older' ones (Cooper 2017; Yalom 1980; Frankl 1994). What becomes an opportunity for authenticity and the actualization of other virtues is found in the uniqueness of the various existential pathways our study participants take as they cope with the happenings in their life stories (Lehmann and Brinkmann 2019a). These existential pathways represent the perspectives we take on what has happened or is happening to us through our attitudes towards the way reality unfolds according to our choices and other uncontrollable events. This coincides with Laceulle's (2017) assumption that virtuous ageing corresponds in great measure with our attitudes towards the vulnerability of life and the practice of virtues that support meaningful actions in society. Therefore, virtuous ageing, in our view, corresponds to the practice of moral attitudes toward one's vulnerability and the vulnerability of others – a shared humanity – as exemplified by Ivar when writing about his friend 'who had to head down the "Huntington Road"'. Now, the Huntington Road is not here a personal life philosophy in itself. Revisiting that party night, sitting next to a friend without knowing of his friend's illness – that is the very image of the fragility of existence, which can give birth to virtues such as compassion, hope and loving-kindness, just to mention a few.

Conclusion

In this chapter, we explored the experienced and imagined effects that writing can have on the lives of a group of Norwegian older adults, as well as their motivations to enrol in writing courses such as the one we arranged in Trondheim in 2019. Although they were not writing with a therapeutic intention or as part of a therapeutic setting, many of our study participants described writing as having therapeutic effects, and they acknowledged that poetry helped them connect with their emotional world – saying and evoking more with fewer words. Exploring their perspectives on belonging to a writing course helped us, as authors, to conceptualize *poiesis* as a process, linking it with its potential for the praxis of virtues. In other words, feeling creative made our study participants feel human and embrace a sense of authenticity, courage, freedom, reciprocity and commitment to a community.

In addition, the process of writing about their life stories was important not necessarily because those who write acquire insights or integrate existential pathways into their personal life philosophies but because these writings become testimonies of the complexities of being human. No matter the outcomes of their life-trajectories, our participants' willingness to join a writing course in which they could write about their lives and share the uniqueness of their stories speaks of belonging, being seen in their authenticity and being accepted – even in their contradictions, their suffering and their vulnerability. Whatever existential pathways our participants have taken throughout their lives, the writing course amplified their sense of freedom to choose, if not a different ending, at least a different attitude towards their life stories.

However, neither the narrative nor the poetic processes of meeting our life stories are 'a given' to all of us. Either because we do not find the possibilities that Lili had with Svend in Denmark or the one that our study participants had with Olga in Norway, but also because such a need for such openness does not always come as a spontaneous motivation. In addition, the potential benefits of enrolling in a writing community are not limited to writing itself; there is a crucial human need that our writing course met: the sense of belonging, the possibility to lessen existential loneliness and sharing one's humanity in the beauty of its fragility with peers. As Tina, one of our study participants, said after reading this chapter: 'Also, starting such an endeavour and continuing it represents for the participants a process of new discoveries connected to therapeutic effects, meaning making, transitions in dignity'. Therefore, we argue that both the act of writing and belonging to a writing community support virtuous ageing as a poetic endeavour.

By poetic endeavour, in this context, we mean the aspiration to revisit and edit one's storylines in ways that maintain and restore human dignity, not only because we age, but because we are human beings. Whether or not our study participants or anyone else integrate diverse existential pathways into specific personal life philosophies, the aspiration to live virtuously is meaningless unless it is relational. Therefore, older adults need and deserve sociocultural spaces where they feel like active members of society, not only because they are old, but also because they still have intellectual skills and want to be challenged to keep learning. The threshold between the value of the community intervention for a specific age and other ages is narrow and needs further exploration. What the data appear to show consistently is the weight of having a common intellectual activity, which possibly they miss in this retirement phase. This has some potential implications for policymaking, as writing courses can become more available as community interventions that promote mental health and well-being and support older adults in their transitions to retirement. More research is needed in collaboration with neuropsychology to address the cognitive effects of such writing communities, which could be addressed in participants with or without dementia.

Having this assessment could serve as a platform to promote more similar community interventions and to contribute to tailoring policies for older adults in Norway that respond to their needs and wants to keep active and feel that they belong and can contribute to different communities in their cities and the country. The challenge for policymakers and health promotion programmes is that older adults need to be actively included in developing and maintaining social arenas for virtuous ageing to flourish (Laceulle 2017), and writing courses, such as the one we discussed in this chapter, serve this purpose.

Acknowledgements

We are especially grateful to each participant who attended the course, as well as the teachers Marte Huke and Cecilie Wold Andersen. Special thanks to Sukhanwar Gulabuddin from the Literature House of Trondheim and the Local Library of Trondheim for their support with logistics and finding a location. We are also grateful to Mark Freeman, William Randall and Oddgeir Synnes for their detailed feedback on earlier versions of this manuscript. Last but not least, we would like to thank Gregory Orr for his generosity in sharing his poem on Whitman with us and giving us permission to use it in this chapter.

References

Alex, J. L. (2010), Older Adults and a Writing Workshop: A Phenomenological Study. (Unpublished doctoral dissertation, dissertation 466). The University of Southern Mississippi, Hattiesburg. https://aquila.usm.edu/dissertations/466

Aadlandsvik, R. (2007), 'Education, Poetry, and the Process of Growing Old', *Educational Gerontology* 33 (8), 665–678.

Argüello Manresa, G. and V. Glăveanu (2017), 'Poetry in and for Society: Poetic Messages, Creativity and Social Change', in O. Lehmann, N. Chaudhary, A. C. Bastos and E. Abbey (eds.), *Poetry and Imagined Worlds*, 43–62, Cham, Switzerland: Palgrave Macmillan.

Bahl, N. K. H., H. E. Nafstad, R. M. Blakar and A. Geirdal (2017), 'Responsibility for Psychological Sense of Community and Well-being in Old Age: A Qualitative Study of Urban Older Adults in Norway', *Open Journal of Social Sciences* 5 (7), 321–338. https://doi.org/10.4236/jss.2017.57020

Bendien, E. (2016), 'Teaching Through Remembering: Using Written Reminiscences in Courses for Older Adults', *Gerontology & Geriatrics Education* 37, 255–272. doi:10.1080/02701960.2016.1152269

Brinkmann, S. (2011), *Psychology as a Moral Science: Perspectives on Normativity*, New York: Springer.

Brinkmann, S. (2021), *Vi er det liv, vi lever: En fortælling om skæbnen* (We Are the Life that We Live: A Story of Fate), Copenhagen: Politikens forlag.

Chamberlin, J. (2014), Retiring Minds Want to Know. *Monitor on Psychology*, 45 (1): 61.

Churchill, S. D. (2022), *Essentials of Existential Phenomenological Research*, Washington, DC: American Psychological Association.

Cooper, M. (2017), *Existential Therapies*, London: SAGE.

de Medeiros, K. (2007), 'Beyond the Memoir: Telling Life Stories Using Multiple Literary Forms', *Journal of Aging, Humanities, and the Arts* 1 (3-4): 159-167.

Dylan, B. (1962), 'Song to Woody', (Produced by J. H. Hammond). *Bob Dylan*. New York: Columbia Records.

Faulkner, S. L. (2005, May), How Do You Know a Good Poem? Poetic Re-presentation and the Case for Criteria. Paper presented at the 1st International Conference of Qualitative Inquiry, University of Illinois at Urbana-Champaign.

Faulkner, S. L. (2009), *Poetry as Method: Reporting Research Through Verse*, Walnut Creek, CA: Left Coast Press.

Frankl, V. (1994), *El hombre doliente. Fundamentos antropológicos de la psicoterapia* (Homo patients. Anthropological foundations of psychotherapy), Barcelona, Spain: Herder. (Original work published 1975)

García Márquez, G. (2002), *Vivir para contarla* (Living to tell the tale), Bogotá: Norma.

Giorgi, A. (2012), 'The Descriptive Phenomenological Psychological Method', *Journal of Phenomenological Psychology* 43 (1), 3-12. https://doi.org/10.1163/156916212X632934

Jackson, M. and A. Piette (2015), *What is Existential Anthropology?*, New York: Berghahn Books.

Laceulle, H. (2017), 'Virtuous aging and existential vulnerability', *Journal of Aging Studies* 43: 1-8. doi:10.1016/j.jaging.2017.08.001

Laceulle, H. (2018), 'Aging and the Ethics of Authenticity', *The Gerontologist* 58 (5), 970-978. doi:10.1093/geront/gnx037

Längle, A. and C. Probst (2000), 'Existential Questions of the Elderly', *International Medical Journal* 7 (3): 193-196.

Lehmann, O. V. (2018a), 'Meaning Focused Perspectives on Suffering, Compassion, and Caregiving for the Elderly. A Commentary on Schulz's & Monin's Model', In, T. Boll., D. Ferring and J. Valsiner (eds), *Cultures of Care in Aging*, 251-269, Charlotte, NC: Information Age Publishing.

Lehmann, O. V. (2018b), 'The cultural psychology of silence: Treasuring the poetics of affect at the core of human existence' (Unpublished doctoral dissertation), NTNU Norwegian University of Science and Technology, Trondheim, Norway. Retrieved from https://brage.bibsys.no/xmlui/handle/11250/2484902

Lehmann, O. V. and S. Brinkmann (2019a), '"Humbled by Life": Poetic Representations of Existential Pathways and Personal Life Philosophies Among Older Adults in Norway', *Qualitative Inquiry*. https://doi.org/10.1177/1077800419885414

Lehmann, O. V. and S. Brinkmann (2019b), 'Revisiting "The Art of Being Fragile": Why Cultural Psychology needs Literature and Poetry', *Culture &Psychology* https://doi.org/10.1177/1354067X19862183.

Lehmann, O. V. and S. Brinkmann (2019c), '"I'm the one who has written this": Reciprocity and existential meaning-making in writing courses for older adults in Norway', *International Journal of Qualitative Studies on Health and Well-being* 14. 10.1080/17482631.2019.1650586

Lehmann, O. V. and S. H. Klempe (2015), 'Psychology and the Notion of the Spirit: Implications of Max Scheler's Anthropological Philosophy in Theory of Psychology', *Integrative Psychological & Behavioral Science* 49 (3), 478-484. doi:10.1007/s12124-015-9295-5

Lehmann, O. V., R. A. Neimeyer, J. Thimm, A. Hjeltnes, R. Lengelle and T. G. Kalstad (2022), 'Experiences of Norwegian Mothers Attending an Online Course of Therapeutic Writing Following the Unexpected Death of a Child', *Frontiers in Psychology* 12, article 809848.

Low, G., A. Molzahn and M. Kalfoss (2014), 'Cultural Frames, Qualities of Life, and the Aging Self', *Western Journal of Nursing Research* 36 (5) 643–663. doi: 10.1177/0193945913507635

Midtsundstad, T. and H. Bogen (2014), 'Active Aging Policies between Individual Needs and Collective Goods: A Study of Active Aging Policies and Practices in Norway', *Nordic Journal of Working Life Studies* 4 (2): 139–158.

Neimeyer, R. (2016), *Techniques of Grief Therapy: Assessment and Intervention*, New York: Routledge.

Osborne, J. W. (1990), 'Some Basic Existential-phenomenological Research Methodology for Counsellors', *Canadian Journal of Counselling* 24 (2), 79–91.

Orr, G. (2022), *Selected Books of the Beloved*, Port Townsend: Copper Canyon Press.

Paz, O. (1956/1999), *El Arco y la lira* (The Bow and the Lyre), Barcelona: Galaxia-Gutemberg.

Pennebaker, J. W. (1999), 'Writing About Emotional Experiences As A Therapeutic Process', *Psychological Science* 8 (3), 162–166.

Pillemer, K. (2012), *30 Lessons for Living: Tried and True Advice from the Wisest Americans*, New York: Plume.

Ruddick, W. (1999), 'Hope and Deception', *Bioethics* 13 (3/4), 343–357, https://pubmed.ncbi.nlm.nih.gov/11657244/.

Saunders, P. (2006), 'Silent No More: Older Adults as Poets: Creative Writing as a Preventative Approach to Cognitive Decline of the Elderly' (Unpublished doctoral dissertation), Union Institute and University.

Synnes, O. (2016), 'Storytelling as a Dignity-preserving Practice in Palliative Care', in O. Tranvåg, O. Synnes and W. McSherry (eds), *Stories of Dignity within Healthcare: Research, Narratives and Theories*, 61–74, Keswick, Cumbria, UK: M&K Publishing.

Synnes, O., M. Råheim, E. Lykkeslet and E. Gjengedal (2021), 'A Complex Reminding: The Ethics of Poetry Writing in Dementia Care', *Dementia* 20 (3): 1025–1043. https://doi.org/10.1177/1471301220922750

Swinnen, A. M. C. (2016), 'Healing words: A study of poetry interventions in dementia care', *Dementia* 15 (6), 1377–1404. https://doi.org/10.1177/1471301214560378

Swinnen, A. and K. de Medeiros (2018), 'Participatory arts programs in residential dementia care: Playing with language differences', *Dementia* 17 (6), 763–774. https://doi.org/10.1177/1471301217729985

Yalom, I. (1980), *Existential psychotherapy*, New York: Basic Books.

Zittoun, T. (2006), *Transitions: Development through Symbolic Resources*, Greenwich: Information Age Publishing.

Zittoun, T. (2017a), 'Imagining Self in a Changing World – An Exploration of "Studies of Marriage"'. In M. Han and C. Cunha (eds.) *The Subjectified and Subjectifying Mind*, 85–116, Charlotte, NC: Information Age Publishing.

Zittoun, T. (2017b). 'The Concern for Poesis and Imagination', in O. V. Lehmann, O. N. Chaudhary, A. C. Bastos and E. Abbey (eds.), *Poetry and Imagined Worlds: Creativity and Everyday Experience*, 81–95, London: Palgrave Macmillan.

Zittoun. T. and A. Baucal (2021), 'The relevance of a sociocultural perspective for understanding learning and development in older age', *Learning, Culture and Social Interaction* 28, https://doi.org/10.1016/j.lcsi.2020.100453

Zittoun, T., J. Valsiner, D. Vedeler, J. Salgado, M. Goncalves, and D. Ferring (2013), *Human Development in the Life Course: Melodies of Living*, Cambridge, UK: Cambridge University Press.

8

The Poetics of Growing Old: Metaphoric Competence and the Philosophic Homework of Later Life

William L. Randall

The wilderness within: An introduction

'Literature is a wilderness, psychology is a garden' (Albright 1994: 19). Straddling these two worlds, literature and psychology, a narrative approach to ageing, or a *narrative gerontology*, takes this blunt assessment very much to heart. In contrast to the medical model that tends to dominate our perceptions of ageing, narrative gerontology takes its cue from the 'root metaphor' of life-as-*story* (Sarbin 1986) and views ageing as more than just a sad saga of disability and disease, more than a 'narrative of decline' (Gullette 2004). Rather, and this constitutes a different starting-point, a different lens, for construing what ageing is,[1] narrative gerontology (or at least my *version* of it) views our lives – as we experience them subjectively – as quasi-literary texts which we ourselves are continually composing, as author, narrator, protagonist, editor, and reader, more or less at once. It sees them not as reducible to what's happening with our bodies but as meandering works of creative non-fiction – or *faction* – that we're forever storying and re-storying in our memory and imagination (Kenyon, Bohlmeijer and Randall 2011). It sees them as novels-in-the-making, which we fashion from within, which to varying degrees we take to be 'true', and which, potentially, grow richer with meaning the nearer we reach The End (Randall and Khurshid 2017). 'As life goes on', echoes the poet, John Hall Wheelock, writing at 90, 'it becomes more intense because there are tremendous numbers of associations, and so many memories' (cited in Sarton 1981: 231).

Composing and comprehending these intricate, multi-layered texts, so inseparable from our sense of who we *are* (Randall 2014), requires an immense amount of '*narrative imagination*' (Andrews 2014). Our exercise of such imagination has to do with *poetics*, a term that I use here in much the same broad sense that Mark Freeman does with his

---

[1] Let me distinguish here briefly between *narrative* gerontology and *literary* gerontology. Though these two fields are linked by virtue of their common leaning toward the humanities over the social sciences, the latter concentrates on the portrayal of the aged, and ageing, in literary texts. The former, at least as I come at it, takes the more radical, conceptual tack of looking at our lives themselves as texts that we are in the middle of, making them up as we go.

notion of the 'poetics of selfhood' (1999), or that Paul Ricoeur does with his vision of 'a poetics of being' (see Synnes, Romm and Bondevik 2021: 177). I use it in the sense, less of poetry per se, in other words, than of (so to speak) 'literariness' in general. As literary scholar Shlomith Rimmon-Kenan (1989) expresses it, poetics 'deals with the question of "What is Literature?" and with all possible questions developed from it' (2).

A literary perspective on later life, then, pulls us from the earnest world of social science, with its emphasis on hypotheses and methodologies, on variables and statistics, and ushers us into the bewildering world of novels, poetry and art, with all the ambiguity and allusion, irony and innuendo, and interpretive possibilities which that world entails. More than mainstream psychology can do justice to, that world mirrors the complexity of what I call our *texistence* (Randall and McKim 2008: 5); that intricate, internal terrain of memories, emotions, and 'associations' that we criss-cross continually, often confusedly, as we age – as we age *biographically*, that is. This inner wilderness can overwhelm us, in other words, with its vastness and depth. How do I even *tell* 'my story', we may find ourselves asking, let alone make sense of it? How can I step back from it sufficiently to assess it, to review it, to reach any sort of conclusions concerning it? Indeed, is it one story or many? And might it reflect many genres besides 'story' itself?

The chronological route of inventorying our lives – which has its place in the 'life review' process that Erikson saw as essential to achieving a measure of 'ego integrity' (Butler 1963) – is a worthy avenue for approaching such questions. In order to examine our lives, we need first to recall them. Says the poet, Malcolm Cowley (1980), writing in his eighties: 'before passing judgment, we have to untangle the plot of the play ... the first step is simply remembering' (72). A next step, I propose, however, is through the medium of metaphor. Following the lead of Ricoeur, for whom narrative and metaphor are closely linked as semantic innovation, in terms of how we come to orient ourselves in the world by way of interpretation (Synnes et al. 2021: 177), my premise in this chapter is that by developing a dimension of our narrative imagination that could be called 'metaphoric competence' (Gardner and Winner 1979) and employing it in the process of 'reading our lives' (Randall and McKim 2008), we can expand our self-awareness, enrich our autobiographical reasoning, strengthen our internal resilience (Randall et al. 2015), and enhance our mental and emotional health overall. We can be helped to make out themes, tease out patterns, toy with possibilities, and arrive at (always provisional) insights into our stories and our selves, a process that leads to the enlargement of our inner life and, with it, an enhanced sense of substance and self-worth, or at the very least, of interestingness. We can be aided, too, in addressing the 'philosophic homework' that later life is said to assign us (Schacter-Shalomi and Miller 1995: 124–7). We can be aided to truly *grow* old, as I like to put it, and not just *get* old.

In this chapter, my overarching aim is to contemplate the intimate links between memory, metaphor, meaning, and emotion in later life (see Randall 2011) by sketching a vision of what I have elsewhere (Randall and McKim 2008) called the poetics of growing old. I shall do this by commenting, first, on the element of mystery that runs through the stories of our lives; next, by elaborating on the concept, just mentioned, of 'metaphoric competence'; and then enlarging a little on this idea of the 'philosophic homework' of later life. Finally, and in a more practice-oriented vein, which is my natural bent, I'll look at various ways of exploring and expanding older people's storyworlds (including our own) through the medium of metaphorical reflection – or more precisely perhaps, of metaphorical *play*.

The mystery in my story

Much of my scholarly career has been devoted to playing with one metaphor in particular in order to shed light on such vital but overlooked topics in the study of ageing as meaning, spirituality, and wisdom. It's the familiar metaphor of *life-as-story*, as in the common expression that we have all at some point uttered or heard: 'the story of my life'. But 'familiar' hardly means straightforward. As one of my students once noted, 'there's nothing simple about a life story!'

For starters, the stories of our lives embrace multiple subplots, chapters, and themes, plus countless little stories (or memories, insofar as memory – *autobiographical memory* – has a narrative dimension (Rubin 1995: 2)) that we are capable of recounting, plus countless others that we aren't. And there are any number of larger, longer stories about our life overall that we can rattle off, depending upon our audience or the point of view we take in telling it. In the words of autobiography scholar, Paul John Eakin (1999): 'there are many stories of Self to tell, and many selves to tell them' (xi). Within the storyworld that is our unique life, or what Arthur Frank (2010) would call our 'narrative habitus' (49), there is all manner of narrative material with seemingly no central thread to provide us with more than occasional tastes of 'narrative coherence' (Hyvärinen et al. 2010). Besides 'small stories' (stories, e.g., about what we did last evening) and 'big stories' about our life as a whole (Bamberg 2006), there are obviously short ones and long ones as well. There are also shared stories and solo stories. There are secret stories, 'nostalgic stories' (Synnes 2015), and 'signature stories' (Kenyon and Randall 1997: 46–9): stories of poignant or important experiences which, for whatever reasons, we enjoy relating to others. There are back stories and 'shadow stories' (de Medeiros and Rubinstein 2015), stories behind stories and stories inside of stories. There are stories about the past and stories about the future, stories of what might have been and of what might still be. And at the edges of this swirl of story stuff lurks all manner of 'narrative debris' (McKendy 2006: 473): bits and shards of memories, such as the novelist Thomas Wolfe (1938/1983) alludes to when he speaks of 'the million little things that we have known all our lives but for which we never found a word . . . all the things remembered and forgotten' (88); 'that . . . will return unbidden in an unexpected moment' (44).

As my student astutely noted, then, a life story is scarcely a straightforward commodity. Nor does it ever stand still. As the poet May Sarton (1981), writing in her seventies, expresses it: 'the past is always changing, is never static, never "placed" forever like a book on a shelf. As we grow and change, we understand things . . . in new ways' (95). This dynamic element to our life stories is captured by psychologist Donald Polkinghorne (1988) in his masterful book, *Narrative Knowing and the Human Sciences*. In it, he paves the way for the perspective that I'm proposing here by 'envision[ing] the primary organizing principles in human experience as more akin to those that construct poetic meaning than to those that construct the proofs of formal logic' (16). Moreover, he sees 'the realm of meaning [as] an open system in which new forms of organization can emerge and new meaning systems can be developed' (16). Put simply, he says, 'we are in the middle of our stories and cannot be sure how they will end. We are constantly having to revise the plot as new events are added to our lives' (150).

An important way into this ever-shifting corpus of narrative material, so impossible to tame yet so inseparable from our sense of self, is *metaphor*. (See also Mazzarella, in this volume). It is a way into what another student on my course on Narrative Gerontology, who throughout the semester found herself growing in awe at the narrative complexity of her own life, described aloud to the class one day as 'the mystery in my story'. It is not the sole way, to be sure, but a potent one nonetheless, opening up fresh avenues of entry into countless corners of our personal storyworld. Before looking at various approaches for employing metaphorical reflection to probe this mystery, let me say more, though, about this concept of *metaphoric competence*.

Metaphoric competence

Metaphor is so central to human experience that it is difficult to state clearly what it is. It's as if we need metaphors to explain what metaphors are and do. At a very basic level, we can think of metaphor as using a familiar, perhaps concrete, thing to illuminate an abstract dimension of some other thing. *My love is a rose, my car is a lemon*, and *my heart is broken* are simple examples. But metaphor is more pervasive than this, for it is not just about inserting flowery phrases to enliven dull prose. Metaphor infuses our conception of virtually anything that we can think of, certainly of grand topics like Time or Life, or even Ageing itself (see Kenyon, Birren and Schroots 1991), and certainly God, plus everything from the solitary atom to the cosmos as a whole. Science, philosophy, theology – all are reliant on metaphors and their 'entailments' (Lakoff and Johnson 1980) to inspire the inquiries that they undertake and to persuade others of their conclusions. Religion, especially, relies on metaphorical expression. We can scarcely get through a passage of scripture, a line in a prayer, or a verse in a hymn without encountering expressions that in any other context would make no sense whatsoever. Meanwhile, of course, literature and art are absolutely rampant with metaphorical allusion – poetry, above all.

For its part, therapy, including *narrative* therapy, revolves around clients and clinicians interrogating the stories by which clients are living (though perhaps not thriving) and trying on more growth-inviting stories instead. Often, in fact, a particular metaphor will surface in their conversations that captures precisely what the client is experiencing, in effect 'creat[ing] an experience that [the client] has never had before' (Schafer 1983: 127). As Roy Schafer (1992) puts it in his book *Retelling a Life: Narrative and Dialogue in Psychoanalysis*, 'metaphor may establish [in the dialogue between analyst and analysand] a storyline, and what is called unpacking a metaphor is … much like laying out the kinds of story that are entailed by the metaphor' (32). This process of metaphorical exploration is encouraged in something explicitly called 'metaphor therapy', where by completing a phrase such as *my life is like* ___ or *I am like*

___, one experiences 'a deeper immersion in one's metaphorical imagination' (Kopp, cited in Chavis 2011: 173). Explaining what is happening in such a process on a cognitive level, Polkinghorne (1988) notes how 'experience makes connections and enlarges itself through the use of metaphoric processes that link together experiences similar but not exactly the same, and it evaluates items according to the positions they hold in relation to larger wholes' (16). Given its central if subtle role, then, in promoting personal change, we might say that metaphor fuels metamorphosis. For all such reasons, Ricoeur is right to honour *The Rule of Metaphor* (1981).

Educators have capitalized on this insight in relation to learning a language. Learning in general, of course, relies implicitly on metaphorical processes, insofar as we can only be said to understand an unfamiliar concept when we can relate it to a familiar one – for example, envisioning the structure of the atom as a miniature solar system, or thinking of the universe as beginning with a Big Bang. But learning a language is doubly metaphorical in that we can only be deemed proficient in it when we are able to grasp the meaning of the metaphors that infuse it, from the level of idiomatic phrases to that of individual words. Key to mastering a language is 'metaphoric competence' (Gardner and Winner 1979; Littlemore 2001).

Metaphoric competence is a complex cognitive capacity that is hardly 'of a single piece' (Gardner and Winner 1979: 136). At the very least, though, it involves *metaphoric comprehension* and *metaphoric production*: the ability both to paraphrase particular figures of speech and to generate fresh metaphors of our own. It is a dimension of so-called 'linguistic intelligence' that certain individuals – poets, for certain – have honed to a tee. But it goes beyond language per se, since it is not merely a turn of phrase but also an action or an object that can perform a metaphorical function (e.g., Randall and Robinson, in press). A handshake can be an expression of friendship. A lock of hair can stand for a cherished relationship. A cross can signify an entire spiritual tradition. And a work of fiction can serve as an extended metaphor for a universe of possibilities into which, by virtue of our (narrative) imaginations, we can insert our own selves.

The concept of metaphoric competence needs to be broadened, however, to embrace the domain of affect as well (see Ricoeur 1981). The comprehension and production of metaphor concerns not just the workings of our thoughts but – often profoundly – of our emotions too. Developing our 'emotional intelligence' (Goleman 1995), for instance, can entail identifying what we are feeling, and why, by summoning some metaphor to assist us. 'It's like I'm drowning in a sea of guilt' or 'My life is always one step forward and two steps back', and so forth. As for the emotional complexity of ageing in general, however, not to mention the intricate links between emotion and memory, and the role of metaphor in mediating between the two, these are relatively underexplored areas within the study of ageing (see Magai and McFadden 1996), though hopefully my line of thinking in this chapter will help modestly to address that gap.

In these various ways then, metaphoric competence, or the metaphorical imagination, is so central to cognition, to emotion, and indeed to development in general, that it would seem to be bred in the bone. It seems logical, therefore, that it evolves from childhood onwards, such that an expression that we may take literally as toddlers (e.g., *my heart is broken*) assumes increasingly symbolic significance as we move through our teens and beyond. That said, few studies to date have examined directly how such competence changes across the lifespan, and into old age in particular. What has been studied, however, is a shift with age in our style of reasoning overall that is known as 'post-formal operational thought' (Csikszentimihalyi and Rathunde 1990; Kramer 1983).

Based on the work of French psychologist, Jean Piaget, post-formal thought is a 'higher-level reasoning' (Cohen 2005: 36) – of *autobiographical* reasoning, in particular (see Habermas 2010) – that we become more capable of in later life. The capacity for such reasoning is due in part, claims gerontologist Gene Cohen (2005), to changes in the functioning of our brains themselves. Among these are increased cooperation between our left hemisphere and our right, which is particularly interesting from a narrative perspective insofar as, for Cohen, greater 'bilateral involvement' leads to an intensification of 'the autobiographical drive' (23). Post-formal thought, he suggests, involves three types of thinking.

First is *relativistic thinking*, which means 'understanding that knowledge sometimes reflects on our subjective perspective, that the context of a situation influences our conclusions, that contexts can change, and that answers are not absolute' (36). In other words, post-formal thinking entails an increased capacity to tolerate ambiguity, in life generally and our own life in particular. Second is *dualistic thinking*, which means 'the ability to uncover and resolve contradictions in opposing and seemingly incompatible views' (37). It means the ability to appreciate the yin and yang of things, to tolerate paradox and irony – in the world, in others, in ourselves. Third is *systematic thinking*, which 'means being able to see the forest instead of the trees. It's an ability to pull back from an idea or situation to take a broader view of the entire system of knowledge, ideas, and context that are involved' (37). It's the ability to step back from the day-to-day minutiae of our lives and take the long view of things.

The emergence of such thinking coincides nicely, it bears noting, with the sheer accumulation of memories and experiences that later life brings. Because of this, I would submit, it can entail the capacity to appreciate not just paradox and contradiction but metaphor and symbol as well. Psychologist Gisela Labouvie-Vief (1990), for example, observes in a published discussion of 'Wisdom as Integrated Thought' that, when presented with pieces of text, there are clear 'qualitative differences in text processing between younger and more mature adults' (69). Specifically, 'the more mature individual construes text not only logically but also psychologically and symbolically' (69). In effect, and in tandem with the changes just noted in our brains, there is 'a balancing of logos [and] mythos' as we continue to age – a trend that, arguably, figures in the 'late style' that is said to characterize the works of ageing painters, musicians, and other highly creative individuals (Said 2006). Paralleling the logos–mythos distinction is of course the one proposed by Bruner (1986) between 'logical thought' and 'narrative thought', a differentiation that has done as much as any to drive the so-called 'narrative turn' whose impact is reaching increasingly throughout the scholarly world. For an assortment of reasons, then, later life may be 'the narrative phase par excellence' (Freeman 1997: 394): the phase in which, to use another of Bruner's (1986) distinctions, we shift from the 'landscape of action' to the 'landscape of consciousness' (14).

Briefly, the landscape of action concerns the setting and events of a story. It is, if you like, the story's outside or objective dimension. The landscape of consciousness, however, concerns the various interpretations – or, if you like, emplotments – that are possible of these various features; for instance, events as viewed or experienced by the narrator, or through the eyes of the different characters, the reader, etc. This landscape corresponds to the *inside* of the story, its subjective dimension. Relating this to *life-story*, it could be said, then, that ageing itself nudges us from the former to the latter, from the objective to the subjective. More to the point, while there is arguably a limit to the scope of the objective or outside dimension (i.e., what happened, happened!), there is none whatsoever to that of the subjective or inner dimension. And it is in this realm that the inner material of our lives, in all its complexity and messiness, is so amenable to multiple readings. As such, metaphor is key.

In *Reminiscence and the Self in Old Age*, psychologist Edmund Sherman (1991) explains how, as we saw with therapy, 'metaphor enables us to take experiences and construct them into larger meaningful wholes', leading to 'valuable new linkages or integrations with other life experiences' (87). Thus, 'the metaphorical suggestibility of memory is revealed...as endless'. This endlessness is rendered all the more complicated, of course, insofar as memories – autobiographical memories, that is – inevitably possess a potent emotional component (Ruth and Vilkko 1996), while emotions themselves are, at once, 'preferred objects of metaphors' (Habermas 2019: 56) and 'narrative constructions' (Singer 1996: 447). Given this intense intertwining of memory, metaphor, emotion, *and* narrative, it is no wonder then that, in Sherman's (1991) words, 'memory is infinite in its metaphorical potential'. If later life is the narrative phase, then it is arguably the *metaphoric* phase as well.

As excited as I am by Sherman's point, I'm certainly not proposing that ageing itself automatically increases our metaphoric competence, making us more open to metaphorical suggestibility. For many as they age, the opposite is true, those in the grip of 'narrative foreclosure', for instance, whose narrative imaginations have been, not inspired but impoverished by the countless challenges, physical and otherwise, that ageing can bring (Bohlmeijer et al. 2011). What I *am* proposing, however, is that such competence can be enhanced. Shortly, I'll be outlining various ways that it can, and along with it, our ability to engage in the type of narrative reflection associated with the philosophic homework that I referred to before. Before this, though, let me say more about what such homework involves.

The philosophic homework of later life

Inquire within ... Know thyself ... Such advice can sound more loudly inside of us as we age, and as we dis-engage, to use a word that gerontologists associate with Disengagement Theory, a theory, it seems, now widely disparaged. I fear, though, that we have thrown out the baby with the bathwater, and that some measure of disengagement is not by nature a bad thing, a theme that Lars Tornstam's (1996) theory of 'gerotranscendence' obviously supports. I don't necessarily mean pulling back from life in an outward way, although for many that occurs for a range of understandable reasons. I mean pulling back in an inward way, or pulling *in* – like the older woman whom I visited one rainy afternoon, an artist by profession, who confided in me that it was an ideal day to 'crawl up inside of myself'. Jung (1976) puts the point still more starkly: 'for the ageing person it is a duty and a necessity to devote serious attention to himself' (17). If you will, there is a special brand of learning that is vital to engage in as we age, something that I've come to call 'autobiographical learning' (Randall 2010), namely learning about and, more importantly perhaps, *from* the stories of our own lives. I see such learning as central to what psychologists might call the 'developmental tasks' that await us in later life, tasks that are subtler and more internal, as it were, than those we face, say, as children or adolescents, but are no less critical to tackle. For me, the phrase 'philosophic homework' captures nicely what they involve.

In using this (to me) enticing phrase, 'philosophic homework', in his popular book, *From Age-ing to Sage-ing*, Rabbi Zalman Schacter-Shalomi, founder of the *Spiritual Eldering Institute*, does not, alas, define it precisely (Schacter-Shalomi and Miller 1995). Nonetheless, in keeping with Erikson's vision of 'life review' as essential to achieving some degree of 'ego integrity' in later life, Schacter-Shalomi sees it as bound up with the need 'to synthesize wisdom from long life experience' (124) and to 'wrestle' intentionally 'with ... transcendent questions' – such as 'What has it all meant?, where did I come from?, and what is my next destination?' (124). Such homework, then, is less about nailing down answers than about keeping open to the questions. It involves what the psychotherapist, Ira Progoff (1975), originator of the *Intensive Journal Process*, calls the 'progressive deepening' (270) or 'progressive enlargement' (99) of our inner worlds. It involves sifting through, and delving into, the mass of narrative material that I talked about before, however inconclusive that process will necessarily be. Inasmuch as we are in the middle of our stories, forever revising the plot, with no end of narrative debris to distract us, our lives, that is, are gloriously open-ended, amenable to multiple readings from multiple angles and thus to multiple meanings. Mark Freeman (1993: 184) sums the matter up beautifully: 'our lives', he writes, '[are] like richly ambiguous texts to be interpreted and understood ... whose meanings are inexhaustible, whose mysterious existence ceaselessly calls forth the desire to know, whose readings cannot ever yield a final closure' (see also Freeman, in this volume).

Exploring our storyworlds through metaphorical play

Envisioning our lives in this open-ended manner may, admittedly, be threatening to some, but it may also inspire 'the thrill of narrative freedom' (Gullette 2004: 158). This is precisely what can happen, in fact, when we play with the narrative root metaphor itself, the first avenue of metaphorical reflection that I'd like to look at now. I've seen it happen time and again, whether with students in my classes or with participants in workshops that I've led. Extracting ourselves temporarily from the landscape of action and viewing our lives through an explicitly 'story' lens can afford us a gently ironic, affectionate detachment (disengagement) from experiences by which we might continue being troubled (Randall 2013). It can free us to view them as but one chapter or one episode in the larger story of our lives – not the *whole* story at all. It can infuse us with curiosity, even wonder, as to what new chapters and adventures might yet await us, what discoveries and learnings, inner and outer, lie ahead, what new themes and characters might enter our storyworld and take it in unforeseeable directions. Researching the impact of keeping a journal in later life on our 'horizon of self-understanding', gerontologist Harry Berman (1994) writes, for instance, that 'as our horizon ... shifts, it may become apparent that we were not in the middle of the story we thought we were in the middle of. Perhaps we thought our life was a tragedy and all along, unbeknownst to us, it was a romance. Or perhaps we thought our life was almost over, at least in terms of the future holding anything new, and it turned out there was a lot more to it' (180).

Dutch gerontologists have implemented an intervention called 'creative reminiscence' (Bohlmeijer et al. 2005) for older adults coping with depression that effects a similar sort of (so to speak) *re-genre-ation*. Participants are invited to create collages, or to engage in poetry-writing or painting, as a means of gaining distance on issues that are dominating their minds. The results, uniformly, are an increased sense of meaning, agency, and purpose in life, not to mention a decrease in their depressive symptomatology. Along the same lines, gerontological social workers, Nancy Kropf and Cindy Tandy (1998), have adapted strategies from narrative therapy to assist depressed older clients, certainly one in particular, in shifting from a characterization of herself as a 'failure' to that of a 'survivor'. In essence, a different metaphor invited her to play with a more positive emplotment of her life's events, to look back upon her struggles and losses, for instance, and re-envision them as important occasions for learning and growth. And with this more positive storyline, there emerged in her sunnier, more self-affirming feelings about her life as a whole.

The late James Birren pioneered a group-based life review programme called 'guided autobiography', which uses a thematic approach to achieve similarly positive results (Birren and Deutchman 1991). The first theme that members are invited to consider concerns 'The major branching points in your life' (67). They are asked to think of their life as, say, 'a branching tree, as a flowing river that has many juncture points, or as a trailing plant that puts down roots at various places and then grows on' (67). This sort of visual cue encourages them to step back from their lives overall and to identify key periods where they made this decision rather than that one – moved here rather than there: turning points 'that significantly affect the direction or flow of our life' (68). As with metaphor therapy, other exercises include having them think of themselves as particular animals (lion, pussycat, turtle, etc.) or flowers (sunflower, dandelion, rose, etc.) (88). The overall aim of such activities is to afford people distance on how they are storying their lives and 'trade in and up the old metaphors that [they] use to characterize [them]selves' (86f). (See Mazzarella, in this volume.)

Comparable reflections have been stimulated as part of a research project that I've been involved in that is exploring the links between the resilience older adults bring to the challenges of ageing and the sorts of stories that they tell about their lives (Randall et al. 2015). Our hunch all along has been that the stronger the story – namely, the more complex or layered it is, the more narrative agency the person experiences in the midst of it, and the more emotionally nuanced their telling and reading of it – then the greater will be their reservoir of 'inner resources' (Dubovska et al. 2017) and thus their internal resilience: their *narrative* resilience, if you will. As part of the project, we held three one-day life-writing workshops in which participants engaged in a number of writing exercises for exploring their life-stories in ever-increasing depth. In one, they were asked to write freely for eight minutes using the prompt 'Once upon a time …'. This invited them to step outside themselves in an imaginary manner and to view their life as if from afar, in the process triggering playful reflections on their whole way of being in the world.

In another project I've been working on, two colleagues and I have been re-visiting fairy tales and other little stories that we've remembered since our childhood – *Sleeping Beauty*, *The Tortoise and the Hare*, *The Ugly Duckling*, and the like – to see what they say to us now that we're in our sixties and seventies (Randall, Lewis and Achenbaum, 2022). Treating these tales as Rorschach blots almost, we've found this to be a fascinating means of probing the mysteries of our respective storyworlds (see, e.g., Bettelheim 1975). It has enticed us to re-visit nooks and crannies of our memories and to ponder issues that have lurked there quietly for years, issues that re-reading these stories has coaxed back to consciousness for us to reflect upon more fully, with decades of experience now under our belts to broaden our perspective and deepen our understanding. The symbols and images in which they abound have had the most amazing sort of ripple effect inside of us, not unlike what metaphors can have within works of fiction, one that reaches down into our psyches and 'generates its own momentum' (Alter 1989: 94). Author Wendy Lesser (2002) writes of such an experience when she re-reads works of literature that have touched her heart deeply, though differently, across the years, works of poetry in particular. 'For poetry', she writes, 'is the form that most invites rereading, its density insuring that you will harvest new meanings at each return and its brevity making such returns manageable' (53).

This calls to mind comments made by an acquaintance of mine in her seventies who lives in the hills of Appalachia, encircled by neighbours whose conservative views clash sharply with her own. Describing her experience of re-reading pieces by her favourite poets, she writes:

> I think I do this in much the same way that some of my neighbours read the Bible, and for perhaps the same reason: for the solace these poets' words bring me, if I concentrate on them, and let the images they paint infuse into me.… The more I read and reread these … poems, the more I am granted a kind of internal peace.
> (E. Hunter, personal communication, 2020)

She goes on, citing other books that she reads, her sentiments paralleling those of Polkinghorne (1988) about how 'experience makes connections and enlarges itself through the use of metaphoric processes' (16):

> I like to read books that seem to resonate not just with my life but with each other, and for whatever reason, these *and* the poetry, do. It all feels *enlarging*, which is REALLY important to me in a world that feels increasingly stifling, and a time of life which inevitably does too.
> (Hunter, personal communication, 2020; emphasis hers)

Hospice chaplain, Robert Mundle (2019), discusses the soulful role that poetry can play in the lives of the terminally ill. In *How To Be An Even Better Listener*, he tells the story of Maria, an older Spanish-speaking woman who had arrived in palliative care 'alone and afraid' (32). On learning from family members that she loved to write poetry, he and his colleagues on the unit presented her with paper and pens. After some time, the poems 'began to tumble out of her' (33), two of which she made a point of presenting to him as a gift, works by well-known writers in her native Nicaragua that she had committed to memory years ago. While Mundle admits that 'Maria's relationship to poetry raised many questions for me' – above all, 'what did she wish to express to me through them at the end of her life?' – it was clear to him that 'poetry and metaphor can connect us to the seriously ill, and that such connection can be central to healing at the end of life in a holistic approach to care' (36). (See also Lehmann & Brinkmann, in this volume.)

While reading and re-reading poetry and fiction can surely enlarge our horizon of self-understanding in later life, including the end of life, so too can reading autobiography. In *Speaking in Parables: A Study in Metaphor and Theology*, Sallie TeSelle (1975) writes that: 'Like a good story, a good autobiography deals with a great unfamiliar, the mystery of the self, in and through the familiar, a multitude of events and circumstances. If the autobiography is true', she goes on, 'it points to the self elliptically through these events and circumstances; in other words, a successful autobiography is very similar to a parable' (145). While words like 'successful' and 'true' can be controversial to employ in relation to autobiography, her follow-up point seems obvious: 'We read autobiographies to find out about ourselves. The other is a medium, a metaphor, into that desert, *myself*' (146). That an autobiography is parabolic can be expressed, of course, in still more basic terms, insofar as any given autobiography exists in a metaphorical relationship to the life that it purports to sketch the story of. However, probing it might be, a 200–300-page memoir can scarcely mirror the full stream of events and emotions that the author experienced in living that life (see also Lehmann and Brinkmann, as well as Mazzarella, in this volume).

Reading about others' lives is one thing, but so, too, is writing about our own. Whether it be in a life-writing group where we turn particular experiences into entertaining tales, in keeping a journal such as a Progoff recommends, or in giving into the autobiographical drive and endeavouring to write *The Story of My Life* as a whole, it can have a similar parabolic impact. It can set off all manner of inner reflections, perhaps inspiring us to 'recontextualize' (Schachter-Shalomi and Miller 1995: 94–6), or re-genre-ate, apparent tragedies in our past – an aborted adventure, an unfulfilled dream, or a broken heart – as invaluable, if not needed, occasions for growth.

Obviously, such recontextualizing can sometimes go the other way, resulting in a sense not of resolution as regards the past but of regret and despair, a sense that the past is, so to speak, unredeemable. In such cases, a fitting intervention could be 'life review therapy' (Bohlmeijer and Westerhof 2011: 277–8), where a trained professional helps older adults suffering from depression to focus on, and flesh out, more positive memories than those negative ones on which they are otherwise obsessing. This risk acknowledged, and along with it, the need for a suitable intervention, I would nonetheless suggest that in the vast majority of instances – outside of clinical contexts, at least – autobiographical reflection can open us to the full complexity of our inner narrative world, its positive and negative dimensions alike; to how intriguing our lives have actually been; and to how wondrously open our memories can be. It can have the effect less of laying out the facts of our lives than of opening out the depths of our selves. Indeed, this is the inevitable by-product of autobiographical reflection, a process that Freeman (1993) perceives as 'fundamentally metaphorical' in nature, insofar as 'a new relationship is being created between the past and present, a new poetic configuration, designed to give greater form to one's previous – and present – experience. The text of the self is thus being rewritten' (30). Narrative development is thus, he says, 'a potentially infinite process' (Freeman 1991: 90).

Freeman's point calls to mind for me a participant in a workshop that I once helped to facilitate. A woman in her eighties, she announced proudly to the group over lunch that, just a few weeks beforehand, she had finished writing her memoir. As soon as our applause subsided, she made this follow-up announcement: 'and now I'm ready to start all over again!' It was as if, in penning the first version, not only had she recalled more details to include, but also, perhaps, had stumbled upon chapters that she'd forgotten altogether. Rather than tidying things up, writing her life had *opened* things up, enlarging her storyworld all the more. Memoirist Patricia Hampl (1999) has much the same experience in mind when she makes the observation that 'if we learn not only to tell our stories, but to listen to what our stories tell us – to write the first draft and then return for the second draft – we are doing the work of memory' (33). The 'work of memory', as Hampl puts it, is pivotal, I submit to the *home*work of later life.

A personal anecdote might help to illustrate how this homework – this *story*work, as I call it (Randall 2010) – can be tackled. One of my own signature stories is about how, at the age of two, I came down with polio, the 1950s counterpart to Covid-19. Because the disease had compromised the functioning of my diaphragm, I was placed for two weeks in an iron lung. For many years to follow, I heard myself regaling various friends and colleagues, sometimes even total strangers, with my little tale of being in the iron lung, garnering much-welcomed attention whenever I did: *Poor you. That must have been so hard* . . . It was not until I was in my mid-forties, however, that my parents sat me down and set me straight. The story, it turns out, isn't true. Oh sure, I had polio alright, and they were genuinely concerned. But it was no iron lung in which I was placed, but an oxygen tent – not nearly so epic a prop! Such a stinging challenge to this cornerstone of my narrative identity prompted me to enter upon a playful, often amusing, course of reflection as to why I'd come up with the story in the first place. What was *in* it, in other words? What metaphorical significance has it held for me? I suspect that I'll keep mining this tale for meaning, but here is what I wrote recently about the role that it's played in my life:

> . . . my iron lung story has been a secret source of psychic strength, enabling me to see myself as a hero at heart, albeit a passive, long-suffering one, yet a hero all the same. Or at the very least, different. Like an ace I've kept up my sleeve, it has served as a refuge, a shield, a line of last defence whenever my sense of self-worth has felt under assault.... But [when my parents set me straight], at nearly 45, with accomplishments under my belt and a self-assurance that I'd been lacking in the past, I could bid fond farewell to my beloved iron lung, thankful for the countless times that I'd enlisted it to come to my aid.
>
> (Randall 2019: 153f)

Concluding considerations

Let me conclude – to the extent that 'conclusions' are ever possible where a narrative perspective is concerned – by offering a metaphor or two for how metaphor works, in later life especially.

In pointing to memory's 'infinite metaphorical potential', Sherman implies that any metaphor, whatever its source (a poem, a memoir, a novel, a fairy tale, a therapist's suggestion, a prompt in a workshop, an image in a dream, a thought jotted in our journal), has the power to reach into our storyworld and, like a magnet, attract towards it all manner of narrative material. And different metaphors will attract different material around different themes, each unveiling a different pattern in the process – as happens each time we give a kid's kaleidoscope a twist. Each provides a partial, always provisional, experience of coherence, of meaning, of truth, where 'truth' is understood in narrative or poetic terms more than factual or historical ones (Spence 1982; Lehmann and Brinkmann, 2019), as something open-ended, not settled or final. With enough such experiences, our sense of meaning-full-ness in general can, potentially, accelerate. As we open ourselves to the richness of our inner world and 'its full metaphoric possibilities' (Booth 1992: 143), we can experience ageing less as merely a narrative of decline than as a time of discovery, of adventure even.

As I see it, there is no inherent end to what we can learn, no end of versions of 'our story' to reflect upon, and thus no end of insights to savour, of questions to consider. And what this leads to, as we give vent to our innate capacity for post-formal thought, as our comfort with metaphors increases, and as we allow them to ripple through the layers of our lives, is the 'enlarging' of our hearts and minds. If this is not a recipe for mental and emotional health in later life, I'm not sure what is. It is a means of heightening our awe at the mystery of our storyworld, with its endless potential for meaning. It is a means of raising our tolerance for ambiguity, of instilling a quality of positive uncertainty (Gordon 2003), of (ironically) widening our sense of self-esteem, and, I would argue, of strengthening our resilience overall. In a word, it is *therapoetic*. But it is a means not just of heightening and widening but of lightening too; in other words, a means of *play*.

Throughout this chapter I've been using the word 'work', as in home*work* and story*work*. But as I've learned from reflecting on my iron lung, and from entertaining the significance that such stories generally can hold for us, 'play' is perhaps the better term. For it may be best to engage in such reflection in an ironic, affectionate, light-hearted manner (Randall 2013); best to see it not as navel-gazing, so introspective and intense, as much as (pardon the pun!) *novel-grazing*: drifting back and forth, affectionately and open-heartedly, across the vast 'emotional terrain' (Pipher 1999) of our inner worlds.

This kind of reflection, I suggest, is a means to *wisdom* as well, where wisdom itself is conceived in narrative terms, and where the element of irony, of openness, of detachment is key. 'A person is truly "wise"', writes gerontologist Ruth Ray (2000), 'when she is able to see life as an evolving story and to create distance between self and story by reflecting on it from multiple perspectives' (29). Reflection of this kind may not be the only means to wisdom, to be sure. Indeed, some would question whether older adults should even be encouraged to cultivate such an open-ended orientation towards their lives, lest it lead to dis-orientation instead, and a kind of existential despair, what sociologist Peter Berger (1963) provocatively refers to as a 'metaphysical agoraphobia before the endlessly overlapping horizons of one's possible being' (63). Once again though, while acknowledging that this is a danger, I wish to differ. For I fear that we have unwittingly internalized the narrative of decline to the point where we expect too little of later life, the idea of older adults as in any way 'Elders' being a sad casualty of this trend. As a result, we can shrink from keeping ourselves (narratively) open, and growing, in the ways that I've been looking into here.

No doubt, given the several strands of thinking that I've attempted to weave together, I've raised more issues than I've resolved, to say nothing of those that I've skirted around entirely. There is the matter, for instance, of how metaphor works where dementia is involved, which rightly requires a chapter of its own (see Freeman, in this volume), although Jane Crisp's (1995) view of the confusing confabulations that her mother would tell as 'waking dreams' that were to be appreciated accordingly, is a step in this direction. Nor have I addressed fairly how, in advanced age, 'frailty affects one's narrative capacity' (de Lange 2017: 100). As Frits de Lange argues in *Loving Later Life*, 'the construction of narrative identity requires an active subject, creating a coherent and enduring "self" in its imagination'. However, 'some older adults may lack the courage and energy to take up that task' (97). Thus, he advises, we should scale back our expectations concerning the storywork (or play) that they are capable of and settle for 'narrative identity, version light', which 'requires only modest narrative power and energy' to sustain (100).

These two issues – concerning frailty and dementia (see also in this volume: Freeman; Swinnen; Synnes, Gjengedal and Råheim; Morrison) – are critical, no doubt. But even those that I've looked into in this chapter demand more coordinated consideration than I've been able to give them here. Going forward, for instance, I shall be continuing to inquire into the complexity of autobiographical reasoning in later life; the links between memory, metaphor, emotion, and meaning (Randall 2011); and the connection between metaphorical suggestibility and spirituality, even in – and maybe particularly in – advanced old age. All of these issues are intimately entwined whenever we ponder the poetics of the ageing self and therefore beg a larger forum to properly explore. That said, I hope to have shed at least a little light on a few of them here and, in so doing, drawn attention to the philosophic homework of later life, a process in which metaphorical play, I suggest, plays no small role.

References

Albright, D. (1994), 'Literary and Psychological Models of the Self', in U. Neisser and R. Fivush (eds), *The Remembering Self: Construction and Accuracy in the Self-Narrative*, 19–40. New York: Cambridge University Press.

Alter, R. (1989), *The Pleasures of Reading in an Ideological Age*, New York: Simon & Schuster.

Andrews, M. (2014), *Narrative Imagination and Everyday Life*, New York: Oxford University Press.

Bamberg, M. (2006), 'Stories: Big or Small – Why Do We Care?', *Narrative Inquiry* 16: 139–147.
Berger, P. (1963), *Invitation to Sociology: A Humanistic Perspective*, Garden City, NY: Anchor.
Berman, H. (1994), *Interpreting the Aging Self: Personal Journals of Later Life*, New York: Springer.
Bettelheim, B. (1975), *The Uses of Enchantment: The Meaning and Importance of Fairy Tales*, New York: Vintage.
Birren, J. and D. Deutchman (1991), *Guiding Autobiography Groups for Older Adults: Exploring the Fabric of Life*, Baltimore, MD: Johns Hopkins University Press.
Bohlmeijer, E., M. Valenkamp, G. Westerhof, G. Smit and P. Cuijpers (2005), 'Creative Reminiscence as an Early Intervention for Depression: Results of a Pilot Project', *Aging & Mental Health* 9 (4): 302–304.
Bohlmeijer, E., G. Westerhof, W. Randall, T. Tromp and G. Kenyon (2011), 'Narrative Foreclosure: Preliminary Considerations for a New Sensitizing Concept', *Journal of Aging Studies* 25(4): 364–370.
Bohlmeijer, E. and G. Westerhof (2011), 'Reminiscence Interventions: Bringing Narrative Gerontology into Practice', in G. Kenyon, E. Bohlmeijer and W. Randall (eds), *Storying Later Life: Issues, Investigations, and Interventions in Narrative Gerontology*, 273–289, New York: Oxford University Press.
Booth, W. (1992), *The Art of Growing Older: Writers on Living and Aging*, Chicago: University of Chicago Press.
Bruner, J. (1986), *Actual Minds, Possible Worlds*, Cambridge, MA: Harvard University Press.
Butler, R. (1963), 'The Life Review: An Interpretation of Reminiscence in the Aged', *Psychiatry* 26: 65–76.
Chavis, G. (2011), *Poetry and Story Therapy: The Healing Power of Creative Expression*, London: Jessica Kingsley.
Cohen, G. (2005), *The Mature Mind: The Positive Power of the Aging Brain*, Boston, MA: Basic Books.
Cowley, M. (1980), *The View from 80*, New York: Viking.
Crisp, J. (1995), 'Making Sense of the Stories that People with Alzheimer's Tell: A Journey with My Mother', *Nursing Inquiry* 2: 133–140.
Csikszentmihalyi, M. and K. Rathunde (1990), 'The Psychology of Wisdom: An Evolutionary Interpretation', in R. Sternberg (ed.), *Wisdom: Its Nature, Origins, and Development*, 25–51. Cambridge: Cambridge University Press
de Lange, F. (2017), *Loving Later Life: An Ethics of Aging*, Grand Rapids, MI: Eerdmans.
De Medeiros, K. and Rubinstein, R. (2015), "'Shadow Stories' in Oral Interviews: Narrative Care Through Careful Listening', *Journal of Aging Studies* 34: 162–168.
Dubovska, E., V. Chrz, P. Tavel, I. Solcova and J Ruzicka (2017), 'Narrative Construction of Resilience: Stories of Czech Adults', *Ageing and Society* 37 (9): 1849–1873.
Eakin, P. J. (1999), *How Our Lives Become Stories: Making Selves*, Ithaca, NY: Cornell University Press.
Frank, A. (2010), *Letting Stories Breathe: A Socio-Narratology*, Chicago, IL: University of Chicago Press.
Freeman, M. (1991), 'Rewriting the Self: Development as Moral Practice', in M. Tappan and M. Packer (eds), *Narrative and Storytelling: Implications for Understanding Moral Development*, 83–101, San Francisco: Jossey-Bass.
Freeman, M. (1993), *Rewriting the Self: History, Memory, Narrative*, London: Routledge.

Freeman, M. (1997), 'Death, Narrative Integrity, and the Radical Challenge of Self-Understanding: A Reading of Tolstoy's *Death of Ivan Ilych*', *Ageing and Society* 17: 373–398.

Freeman, M. (1999), 'Life Narratives, the Poetics of Selfhood, and the Redefinition of Psychological Theory', in W. Maiers, B. Bayer, B. Esgalhado, R. Jorna and E. Schraube (eds), *Challenges to Theoretical Psychology*, 245–250, Toronto: Captus University Publications.

Gardner, H. and E. Winner (1979), 'The Development of Metaphoric Competence: Implications for Humanistic Disciplines', in S. Sacks (ed.), *On Metaphor*, 121–139, Chicago: The University of Chicago Press.

Goleman, D. (1995), *Emotional Intelligence: Why It Can Matter More Than IQ*, New York: Bantam.

Gordon, K. (2003), 'The Impermanence of Being: Toward a Psychology of Uncertainty', *Journal of Humanistic Psychology* 43 (2): 96–117.

Gullette, M. (2004), *Aged by Culture*, Chicago: University of Chicago Press.

Habermas, T. (2019), *Emotion and Narrative: Perspectives on Autobiographical Storytelling*, Cambridge: Cambridge University Press.

Habermas, T. (2010), 'Autobiographical Reasoning: Arguing and Narrating from a Biographical Perspective', *New Directions for Child and Adolescent Development* 131: 1–17.

Hampl, P. (1999), *I Could Tell You Stories: Sojourns in the Land of Memory*, New York: Norton.

Hyvärinen, M., L.-C. Hydén, M. Saarenheimo and M. Tamboukou, eds (2010), *Beyond Narrative Coherence*, Amsterdam: John Benjamins.

Jung, C. G. (1976), 'The Stages of Life', in J. Campbell (ed.), *The Portable Jung*, 3–22, London: Penguin.

Kenyon, G., J. Birren and J. Schroots, eds (1991), *Metaphors of Aging in Science and the Humanities*, New York: Springer.

Kenyon, G., E. Bohlmeijer and W. Randall, eds (2011), *Storying Later Life: Issues, Investigations, and Interventions in Narrative Gerontology*, New York: Oxford University Press.

Kenyon, G. and W. Randall (1997), *Restorying Our Lives: Personal Growth Through Autobiographical Reflection*, Westport, CT: Praeger.

Kramer, D. A. (1983), 'Postformal Operations? A Need for Further Conceptualization', *Human Development* 26: 91–105.

Kropf, N. and C. Tandy (1998), 'Narrative Therapy with Older Clients: The Use of a "Meaning Making" Approach'. *Clinical Gerontologist* 18 (4): 3–16.

Labouvie-Vief, G. (1990), 'Wisdom as Integrated Thought: Historical and Developmental Perspectives', in R. Sternberg (ed.), *Wisdom: Its Nature, Origins, and Development*, 52–83, New York: Cambridge University Press.

Lakoff, G. and M. Johnson (1980), *Metaphors We Live By*, Chicago: University of Chicago Press.

Lehmann, O. V. and S. Brinkmann (2019), '"Humbled by Life": Poetic Representations of Existential Pathways and Personal Life Philosophies Among Older Adults in Norway'. *Qualitative Inquiry*. https://doi.org/10.1177/1077800419885414

Lesser, W. (2002), *Nothing Remains the Same: Rereading and Remembering*, Boston, MA: Houghton Mifflin.

Littlemore, J. (2001), 'Metaphoric Competence: A Language Learning Strength of Students with a Holistic Cognitive Style?', *TESOL Quarterly* 35 (3): 459–491.

Magai, C. and S. McFadden, eds (1996), *Handbook of Emotion, Adult Development, and Aging*, San Diego: Academic Press.

McKendy, J. (2006), '"I'm Very Careful About That": Narrative Agency of Men in Prison', *Discourse & Society* 17(4): 473–502.

Mundle, R. (2019), *How to Be an Even Better Listener: A Practical Guide for Hospice and Palliative Care Volunteers*, Philadelphia: Jessica Kingsley.

Pipher, M. (1999), *Another Country: Navigating the Emotional Terrain of Our Elders*, New York: Riverhead.

Polkinghorne, D. (1988), *Narrative Knowing and the Human Sciences*, Albany, NY: State University of New York Press.

Progoff, I. (1975), *At a Journal Workshop: The Basic Text and Guide for Using the Intensive Journal*, New York: Dialogue House Library.

Randall, W. (2010), 'Storywork: Autobiographical Learning in Later Life', in C. Clark and M. Rossiter (eds), *Narrative Perspectives on Adult Education: New Directions for Adult and Continuing Education* 126: 25–36, San Francisco: Jossey-Bass.

Randall, W. (2011), 'Memory, Metaphor, and Meaning: Reading for Wisdom in the Stories of Our Lives', in G. Kenyon, E. Bohlmeijer and W. Randall (eds), *Storying Later Life: Issues, Investigations, and Interventions in Narrative Gerontology*, 20–38. New York: Oxford University Press.

Randall, W. (2013), 'The Importance of Being Ironic: Narrative Openness and Personal Resilience in Later Life', *The Gerontologist* 53(1): 9–16.

Randall, W. (2014), *The Stories We Are: An Essay on Self-Creation*, 2nd edn, Toronto, ON: University of Toronto Press.

Randall, W. (2019), *In Our Stories Lies Our Strength: Aging, Spirituality, and Narrative*, Kindle Direct Publishing.

Randall, W., C. Baldwin, S. McKenzie-Mohr, E. McKim and D. Furlong (2015), 'Narrative and Resilience: A Comparative Analysis of How Older Adults Story Their Lives', *Journal of Aging Studies* 34: 155–161.

Randall, W. and G. Kenyon (2001), *Ordinary Wisdom: Biographical Aging and the Journey of Life*, Westport, CT: Praeger.

Randall, W. and K. Khurshid (2017), 'Narrative Development in Later Life: A Novel Perspective', *Age, Culture, Humanities: An Interdisciplinary Journal* 3.

Randall, W., B. Lewis and A. Achenbaum (2022), *Fairy Tale Wisdom: Stories for the Second Half of Life*, ElderPress Books.

Randall, W. and E. McKim (2008), *Reading Our Lives: The Poetics of Growing Old*, New York: Oxford University Press.

Randall, W. and M. Robinson, eds (in press), *Things That Matter: The Role of Special Objects in Our Stories As We Age*, Toronto: University of Toronto Press.

Ray, R. (2000), *Beyond Nostalgia: Aging and Life-Story Writing*, Charlottesville, VA: University Press of Virginia.

Ricoeur, P. (1981), *The Rule of Metaphor: Multidisciplinary Studies of the Creation of Meaning in Language*, trans. R. Czerny, Chicago: The University of Chicago Press.

Rimmon-Kenan, S. (1989), *Narrative Fiction: Contemporary Poetics*, London: Routledge.

Rubin, D., ed. (1995), *Remembering Our Past: Studies in Autobiographical Memory*, New York: Cambridge University Press.

Ruth, J.-E. and A. Vilkko (1996), 'Emotions in the Construction of Autobiography', in C. Magai and S. McFadden (eds.), *Handbook of Emotion, Adult Development, and Aging*, 167–181. San Diego, CA: Academic Press.

Said, E. (2006), *On Late Style: Music and Literature Against the Grain*, New York: Vintage.
Sarbin, T. (1986), 'The Narrative as a Root Metaphor for Psychology', in T. Sarbin (ed.), *Narrative Psychology: The Storied Nature of Human Conduct*, 3–21, New York: Praeger.
Sarton, M. (1981), *House by the Sea: A Journal*, New York: W. W. Norton.
Schachter-Shalomi, Z. and R. Miller (1995), *From Age-ing to Sage-ing: A Profound New Vision of Growing Older*, New York: Warner.
Schafer, R. (1983), *The Analytic Attitude*, New York: Basic Books.
Schafer, R. (1992), *Retelling a Life: Narration and Dialogue in Psychoanalysis*, New York: Basic Books.
Sherman, E. (1991), *Reminiscence and the Self in Old Age*, New York: Springer.
Singer, J. (1996), 'The Story of Your Life: A Process Perspective on Narrative and Emotion in Adult Development', in C. Magai and S. McFadden (eds), *Handbook of Emotion, Adult Development, and Aging*, 443–463. San Diego: Academic Press.
Spence, D. (1982), *Narrative Truth and Historical Truth: Meaning and Interpretation in Psychoanalysis*, New York: W. W. Norton.
Synnes, O. (2015), 'Narratives of Nostalgia in the Face of Death: The Importance of Lighter Stories of the Past in Palliative Care', *Journal of Aging Studies* 34: 169–176.
Synnes, O., K. L. Romm and H. Bondevik (2021), 'The Poetics of Vulnerability: Creative Writing among Young Adults in Treatment for Psychosis in light of Ricoeur's and Kristeva's Philosophy of Language and Subjectivity', *Medicine, Health Care and Philosophy* 24 (2): 173–187.
TeSelle, S. (1975), *Speaking in Parables: A Study in Metaphor and Theology*, Philadelphia: Fortress.
Tornstam, L. (1996), 'Gerotranscendence: A Theory about Maturing into Old Age', *Journal of Aging and Identity* 1, 37–50.
Wolfe, T. ([1938] 1983), *The Autobiography of an American Novelist*, Cambridge, MA: Harvard University Press.

9

Poetry, Science, and a Science of Poetry: With an Illustration of Poetry and Ageing

Steven R. Brown

An ambivalence ranging from warm embrace to hostility has often characterized the relationship between science and the humanities. Poet E. E. Cummings (1972: 264), for example, expressed disdain for 'some one-eyed son of a bitch' who tries to measure Spring, and John Donne (1952: 11) put the natural world on notice when he asked of the sun, 'Must to thy motions lovers' seasons run?' By the same token, mathematician Jacob Bronowski (1966) regarded science and poetry as having a common source in the quality of imagination, albeit reaching us in different ways, and Aldous Huxley (1963) defended not only his scientist grandfather, but also a string of luminaries on both sides – poet Matthew Arnold, literary critic Lionel Trilling, and physicists Robert Oppenheimer and Arthur Eddington – for having advocated a balanced and mutually enriching education of both science and the humanities. Huxley was responding in part to the mid-century debate between C. P. Snow (1959) and F. R. Leavis (1962) concerning the alleged gulf between the two cultures, a hyperbolic stir that continues to attract attention (e.g., Collini 2013; Krauss 2009) and may still be just below the politer and more tolerant surface that manifests itself, for instance, in recent recordings bringing poets and scientists together (Illingworth and Simpson, 2021) and in Popova's (2019) impressive compendium of scientists, artists, sculptors, and poets expressing their admiration of the wonders of the universe.

It is a rather effortless matter for physicists and biologists to attend symphony concerts and for novelists and musicians to keep up on the popular developments in astronomy, but it would be a more serious undertaking to develop the necessary skills and methods for the systematic appraisal of the humanities that would be viewed as valuable by those who contribute to the humanities. Most such efforts consequently lack credibility, as when Wilson (1940) sought to assess literary style by measuring sentence length and Hanauer (2011) lapsed into psycholinguistics, with measurability trumping meaning and feeling, which are often regarded as the hallmarks of poetry. The structures and procedures of universities, of course, conspire against intellectual interbreeding of the kind required, and those already firmly in one camp have little incentive to develop capacities needed to make contributions in the other; in addition, those in the humanities, usually lacking scientific training, have little ability to distinguish useful from less useful efforts to reach across the aisle. Little wonder, then, that those on both sides of the debate are left in a state of trained incapacity that duplicates itself in each succeeding generation.

There is a possible exception in the writings of William Stephenson (1902–1989), an Englishman with an unusual pedigree, having earned doctorates in both physics and in psychology. Stephenson's first doctorate came at a time when physics was in upheaval and in the midst of the debates between Einstein and Bohr concerning the fundamental nature of reality, a debate in which Bohr's new quantum theory eventually prevailed. It was also during this time that the field of psychology was more or less considered part of the humanities, as a philosophy of mind. Stephenson was therefore educated to some extent with a foot both in the sciences and the humanities. In addition, it is worth noting that he was involved in old-age research dating from the mid-1930s when he was on the faculty at Oxford, and that he was a co-founder of Britain's Club for the Study of Ageing in the early 1940s (Good 2011; Stephenson [1950] 1979, 2011); moreover, that the method that he innovated has been used from time to time to study various problems of old age (e.g., Robinson et al. 2003, 2008).

It is the purpose of this chapter to introduce Stephenson's methodological innovation, an unusual blend of subjectivity and mathematics, and to suggest its value to the study of poetry in terms of an illustration provided by later-life readers of poems focused on old age. It is important to emphasize that the method is in no way to be considered a competitor to the poet; rather, it is a philosophy and set of technical procedures designed, for example, to help reveal the diversity of poetic understandings, in this case among individuals in their later years. It is therefore a method to be considered more by scholars of the art than by its practitioners.

Introducing Q methodology

Stephenson's mentor was Sir Charles Spearman, who invented the statistical method of factor analysis and who characterized his protégé as the most creative statistician in contemporary psychology. Spearman's version of factor analysis was used for the study of so-called objective characteristics of behaviour, such as intelligence and abilities, and came to be referred to as *R methodology*, but in a flash of insight it occurred to Stephenson that by turning factor analysis on its head, the whole world of subjectivity could be made available for rigorous examination, and this inversion has come to be referred to as *Q methodology*. In this regard, we are reminded of a youthful Sylvia Plath's (1975: 34) remark that 'once a poem is made available to the public, the right of interpretation belongs to the reader', and of Sartre's (1950: 31) continuation of this line of thought by noting that the meaning of a poem has 'no other substance than the reader's subjectivity'. It is at this point that the baton is passed on to Q methodology to show how subjective understandings can be revealed and clarified.

In a nutshell, Q methodology consists of presenting a person with a set of items along with instructions to rank-order them from, say, agree to disagree, a procedure that Stephenson referred to as *Q sorting*. To facilitate this task, the person is usually provided with a numerical continuum, e.g., from agree to disagree, with neutral in the centre. The 'items' to be placed in an order could be anything, really: a set of photographs, for example, or songs, or odours, or sculptures, etc. In most studies, the items are a set of opinions about anything under the sun – e.g., about the pandemic, or the latest movie sensation, or what to do about bullying in the public schools, or about what colour to paint the living room, ... or about a poem.

In one of his many studies, for instance, Stephenson (1972) provided a group of graduate students majoring in English literature with a set of *statements* about Keats's 'Ode on a Grecian Urn', the statements having been drawn from comments by writers such as Edgar Allan Poe and T. S. Eliot; and Brown and Mathieson (1990) administered a set of critical remarks about D. H. Lawrence's 'Piano' (drawn from Richards 1929), also to a group of graduate students in English literature. By constructing their separate Q sorts, the students were displaying their own subjective understandings of Keats's 'Ode' or Lawrence's 'Piano'. In the case of the former, four separate classes of response emerged, three of which corresponded with Dickstein's (1971) interpretation of Keats's own development – from a naïve romanticism, to a more conflicted view of life, and finally to a more mature vantage point in which both beauty and tragedy are accepted as 'all ye know ... and all ye need to know'. A fourth response emerging from Stephenson's study was more logical and empty of beauty, and a kind of distortion that is common among those who in general fail to achieve an understanding. Thus, readers at various levels of sophistication projected their own understandings of the 'Ode' that reflected Keats's own course of intellectual development.

Factor analysis in Spearman's R methodology leads to clusters of *variables* that are similar to one another, and this is the overwhelmingly predominant way in which factor analysis is used in the psychological and social sciences; in Stephenson's Q methodology, however, factor analysis leads to groups of *people* who have sorted the items in a similar order, under the assumption initially that they share a common outlook, understanding, or perspective. It is assumed, for example, that individuals who belong to the same Q factor share essentially the same understanding of Keats's 'Ode' or of Lawrence's 'Piano', and that their understanding is unlike the understanding of a group of individuals who constitute a different factor. The factors, like the Q sorts that define them, are therefore a reflection of the diversity in subjectivity that led to them, and the number of factors is a purely empirical matter: if there is only one consensual understanding of a poem, only one factor will appear; if there are four separate understandings, four factors will emerge. A simplified description of Q methodology is presented elsewhere (Brown 1993).

An illustration: Responses to poetry in later life

Rather than present participants with statements about a poem, the Q set used in this present illustration comprised 20 poems (in most instances of poetic fragments), such as the following:

> When you are old and grey and full of sleep,
> And nodding by the fire, take down this book
> And slowly read and dream of the soft look

> Your eyes had once, and of their shadows deep.
> (William Butler Yeats [1956: 40], 'When You Are Old')

> It is to spend long days
> And not once feel that we were ever young.
> It is to add, immured
> In the hot prison of the present, month
> To month with weary pain.
> (Matthew Arnold [1884: 213], 'Growing Old')

The poems for the most part addressed issues of later life and included text only, i.e., none carried a title or author's name. In the interest of breadth, efforts were made to diversify the sample of poems by avoiding similarities in focus and expression, by choosing some poems that were optimistic as well as pessimistic about the ageing process, and by assuring that some were more recent while others (like the above) were from the canon. An effort was also made to avoid poems that were apt to be recognized (such as Dylan Thomas's [1971: 207–8] 'Do Not Go Gentle into That Good Night' or Stevie Smith's [1983: 303] 'Not Waving but Drowning') and that might then be accepted or rejected on that account. The universe of poetry about ageing is varied and the goal was to select a small sample that approximated that diversity.[1] It is important to note, however, that the results obtained from an exercise such as this are to a large extent independent of the poems actually selected – a consequence of the well-documented principle of the *indifference of the indicator* (Spearman 1927) – and that comparable findings would be expected from a parallel set of verses of comparable variety. What is at issue is readers' *self-referentiality*, i.e., the meanings and saliences that readers impose on the set of poems. As Stephenson (2011: 218) said in this regard, 'Q methodology is a scientific, objective approach to the investigation of *self*, and more to the point of this specific study, that 'studying the feelings of a person in the subjective context can be central to old age research' (230). It is the existence and nature of these different forms of self-referentiality that Q methodology brings to light.

The poems were of variable length and in most instances only a fragment of a poem could be utilized so as to fit on standard-size rectangular paper (4.25″ × 3.25″) and so that all of the poems when spread out would fit within the space of a tabletop. Once selected and formatted, the entire packet of 20 poems was forwarded to each of approximately 15 personal acquaintances who had agreed to participate, virtually all of whom were retired and in their sixties, seventies, or eighties. Out of curiosity, most participants also solicited responses from their spouses, which thereby provided balance from the standpoint of gender and ultimately resulted in a total of 28 responses. The condition of instruction was straightforward: to read all 20 poems and to rank them on a tabletop from pleasing (+2) to unpleasing (−2). The Q sorts were then factor analysed, resulting in three identifiable classes of response. There are software computer programs dedicated to Q-methodology studies (e.g., Banasick 2019; Schmolck 2014)

---

[1] The set of 20 poems employed can be obtained from the author (sbrown@kent.edu). In keeping with the rules of fair use, the poems reported in this paper constitute less than 25 per cent of the total text or are from an author who died more than 75 years ago.

that serve to ferret out and combine all individual Q sorts that are alike in kind (referred to in technical terms as a *factor*) into a single common Q sort that is a composite of the responses of those individuals comprising it. What began as Q sorts from 28 individuals, therefore, condensed into three generalized Q sorts that subsumed virtually all the others. By way of overview, the three can be characterized as follows:

> *Group I* comprised persons who appeared to be motivated by sentimental devotion and who displayed a preference for poems expressing ageing along with a companion.
> *Group II* was a smaller group of individuals who preferred poems that testified to remaining personal worth and with much yet to give despite ageing.
> *Group III* comprised only two persons who were mirror opposites and drawn to poems due largely to their technical features, one preferring poems with rhyme and meter and the other preferring those in free verse.

The factors that materialize in any study must be interpreted, as will be demonstrated, but it is important to grasp how the factors are to be understood. Each of the three model Q sorts is an abstraction comparable to a Weberian ideal type: None of the individual Q sorts that comprise a factor Q sort is exactly like the type, but each of them tends toward this idealization. Moreover, each idealization, like the Q sorts it represents, has a *schema* running throughout – a common feeling that is most evident in those poems judged most pleasing (+2) and that is most negated by those poems judged most unpleasing (–2), with relative absence of feeling toward the centre (score 0). This comports with Charles Peirce's ([1892] 1940: 340) 'Law of Mind', to the effect that 'ideas tend to spread continuously and to affect certain others which stand to them in a peculiar relation of affectability'.

Group I: Ageing Together

Of the 28 original Q sorts, 15 turned out to be primarily associated with factor I, to which the theme of 'Ageing Together' has been tentatively appended in light of some of the poems that received the highest scores (indicating that this group of readers collectively found these to be the most pleasing), among them the following:

> Let us be lovers to the end
> And, growing blind as we grow old,
> Refuse forever to behold
> How age has made the shoulders bend
> And Winter blanched the hair's young gold.
> Let us be lovers to the end.
> (14)   1.73   0.66   0.33

This stanza is from 'Song' by Edith Wharton (2019), not published until after her death, and is poem no. 14 in the set of twenty poems used here, as indicated by the number that appears in parentheses above. The other three numbers are *factor scores* (for factors

I, II, and III, respectively), as produced by the computer program, and indicate the relative pleasure experienced upon reading the poem on the part of the persons within each of the groups.[2] In this instance, for example, poem no. 14 was judged highly pleasing (score 1.73) by those readers comprising group I and as significantly less pleasing (but not displeasing) by those persons comprising groups II and III (scores 0.66 and 0.33, respectively). The extent to which group I embrace this poem is the first evidence that *togetherness* is a salient consideration that distinguishes these readers from the others (i.e., that factor I is thinking of growing old *with* someone), and it is noteworthy that all persons associated with this factor are currently married and presumably content to continue growing old with their partners.

This theme of closeness and attachment becomes more compelling when we consider additional poems at the most-pleasing pole of factor I. The Wharton stanza above received the highest score, and the second highest was associated with Clarence Major's poem 'Ageing Together' (1998), the title of which alone adds validity to the theme and concludes as follows (scores for factors I–III):

> In the morning we climb all the way
> to the top of the hill for a panoramic view.
> We see our village below by the bay.
> We are growing older gracefully together.
> We've taken to ageing like a dog to its collar.
> (8)   1.44   –0.56   1.23

The participants, of course, did not have access to poem titles and authorship, and were responding solely to the lines of text. As with the Wharton poem above, Major's poem received its own factor scores, again showing how attracted factor I was to poetic expressions of this we-ness variety, especially when compared to factor II.

A supplementary source of verification is to be found in comments voluntarily provided by some of the participants associated with factor I. Barbara,[3] for instance, wrote on her score sheet, 'Of the twenty poems dealing with ageing and approaching death, I preferred those that described a couple ageing gracefully and with forgiveness of each other's decline', and Larry voiced an appreciation for the Edith Wharton poem above, stating that 'it hit a chord because one of my all-time favourite songs ... is called "Twilight of Our Years" and this is reminiscent of that. Plus, it coincides with my hopes and dreams'. Michael, who had recently lost his wife of many years, claimed that he had

---

[2] Technically, the factor scores are reported in normalized z-score form (recording the number of standard deviations from the mean of 0.00, which represents absence of feeling) and typically range from approximately +2.00 to –2.00 within each of the factors. (Stephenson referred to these scores as *quantsal* units, for *quant*ification of *sal*ience.) The scores for no. 14 above indicate that this poem receives a score in factor I that is more than one standard deviation higher than the same poem scores in either factor II or factor III, suggesting that this poem is experienced as substantially more pleasing to persons constituting factor I.

[3] Names assigned to participants are pseudonyms, and comments from these individuals were freely given and not requested, although they had been informed that their responses would be used anonymously in an academic publication. Nonparticipation was always an option, and, in fact, some persons who were originally contacted elected not to respond.

found himself disliking those poems in which 'both members of a love relationship are still living', preferring those matching his current situation; however, his broken heart apparently won out, for although he did give high scores to some poems reflecting loneliness and isolation, he also gave himself away by assigning the highest score to the Edith Wharton poem. And Charlie expressed a fondness for those poems that 'spoke to continued relationships'. William Stephenson once compared Q factors to X-ray plates, and as these spontaneous remarks indicate, permeating these reactions to the poems among factor I participants was a theme of contentment with the prospect of growing old together.

The importance of togetherness for factor I can also be seen through contrast; i.e., by examining those poems that factor I found most displeasing, such as the following two:

> I look into my glass,
> And view my wasting skin,
> And say, 'Would God it came to pass
> My heart had shrunk as thin!'
> For then I, undistrest
> By hearts grown cold to me,
> Could lonely wait my endless rest
> With equanimity.
> But Time, to make me grieve,
> Part steals, lets part abide;
> And shakes this fragile frame at eve
> With throbbings of noontide.

(13)   −1.41   −0.05   0.29

> It is to spend long days
> And not once feel that we were ever young.
> It is to add, immured
> In the hot prison of the present, month
> To month with weary pain.

(15)   −1.25   −1.43   −0.66

Poem no. 13 is by Thomas Hardy (1994) and no. 15 by Matthew Arnold (1884), and the scores for factors I, II, and III indicate that neither of these was experienced as pleasing by the participants. In this regard, several of the readers also mentioned what they regarded as unappealing and archaic language and poetic forms, but poetic technique aside, it is difficult to overlook the isolated, pessimistic, and first-person character in Hardy's and Arnold's voice at the negative end of factor I, which provides thematic counterpoint to the more optimistic poems at the positive end, and it is the coherence of the pleasantness of companionship to the unpleasantness of isolation and aloneness that produces the 'wave in the mind' (to quote Virginia Woolf, cited by Le Guin 2004) that provides the synthetic consistency of the factor array as a whole. For the most part, persons comprising group I have spent a lifetime with their spouses and are looking forward to continuing the arrangement.

There is a potentially dynamic feature to factor I that is related to its rejection of isolation and solitude; namely, a denial of regret. The Hardy and Arnold stanzas above foreshadow this, but there are other poems in the Q set that more openly express regret – e.g., Philip Larkin's 'Dockery and Son' (1988), which concludes as follows (with scores for factors I, II, and III, respectively):

> Life is first boredom, then fear.
> Whether or not we use it, it goes,
> And leaves what something hidden from us chose,
> And age, and then the only end of age.
> (19)   −1.47   −0.23   0.29

Larkin's lament that life is boredom, then fear, then the end of age itself is rejected by factor I in particular (score −1.47); as is the sentiment in 'Provide, Provide' by Robert Frost (1979), which says that at the end, it is better to have 'boughten friendship at your side than none at all', which received a score of −1.02 in factor I. There is similar regret in this fragment from Samuel Taylor Coleridge's (1852) 'Youth and Age', which factor I rejects as well:

> Where no hope is, life's a warning
> That only serves to make us grieve,
> When we are old:
> That only serves to make us grieve
> With oft and tedious taking-leave,
> Like some poor nigh-related guest,
> That may not rudely be dismist;
> Yet hath outstay'd his welcome while,
> And tells the jest without the smile.
> (12)   −1.03   −0.55   1.23

A member of factor I, Ann was explicit about regret and wrote on her score sheet, 'The poems I rated negatively [which included Coleridge's] were ones I felt dwell too much on regret and mistakes of youth, or of how much better it was to be young. To me, it is a sad perspective', and this denial of regret (or at least of holding regret at bay) is an integral part of factor I's approach to the poetics of later years.

To reiterate, interpretation is a necessary function in Q methodology since we do not know a priori the meanings and the degree of prominence with which the various poems are going to be endowed, but Peirce's 'Law of Mind' alerts us to the likelihood that some coherent theme or storyline will characterize the poems' order and that this will be based on feelings (such as about growing old together without regret) that will be apparent in the poems and the statement scores that are attached to them. Caution is advisable, however, since it is often possible that there are alternative explanations for the same arrangement of poems. The celebration of togetherness and denial of regret noted above, for instance, might also conceivably serve to suppress anxieties associated with unresolved past grievances that, if permitted resurgence, might at this late date in life leave too little time for resolution, hence the need to keep potential sources of conflict under wraps.

Group II: Affirmation and Convention

It is in the nature of factors in Q methodology that if one factor (X) is shown to exist, then if some other factor (Y) is also shown to exist, X and Y must be different from one another. The technical term for this is *orthogonality*, which means that X and Y must be uncorrelated with one another. In this particular case, for instance, factor I appears on the surface to be organized around a theme of ageing together, so factor II must necessarily be organized around some other principle, or what Lehmann and Brinkmann (2021) might refer to as a different 'virtue'.

It was admittedly difficult to divine an organizing principle for factor II, and this raises an important methodological matter. In the interests of transparency, I must acknowledge that my own Q sort was firmly associated with factor I and this implies that it should be easier for me to understand factor I since I arranged the statements in an order markedly similar to the factor: In a sense, factor I is me. However, it also implies that factor II should be more difficult for me to grasp since it is demonstrably outside my frame of reference. As a consequence, I confess to having less confidence in the interpretation of factor II to follow.[4]

By the phrase 'Affirmation and Convention', which has been proposed as a label for factor II, reference is being made to the general emotional response of these participants toward some of the poems, plus the attitude they seem to have about the craft of poetry itself. Take as an example the poem 'Young and Old' by Charles Kingsley (1884), the quantsal scores below the text reflecting, as previously, the salience of the poem in factors I, II, and III, respectively (see footnote 2):

> When all the world is old, lad,
> And all the trees are brown;
> And all the sport is stale, lad,
> And all the wheels run down:
> Creep home, and take your place there,
> The spent and maimed among:
> God grant you find one face there
> You loved when all was young.

(9)   0.34   0.97   −0.90

Factor II experienced this poem as more pleasant than did either of the other two factors, one of its characteristics being that it follows the kind of rhythm (an altered

---

[4] The relativity of reference frames is comparable to the relativity of coordinate systems in Einstein's theory of special relativity (Brown and Taylor 1973), of which Stephenson, given his physics background, was well aware. Being able to accurately specify the location of the observer within the observational field is one of the advantages of Q methodology compared to other methods within the hermeneutical sciences, and for this reason it is common practice for Q methodologists to add their own Q sorts alongside all others.

iambic trimeter in this instance) and rhyme scheme (ABAB CDCD) often expected in poetry. Why this preference exists can only be speculated about at this point: perhaps due to a conventional personal style that manifests itself in poetry as in other areas of life; or perhaps due to a lack of broad experience with poetry; or, alternatively, perhaps due to a sophisticated choice rooted in deep and prolonged study.[5] Several persons associated with this factor were explicit about this. Mike, for example, although he did not give this specific statement a high score, stated that '[I] found myself liking rhymes and (positive) sentimentality', and Larry remarked that 'I like those that rhyme, that have a pattern, that follow a pre-existing design like poems should'.

So much for convention in the shape, or form, of poems judged pleasing by persons comprising group II, but self-affirmation is even more important to these readers and can also be seen in the Kingsley poem above and in the hope that 'you find one face there / You loved when all was young'. This self-affirmative disposition is even more apparent in contemporary poems, which factor II seems more inclined to embrace. In 'I Still Matter', for instance, Patricia Fleming (2017) acknowledges that she is older and may 'look ugly and old', but proclaims that there is 'beauty inside', and concludes as follows and in a way to which factor II is far more receptive, as evidenced by group II's strong factor score:

> So although not as strong and no beauty, it's true,
> I'm still here and want so much to live,
> And I know that there's no one in this world quite like me,
> And no one who has more to give.
> (17)   0.56   1.80   0.00

Factor II is optimistic about the self, but also realistic: The signs of ageing are obvious and not to be denied, but the important point is that the glass is half full rather than half empty and with much of value remaining.

There is affirmation as well in Mike Hauser's 'The Incredible Ageing Man' (2020) that refers on the one hand to the appearance of wrinkles, thinning hair, enlarged ears, and loss of patience, but then ends in what might be taken as a spirit of hopefulness:

> Sit with me here as into the distance I stare
> Forgetting now who it is I am
> I do so hope you enjoy the show
> Of this 'The Incredible Ageing Man'.
> (7)   −0.50   1.18   −0.33

---

[5] The urge to explain poetic preference is difficult to resist, but it is wise to do so in favour of description in the early stages of inquiry when little is known about alternative hypotheses and their viability. In this regard, we still have much to learn from Newton ([1726] 1934: 547) who was unconvinced of Descartes's vortical whirlpool explanation of gravity and contented himself with advancing descriptions of how gravity actually did operate without feeling compelled to say why that was the case, and ending with his famous comment, *Hypotheses non fingo* (I do not feign hypotheses).

Factor II is obviously the more resonant with this poem (score 1.18) compared to the other two groups, even if it is judged slightly less pleasing than the preceding poem by Fleming (score 1.80). Embracing the two poems points to a common sentiment running through factor II: Age may indeed have taken its toll; however, I remain quite incredible and still have a lot to offer.

But (to anticipate a possible objection), what if Hauser were merely being sardonic when he said, 'I hope you enjoy the show'? This raises another important methodological point. Stephenson was familiar with Gestalt theory and in fact hosted Kurt Koffka, one of the Gestalt founders, at Oxford in the 1930s and subsequently contributed to the Gestalt literature, and one of the central principles of Gestalt psychology – that parts only take on meaning in the context of the whole – is likewise central when it comes to the interpretation of Q factors. Peirce's Law of Mind leads us to look for a common schema in the order among the items within a factor, and the order that suggests itself in factor II is one of affirmation, which makes it unlikely that the individuals comprising this factor suddenly reversed themselves and saw only cynical self-denigration in this isolated poem. It is, of course, conceivable that factor II participants experienced both affirmation and cynicism – in a kind of dialectical dance – but the meaning that is assumed most likely to be at issue with regard to any particular item is the one that conforms with the other items within which it is imbedded.

And finally, poems at the negative end of the array served to affirm much of what has already been reported, as shown, for example, in reaction to Matthew Arnold's 'Growing Old', introduced above (with a score of −1.43 for factor II), which led to this written reply by Larry:

> There's too much work here. Reminds me of the days in English class where we would spend an entire class trying to grasp the deeper meanings of one poem or even a line in a poem. When I had to read a poem here several times just to begin to figure out what it means, then it's not pleasing.

Philip Larkin's poem (also introduced previously) earned a similar response: 'It's a dark message, or what I understand of it – unless there is a deeper meaning here, is not really pleasing'. Both puzzling poetic mechanics and repudiation of hope were important considerations that entered into the response of persons comprising factor II.

Group III: Verse vs. prose

Of the 28 individuals who completed this Q sort, only one of them was relatively young (in her late twenties, the daughter of one of the other participants), and it was intriguing to find her on a factor separate from everyone else, except for one other older participant who was at the opposite end of the same factor. That is, factor III is bipolar with the young person's Q sort being largely the mirror opposite of the older person's Q sort, and with both of them on a factor separate from all the other participants. This usually means that there is a central theme running through both of their Q sorts – and a theme wholly separate from those themes (such as togetherness and affirmation) that preoccupy the other factors – but that these polar opposites have resolved this new theme in essentially opposite ways. It will be recalled that factor II also preferred verse, but that was mixed in with concerns about self-affirmation that are absent in factor III.

Of the available poems, Taylor, not yet out of her twenties, expressed a preference for 'those with rhyme/beat', and she saved her most negative scores for those poems that she judged 'felt like closer to prose than poetry'. Among factor III's favoured poems were those by Samuel Taylor Coleridge and Clarence Major, both referred to previously in the description of factor I, and both (especially Coleridge) with definable meter and rhyme scheme. Also strongly favoured was poem no. 20, 'To Virgins, to Make Much of Time', by seventeenth-century poet Robert Herrick (1963), scores below for factors I, II, and III, respectively:

> That age is best which is the first,
> When youth and blood are warmer;
> But being spent, the worse, and worst
> Times still succeed the former.
> Then be not coy, but use your time,
> And while ye may, go marry;
> For, having lost but once your prime,
> You may forever tarry.
> (20)   0.32   0.42   0.95

It is this kind of poem, with clear rhyme scheme and definite meter, that appeals to factor III.

But most strongly favoured by factor III were the lyrics to 'Hurt', by Trent Reznor, vocalist for the rock band Nine Inch Nails, which was nominated for a Grammy Award for best rock song when Taylor was still a child, but which gained additional notoriety a few years later when covered in a music video by country singer Johnny Cash (2002) that was considered by some as one of the best music videos of all-time. The lyrics are quite dark and ominous at points, ending with '… you could have it all, my empire of dirt; I will let you down, I will make you hurt', which received quantsal scores of −1.10, 0. 23, and 1.90 in groups I through III, respectively, attesting to a much higher level of pleasingness at Taylor's end of factor III. Whether or not Taylor was aware of the authorship of the poem, the text as a whole had a definite rhyme scheme and meter that appealed to her in her adulthood.

Poems such as 'Hurt', however, were judged unpleasant by Aileen, who was at the negative pole of the same factor III and whose preferences were therefore generally the reverse of Taylor's. Poems judged pleasing to Aileen (and unpleasing to Taylor) were, as Taylor said, 'closer to prose than poetry', although it is not clear that this distinction entered directly into Aileen's poetic judgement. Aileen was more inclined to gravitate to poetry in free verse, such as the following more contemporary poems (Roger McGough's [2004] 'Let Me Die a Youngman's Death' and David Wright's [2005] 'Lines on Retirement, After Reading Lear', scores for factors I, II, and the negative pole of III):

> Let me die a youngman's death
> not a free from sin tiptoe in

>   candle wax and waning death
>   not a curtains drawn by angels borne
>   'what a nice way to go' death
> (6)   −0.13   −0.99   1.90

>   In the end, no one leaves
>   the stage in character—we never see
>   the feather, the mirror held to our lips.
>   So don't wait for skies to crack with sun. Feel
>   the storm's sweet sting invade you to the skin,
>   the strange, sore comforts of the wind. Embrace
>   your children's ragged praise and that of friends.
> (11)   0.90   −1.17   1.28

Both of these were without rhyme and consistent metric. However, Aileen also gave one of her highest scores to Kingsley's 'Young and Old' (presented in the above discussion of factor II) with its conventional ABAB CDCD rhyme scheme and its 'perfect cadence; I read it several times', so it is doubtful that Aileen was consciously and solely drawn to free verse.

There is an additional feature of importance in the negative pole of factor III and that likely relates to age – namely, an apparent desire on Aileen's part for a more enlivened old age, perhaps one that would end more like a bang than a whimper. McGough's poem in particular speaks to this (of wanting to die a youngman's death), as does Wright's to some extent (e.g., in his appeal to enjoy the wind and sun and also one's children and friends) – in short, to take time to smell the roses. The fact that Taylor is so much closer to the beginning than the end of life may help account for why she rejects rather than embraces poems like these.

Coda

There is one technical matter that is especially pertinent to factor III, but with implications for all factors in any and all studies – namely, that factor III was only defined by two persons' responses, hence is of lower statistical reliability, which means that we cannot be as certain of our understanding of it compared to our understandings of factor I (comprising twelve persons) and factor II (four persons). Factor stability is tied in part to frequency, and this is a statistical analogue to human experience generally. The person who has tasted a dozen different wines should be more sophisticated about wine than someone who has tasted two only, and the surgeon who has performed a dozen operations should be more skilled than the surgeon who has performed two only. The same holds for the study of poetic preferences: We expect to have a better grasp of preference X than preference Y if we have had the opportunity to examine a dozen of the former compared to only two of the latter.

It is also to be noted that most of the interpretations above were of persons who were relatively 'pure' types, e.g., who were preoccupied with poems that emphasized ageing together (factor I) or who gravitated instead toward poems that emphasized self-affirmation (factor II). However, there were several participants who were of 'mixed' types, i.e., whose Q sorts overlapped with two of the factors at the same time, indicating a blended attraction to the poems (e.g., favouring poems about ageing together as well as poems that were self-affirmative). Moreover, there were also a handful of participants who were not affiliated with any of the factors at all ('null' types), suggesting that their preferences followed criteria for determining poetic pleasure that were relatively idiosyncratic and different from those criteria underlying the three factors described above. One of the participants, for instance, was not significantly associated with any of the three factors, but she had spent much of her early life in the Far East as the child of non-American parents and was therefore not exposed to the same Anglo-American literary influences during her formal education that may be prerequisite for poetic sensitivities necessary for responding like others in this study.

Finally, there is the issue of *consensus*. The three factors emphasize differences in poetic appraisal but buried among the differences were also isolated instances of agreement, foremost among them being the poem 'The Little Boy and the Old Man' by Sheldon Silverstein (1981), which gained scores of 1.19, 2.00, and 0.05 in factors I, II, and III, respectively. This charming little poem is a conversation in which a little boy complains about his life – about dropping things, of wetting his pants, of sometimes crying, and about grown-ups not paying any attention to him – to which the old man replies, 'I know what you mean, I do that, too'. An advantage of Q methodology is that the analysis that it provides can oftentimes reveal the structure behind consensus in art, literature, politics, and other societal activities. In the case of this particular poem, we can see in retrospect why it would appeal to factor I, with its emphasis on growth and development in the company of another person; and to factor II, with its emphasis on affirmation; and perhaps to factor III simply because it is a charming little poem, irrespective of poetic device.[6]

This contrasts with the consensus shown in reaction to the poem by Yeats (1956), 'Down by the Salley Gardens' (scores below for factors I to III):

> In a field by the river
> my love and I did stand,
> And on my leaning shoulder
> she laid her snow-white hand.
> She bid me take life easy,
> as the grass grows on the weirs;
> But I was young and foolish,
> and now am full of tears.
>
> (4)   −0.18   −0.19   0.00

Unlike the positive consensus in reaction to Silverstein's poem, the consensual reaction to Yeats's poem (with quantsal scores at or near zero) was due to the fact that it was

---

[6] The fact that the score was zero in factor III was due to Taylor and Aileen both experiencing the poem as among the most pleasing, but since they otherwise stood in bipolar relationship to one another, this agreeable poem was pulled in opposite directions, resulting in a factor score midway between the two poles.

experienced as neither pleasing nor unpleasing across the board, including by both participants at opposite ends in factor III. In short, there are different ways in which diverse minds can converge on a poem or other event and Q methodology can help unravel the different routes through which this convergence has occurred.

The way ahead: Ascending downward

The study reported in this chapter has been mainly descriptive and designed to show how Q methodology operates at the surface level – i.e., how it serves to reveal the structures of subjective preference among many readers, showing that some have responded one way and others another way – but the methodology is quite capable of more penetrating probes that can help shed light on deeper and more motivational aspects related to the appreciation of poetry.

Space precludes going into detail, but consider for illustrative purposes the study by Swinnen and de Medeiros (2018a) who endeavoured to place the reading of poetry within the framework of Huizinga's (1949) theory of cultural play, which the authors define as voluntary, purposeful, imaginative, based on rules, and lacking in competition – yet Huizinga regarded competition as the epitome of play – and that includes 'joy, humour, and vulnerability through the intimacy of exchange' (Swinnen and de Medeiros, 2018b: 263). Stephenson, too, devoted considerable attention to Huizinga's insights about play (Logan 2022; Stephenson 1964, 1967, 1979; Zong 2017) but, in agreement with Huizinga, did not regard play as the opposite of seriousness: rather, as the opposite of reality and as involving voluntary activity, a temporary stepping out of real life, as absorbing and limited to its own boundaries, without material interest, supportive of social groupings, repetitive, and ordered (Stephenson also added self-enhancing). It is noteworthy that Huizinga devoted an entire chapter to poetry and play, concluding that 'only poetry remains as the stronghold of living and noble play' (Huizinga, 1949: 134). Given the above propositions about play, therefore, we might ask how we could sharpen the focus on poetry *in re* play in Huizinga's sense?

Ponder the following thought experiment. With this same set of 20 poems, any participant (e.g., Swinnen and de Medeiros's case of Mrs. R) could be invited to provide her assessment of them under a variety of conditions of instruction, i.e., to rank these 20 poems from +2 to –2 according to the following criteria:

1. Which of these poems would you find most enjoyable if you had nothing better to do (voluntary activity)? That is, rank-order these poems from those that you would experience as most enjoyable (+2) to most unenjoyable (–2) were you to cease your usual work temporarily and take time for yourself, perhaps over a cup of coffee.

Huizinga (1949: 9) regarded this 'intermezzo, an *interlude* in our daily lives' as a formal characteristic of play and operating with these particular poems under this condition could potentially provide us with a window into a different side of Mrs. R or anyone else who might be chosen for study. And the following additional conditions, each one accompanied by a Q sorting of the same poems, would likewise provide the possibility of seeing Mrs. R from a different angle:

2. Which of these poems do you find the most captivating (absorption)?
3. Which has least to do with you personally (material interest)?
4. Which are you most apt to discuss with others (social grouping)?
5. Which would you be most apt to read over again and perhaps try to memorize (repetitive)?
6. Which would you bring to the attention of a friend, as a kind of 'find' or treasure (agonistic, competitive)?
7. Which of these do you experience as uplifting, that make you feel like you are a better person (self-enhancement)?

And so forth, including any other conditions that might suggest themselves based on the writings of Huizinga (1949), Swinnen and de Medeiros (2018b), Lehmann and Brinkmann (2021), and other relevant authors.

Were only the above seven Q sorts employed, this would result in a 7 × 7 correlation matrix, the factor analysis of which would reveal the structure of response tendencies within Mrs. R and place us in a better position to judge the extent to which playfulness was applicable in her case, and perhaps to cast light on Huizinga's (1949) dismal conclusion that play began to wane onward from its high point in the eighteenth century. The history of Q methodology is replete with single-case studies of this kind (Rhoads 2017) that have served to illuminate behaviour at deeper levels.

One of the advantages of Q methodology is that it documents the diversity in poetic appreciation: From among 28 readers in the case reported above, three diverse classes of preference emerged, plus a handful of participants whose views depart from the main three. It is also advantageous in that it reveals limits that suggest something of an objective substructure within the subjectivity that is so central to the humanities: The 28 responses, each unique to some extent, do not scatter into 28 discrete categories, but into only three (one of which is bipolar), testifying to a constraint in independent variety and perhaps serving as peepholes into what Lehmann and Brinkmann (2019, see also their chapter in this volume) refer to as 'existential pathways'; most responses emphasizing one of the central virtues to which they refer – *love* (the celebration of togetherness and absence of regret in factor I), *authenticity* (the search for self-affirmation on the part of factor II), and *self-exploration* (the openness to adventure in the case of factor III-negative). Finally, Q methodology has the facility for systematic examination of deeper structures of poetic interpretation and appreciation through the intensive study of single cases, thus opening to observation the complexity below the relative order at the surface and supporting parallels to the quantum theory of material reality (Stephenson 1988).

Many years ago, a teacher of literature came upon Stephenson's (1972) study of Keats's 'Ode' and enthusiastically claimed that it provided 'startling results on readers' responses' (Strenski, 1979: 228); however, nothing came of it. As suggested in the opening paragraphs, this non-response is likely due to lack of methodological receptivity and preparation within the humanities, but developments (especially technological developments) in the intervening half century have reduced technical and mathematical barriers, thereby undermining the justification for reticence and rendering the scientific study of poetry more accessible. The door therefore stands ajar.

References

Arnold, M. (1884), *Poems by Matthew Arnold*, New York: Macmillan.
Banasick, S. (2019), 'KADE: A Desktop Application for Q Methodology', *Journal of Open Source Software* 4 (36): art. 1360.
Bronowski, J. (1966), *The Poet's Defence: The Concept of Poetry from Sidney to Yeats*, new edn, Cleveland, OH: World.
Brown, S. R. (1993), 'A Primer on Q Methodology', *Operant Subjectivity* 16: 91–138.
Brown, S. R. and M. Mathieson (1990), 'The Operantcy of Practical Criticism', *Electronic Journal of Communication/La Revue Electronique de Communication* 1 (1). Troy, NY. Available online: http://www.cios.org/www/ejc/v1n190.htm
Brown, S. R. and R. W. Taylor (1973), 'Frames of Reference and the Observation of Behaviour', *Social Science Quarterly* 54: 29–40
Cash, J. (2002), 'Hurt' [music video], Available online: https://www.youtube.com/watch?v=8AHCfZTRGiI (accessed 1 November 2021).
Coleridge, S. T. (1852), *The Poems of Samuel Taylor Coleridge* (D. & S. Coleridge, eds), London: Edward Moxon.
Collini, S. (2013), 'Leavis v Snow: The Two-Cultures Bust-up 50 Years On', *The Guardian*, August 16. Available online: https://www.theguardian.com/books/2013/aug/16/leavis-snow-two-cultures-bust
Cummings, E. E. (1972), *Complete Poems, 1913-1962*, New York: Harcourt Brace Jovanovich.
Dickstein, M. (1971), *Keats and His Poetry: A Study in Development*, Chicago: University of Chicago Press.
Donne, J. (1952), *The Complete Poetry and Selected Prose of John Donne* (ed. C. M. Coffin), New York: Modern Library.
Fleming, P. A. (2017), *I Still Matter*. Available online: https://familyfriendpoems.com/poem/107408 (accessed 1 November 2021).
Frost, R. (1979), *The Poetry of Robert Frost: The Collected Poems* (ed. E. C. Lathem), New York: Henry Holt.
Good, J. M. M. (2011), 'Some Contextualizing Notes on William Stephenson's "Old Age Research"', *Operant Subjectivity* 34: 215–216.
Hanauer, D. I. (2011), 'The Scientific Study of Poetic Writing', *Scientific Study of Literature* 1 (1): 79–87.
Hardy, T. (1994), *The Works of Thomas Hardy*, Ware, UK: Wordsworth Editions.
Hauser, M. (2020), 'The Incredible Ageing Man'. Available online: https://hellopoetry.com/poem/4013304/the-incredible-aging-man/ (accessed 1 November 2021).
Herrick, R. (1963), *The Complete Poetry of Robert Herrick*, New York: New York University Press.
Huizinga, J. (1949), *Homo Ludens: A Study of the Play-Element in Culture*, London: Routledge & Kegan Paul.
Huxley, A. (1963), *Literature and Science*, New York: Harper & Row.
Illingworth, S. and D. Simpson (Producers) (2021), *Experimental Words*. Recording, Arts Council England. https://experimentalwords.com/

Kingsley, C. (1884), *The Works* (Vol. I), London: Macmillan. Available online http://www.potw.org/archive/potw365.html (accessed 1 November 2021).

Krauss, L. M. (2009), 'C. P. Snow in New York', *Scientific American*, September. Available online: https://www.scientificamerican.com/article/an-update-on-cp-snows-two-cultures/)

Larkin, P. (1988), *Philip Larkin: Collected Poems* (ed. A. Thwaite), London: Marvell Press.

Le Guin, U. K. (2004), *The Wave in the Mind*, Boulder, CO: Shambhala.

Leavis, F. R. (1962), *Two Cultures? The Significance of C. P. Snow*, London: Chatto & Windus.

Lehmann, O. V. and S. Brinkmann (2021), '"Humbled by Life": Poetic Representations of Existential Pathway and Personal Life Philosophies among Older Adults in Norway', *Qualitative Inquiry* 27: 102–113.

Logan, R. A. (2022), 'The Arts, Health Literacy, Health Disparities, and Play Theory', in J. C. Rhoads, D. B. Thomas, and S. E. Ramlo (eds.), *Cultivating Q Methodology: Essays Honoring Steven R. Brown*, 118–144, Columbia, MO: International Society for the Scientific Study of Subjectivity.

Major, C. (1998), *Configurations: New and Selected Poems, 1958–1998*, Townsend, WA: Copper Canyon Press.

McGough, R. (2004), *Collected Poems*, London: Penguin. Available online: https://www.best-poems.net/roger_mcgough/index.html (accessed 1 November 2021).

Newton, I. ([1726] 1934), *Mathematical Principles of Natural Philosophy* (rev. trans., F. Cajori), 3rd edn, Berkeley: University of California Press.

Peirce, C. S. ([1892] 1940), 'The Law of Mind', in J. Buchler (ed.), *The Philosophy of Peirce: Selected Writings*, 339–353, London: Routledge & Kegan Paul.

Plath, S. (1975). *Letters Home: Correspondence, 1950–1963* (ed. A. S. Plath). New York: Harper & Row.

Popova, M. (2019), *Figuring*, New York: Pantheon.

Rhoads, J. C. (2017), 'Foreword to the Special Issue: Q Methodology and the Single Case', *Operant Subjectivity* 39 (1–2): 1.

Richards, I. A. (1929), *Practical Criticism: A Study of Literary Judgment*, London: Routledge & Kegan Paul.

Robinson, T., B. Gustafson and M. Popovich (2008), 'Perceptions of Negative Stereotypes of Older People in Magazine Advertisements: Comparing the Perceptions of Older Adults and College Students', *Ageing & Society* 28: 233–251.

Robinson, T. E., M. Popovich, R. Gustafson and C. Fraser (2003), 'Older Adults' Perceptions of Offensive Senior Stereotypes in Magazine Advertisements: Results of a Q-Method Analysis'. *Educational Gerontology* 29: 503–519.

Sartre, J.-P. (1950), *What Is Literature?* London: Methuen.

Schmolck, P. (2014), 'PQMethod' [Computer software], Available online: http://schmolck.org/qmethod/

Silverstein, S. (1981), *A Light in the Attic*, New York: HarperCollins.

Smith, S. (1983), *Collected Poems* (ed. J. MacGibbon), New York: New Directions.

Snow, C. P. (1959), *The Two Cultures and the Scientific Revolution*, Cambridge, UK: Cambridge University Press.

Spearman, C. (1927), *The Abilities of Man*, New York: Macmillan.

Stephenson, W. (1964), 'The Ludenic Theory of Newsreading', *Journalism Quarterly* 41: 367–374.

Stephenson, W. (1967), *The Play Theory of Mass Communication*, Chicago: University of Chicago Press.

Stephenson, W. (1972), 'Applications of Communication Theory: II—Interpretations of Keats' "Ode on a Grecian Urn"', *Psychological Record* 22: 177–192.
Stephenson, W. ([1950] 1979), 'Old Age Research in England', *Operant Subjectivity* 2: 46–50.
Stephenson, W. (1979), 'Homo Ludens: The Play Theory of Advertising', *Rivista Internazionale di Scienze Economiche e Commerciali* 26: 634–653.
Stephenson, W. (1988), 'Quantum Theory of Subjectivity', *Integrative Psychiatry* 6: 180–187.
Stephenson, W. (2011), 'Old Age Research', *Operant Subjectivity* 34: 217–233.
Strenski, E. (1979), 'A Comment on Alan Purves' Model for Research in Reader Response', *College English* 41: 228–229.
Swinnen, A. K. de Medeiros (2018a), 'Participatory Arts Programs in Residential Dementia Care: Playing with Language Differences', *Dementia* 17: 763–774.
Swinnen, A. and K. de Medeiros (2018b), '"Play" and People Living with Dementia: A Humanities-Based Inquiry of TimeSlips and the Alzheimer's Poetry Project', *The Gerontologist* 58: 261–269.
Thomas, D. (1971), *The Poems of Dylan Thomas* (ed. D. Jones), New York: New Directions.
Wharton, E. (2019), *Selected Poems of Edith Wharton* (ed. I. Goldman-Price), New York: Scribner.
Wilson, C. B. (1940), 'A Note on the Statistical Analysis of Sentence-Length as a Criterion of Literary Style', *Biometrika* 31: 356–361.
Wright, D. (2005), *Fine Frenzy*, Iowa City: University of Iowa Press. Available online: https://poets.org/poem/lines-retirement-after-reading-lear (accessed 1 November 2021).
Yeats, W. B. (1956), *The Collected Poems of W. B. Yeats* (definitive edn), New York: Macmillan.
Zong, Y. S. (2017), *Homo Ludens & Q-Methodology & Communication: A Study of William Stephenson's Play Theory of Mass Communication*, Beijing: China University of Political Science and Law Press. (Chinese)

10

Writing Lives

Merete Mazzarella

I have spent my working life in the academy but am writing this not as an academic but out of my own experience as a practitioner of life writing and as someone who has taught it for thirty years. Interestingly, many older people see the very idea of autobiographical writing or even oral storytelling as embarrassingly self-absorbed. At best, they can see that it might be worth doing it for the sake of their children and grandchildren or other younger relatives or friends. Some older people proudly say that their children and grandchildren have shown great interest in their lives or even asked them to write, others say that their offspring have shown no curiosity whatsoever. I would argue that writing is worthwhile in either case: children and grandchildren who have already shown an interest will eventually discover that there is much they have forgotten or never fully took in, those who right now may be too busy with their own lives to take an interest will quite possibly change, if not before then when the parent or grandparent has died. Through writing we can all hope to be seen more clearly and understood more fully. But the most important reason for trying to talk people into autobiographical writing is that it is worthwhile for their own sakes.

Older people inevitably face a variety of life crises, retirement, loss of a partner, serious illness or disability (see also Lehmann and Brinkmann, in this volume). Sooner or later, we will all need to reconstruct our identity, our sense of who we are and what we wish – and are able – to do with our remaining years. As many philosophers – the best-known of them probably Søren Kierkegaard – have pointed out, life must be lived forwards but can only be understood backwards. Writing autobiographically is about self-reflection, about trying to understand ourselves better by retrieving lost memories and coming to grips with past events.

Autobiographical narrative can be about a desire for coming to terms with the way things turned out or achieving closure by seeing one's life as a story with a definite shape. My motivation for teaching this kind of writing came from what happened during the last months of my mother's life. My mother had always said that she was going to write her life story but at 71 she was diagnosed with cancer of the pancreas and three months later she was dead. During these months I spent as much time with her as possible and, knowing that I was about to lose her, I started interviewing her about her life. This way the story she had never had time to write was told, from her childhood in the Danish countryside through her early career as a journalist and writer (which – to her lasting regret, I had always sensed – came to a dead end when she married my father, a Finnish diplomat) and from there on to 15 contented and self-fulfilling widowed years of painting and teaching yoga. A week before she died, in the summer, at her country home, she said: 'I have had a good life and it feels like it has come full circle, it started in the countryside; it allowed me to travel and see the world and now it ends in a place very like the one where it began.'

The point I want to make here is that telling her story had brought her not only existential satisfaction but aesthetic satisfaction, too, through the structure that she suddenly perceived.

My most important book is the one I wrote about her life and death, *Hem från festen (Home from the Party)*, published in 1992. The title is a quote from a comment of hers: 'I actually thought I would live for another ten years or so but as it is, dying before I expected to is really no worse than going home from a party earlier than I expected to. The important thing is that the party was good while I was there.'

When *Home from the Party* was published, I began to receive requests for speaking engagements. Some were to speak to medical staff about the role of family in terminal care, but by far the majority were invitations to teach life writing. Twenty-five years later, when my granddaughter Amelia graduated from Columbia, my son William gave her his own English translation of the book as a present. William – who by this time was a professor of anthropology at the University of Chicago – had lived in the US since the nineties and my two grandchildren were totally American with no knowledge of my language, Swedish. Once again, the book made a vital difference in my life: my grandchildren had never known my mother, but the book brought her to life for them and helped them develop a whole new understanding of me and my background.

If asked what exactly they want to achieve by writing about their lives most older people will simply say that they want to leave a record of places, events, experiences that have been important to them. It is unlikely that there will be any mention of new insights or emotional processes. Many will spontaneously produce something that looks like a CV. They will say exactly when and where they were born, went to school, got their first job, got married, had their children, moved house. There may be descriptions of places, of what they played as children, of family routines and festivities such as Christmas but it will mostly be a very prosaic record. The purpose of a course in autobiographical writing would, it seems to me, be to shift the focus from outer reality to inner, from the prosaic to the literary (see also Randall, in this volume).

Can a life story in prose be poetic?

Yes, I do believe so, but for those not well-versed in literature, 'poetic' is a difficult word to get a handle on. It could mean anything from 'sentimental' to 'ornamental', it could be (mis)understood as icing on a cake. The American writer Mary McCarthy once met a young woman who was taking a writing class and said that once she had finished her story, she expected help with putting the symbols into it. Above all the 'poetic' may seem pretentious or at least daunting, as something that only 'real' writers can achieve. Personally, I would not feel easy using 'poetic' about any of my own work, however hard I work on style. But a life story in prose – including some of my own work – can certainly be literary and can use a good many of the tools of poetry. And though I would not suggest to a group of older people that they should write 'poetically'

I will tell them that there are tools that can help them do what they want to do *better*, more effectively, more vividly to catch and hold the interest of their readers. To that they will usually respond quite enthusiastically.

Since by no means everyone who takes a life writing class is an avid reader, I will often spend some time discussing what literature – fiction, poetry – is all about. As a vivid example I've often taken a column by Gustaf Mattsson, a Finland-Swedish writer from the early twentieth century. Mattsson was a journalist, a restless man with wide interests – he had studied chemistry, he was an excellent pianist, he dabbled in politics – but like many restless people he was terrified of getting bored. In one of his best-known columns from 1914, he tries to envision what the perfect way to avoid boredom would be. It would be, he concludes, to have human heads constructed like lightbulbs so that the moment boredom threatens you could take hold of your head, twist it round a couple of times (Mattsson is particularly vivid about the moment when the head starts to come loose), then lift it right off your neck – and exchange it for someone else's. That way you would be able to feel new thoughts in your brain and new fillings in your teeth (Mattsson 1914/1994).

When I use the column in a writing class my point is that you can get new thoughts in your brain in any number of ways: by reading a newspaper or a book of non-fiction or simply by talking to a friend, but the physical, sensuous experience of someone else's body is one that literature is eminently able to provide. And another thing: the column in itself is a piece of literature, using the light bulb as a metaphor. Mattsson could have said: 'If you're concerned about getting bored, try a change of perspective!' Had he done so, however, we would not have remembered his column, we might have found it quite trite and simply thrown the newspaper to one side. The purpose of a metaphor is to engage our interest by making us see familiar things with a new awareness, maybe even in a new way, and that is precisely what the light bulb image does. Along with the notion of 'new fillings in your teeth' is also quite specific and concrete – and amusing, yet another effective literary strategy.[1]

So how can a teacher get a workshop group to start writing? One way is through a 'Present moment' exercise. The participants are asked to pick up pencil and paper – or to switch on their laptops – and not to be impatient or rush towards the past that they have set themselves the task of narrating but rather to start here and now, to lean back, make themselves comfortable, look around and then start writing about the present moment, first paying attention to as many sensory impressions as possible, how their bodies feel, what they see, what they hear, what they smell, what the atmosphere in the room is like. From there they can go on to writing about what goes on in their heads, worries in their daily lives that they may be having trouble setting aside or perhaps about what they are hoping to get out of the writing workshop. I always make it clear that at this point they should not feel under any obligation to write well, to structure their text or even produce complete sentences. They should feel free to make a note of

---

[1] By now the attentive reader – like some participants in my workshops and many medical students – may have realized that however effective Mattsson's piece is as an example of literary – even poetic – devices, he is mistaken in a very basic sense: if our heads were so constructed that we could swap heads with someone else, it would not be the contents of the head that would surprise us but the body.

any passing thought however irrelevant it might seem, they should not exercise any self-censorship, they should just keep on writing in stream-of-consciousness fashion.

Above all they should rest assured that at this point they are writing entirely for themselves with no obligation to prove themselves to others or even to share their writing. The benefits are twofold: anxious participants are likely to relax and in the following discussion – which is simply about what the exercise felt like – there is almost always a general sense of wonder at how much the present moment contains, how much they had to say. And how liberating and refreshing it was to say it. The next step is another exercise in writing about the senses. This time the task is to write about a memory of a *smell* – good or bad – and to try and describe both the smell itself and some specific situation in which it has played a part.

Why smell?

There are several reasons: One is that most people, once they start thinking about it, have lots of memories of smells so the exercise will encourage all those who joined the class half-apologetically, saying: 'I'm afraid I have a terrible memory.' If anyone still cannot get started, I offer a very simple prompt: 'Write about the smell of the classroom in your primary school – or of the school lunch.'

Another reason is that experiencing a smell – or a taste – summons up memories of previous experiences of that particular smell or taste. The most famous example of this is, of course the madeleine cake which Proust's protagonist Marcel soaks in his tea and lifts to his lips in the first volume of *In Search of Lost Time, Swann's Way*. From the point of view of writing as a craft, smells are interesting because finding the exact words to describe them is harder than many people think, and the effort forces you away from the intellectual and the abstract into the very mundane and specific. The result is often vivid – and often strikingly *visual* – writing.

Above all smells have emotional power. Just a week or two after 9/11, I was invited to do a writing workshop with a group of American women who had all lived in Finland for many years. While doing this particular exercise a couple of them burst into tears and subsequently explained that they had found themselves writing about smells – or scents – that had to do with their life as children and young adults in the US – smells they now thought they would probably never experience again. Another example: In a writing workshop for Swedish medical students one young man wrote about the first operation he had witnessed: 'As soon as the surgeon had made an incision there was a strong smell of meat.' This surely is a poetic effect, a 'making strange' of a routine surgical procedure, by reminding us of what it really involves, treating human flesh as 'meat'. Here, we are confronted with an honest, gut-reaction and it is all the more effective because it breaks with the demands of medical professionalism. One hugely important reason for medical students to do medical humanities is to be confronted by discourse that is very different from that of medical professionalism. Medical discourse – like any scientific discourse – is abstract, impersonal, unsensuous and rigidly controls feeling.

The medical student willingly volunteered to read his piece aloud to the rest of the class – and the result was a minute's absolute silence. In most writing classes it only takes one person to offer to read for many more to be quite eager to follow. No one who appears genuinely unwilling should ever be pressured to read but the silent ones can at least be asked. Listening to the actual voice of an actual writer in the same room is the perfect starting point for a group discussion about such vital literary matters as voice, tone, and rhythm. I always recommend to would-be writers that they read their work out loud to themselves at home.

How then should discussions start? Initially the discussion had best be kept gentle; the most constructive way of organizing it is not to start with specific criticisms or suggestions for improvement but with each member of the group in turn saying first what they really like about the piece, second what they feel they do not quite understand or what they need (or would like?) to know more about. This way the writer gets a general sense of how well they communicate, what has been picked up on and appreciated, what appears to have been misunderstood, what is simply ignored. Discussion based on listening to a text rather than reading it has the advantage that attention is not drawn to spelling mistakes or faulty punctuation.

After 'the present moment' and the memory of a smell, comes the portrait, either a portrait of another person or a self-portrait. I ask everyone to find a photograph of someone who has been important in their lives and to use the photograph as the starting point for a portrait of that person. Here the challenge is not to give a top to toe description but to look for significant details, to interpret the setting and the situation; but above all it is to catch the person's manner and to see if the photograph is at all helpful in giving at least some idea of the person's character. The value of this exercise lies in the fact that for once everyone can actually *see* what everyone else is writing about since the photos can be passed around at the same time as the writing is shared. This means that there is every opportunity for learning from each other, and for a lively discussion about techniques for representing the relationship between outer appearance and inner life. A general conclusion tends to be that when it comes to recording detail less is usually more. Over the years I have carried with me a line from Mary McCarthy's *Memories of a Catholic Girlhood* where she says that her grandmother had 'a monstrous balcony of a bosom' (2013: 2).

Does this sound like a caricature?

Yes, probably.

Is it unkind?

Not necessarily. It can be read as a child's perspective on an old person, and it will remind many of us, who are now old ourselves, how overwhelming – and sometimes outlandish – an old person can seem to a child. At least to me this one detail really brings Mary McCarthy's grandmother to life: I feel I can see her stand, sit, move, I even feel I can hear her speak.

(The question of how generous to relatives and friends – or enemies – a memoir needs to be is a burning one for many would-be writers but not one I am prepared to expand on here. All I can say is that until you start thinking about publishing you should write absolutely without self-censorship: no good work comes out of writing with a sense of every single relative, friend or acquaintance reading over your shoulder.)

At the end of the very first day of a writing course there is often someone who exclaims: 'My goodness, we already know more about each other than we know about some of the friends we have known for years.' A sense of mutual trust is beginning to be established within the group and it will not be long before everyone is willing to make their writing available to each other either on paper or in digital form. Reading aloud should still be encouraged, but now the discussion can become more detailed, more focused on the actual craftsmanship. Voice, rhythm, and tone remain aspects that need to be considered throughout, but it will also be possible to pay attention to the language, the choice of words. A common fault among amateur writers is repetitiveness or general wordiness, or a tendency to be overly explicit, sometimes caused by an inability to trust their readers to draw their own conclusions. Another is taking refuge in cliché or bland or simply un-specific words as in 'She was *nice* to me', 'I loved my grandmother because she was such a *kind* person.'

It is a good idea to start writing without being too self-critical, to allow yourself to go with the flow. As a starting point bad writing is better than no writing at all, but bad writing is only raw material that is likely to need a lot of work. Sometimes it can be a matter of expanding the original, more often – much more often – it is a matter of paring it down. In her excellent book *Essays* (2019) the American writer Lydia Davis shows how she has revised a single sentence step by step. The final version is: 'She walks around the house balancing on the balls of her feet, sometimes whistling and singing, sometimes talking to herself, sometimes stopping dead in a fencing position.' Davis started with the phrase: 'She is likely to walk around the house lightly on the balls of her feet' but was displeased with the rhyme 'likely/lightly'. The next steps – with Davis's objections to them in brackets – were:

> She walks ...
> ... around the house slowly (doesn't suggest happiness)
> ... around the house slowly but delicately ... (too much explanation)
> ... around the house slowly, carefully ... (not strong enough)
> ... around the house slowly, carefully, balancing on the balls of her feet ... (too wordy)
> ... around the house slowly balancing on the balls of her feet ... (good, I like it, then later I think too much and take out slowly, now the first part of the sentence is finished.)
>
> (Davis 2019: 175–6)

The rest of the sentence gets the same careful attention but what Davis seems clear about all along is that she needs to end with 'fencing position': 'it's the culminating, striking image; it's what made me want to write the sentence down in the first place.'

Davis is useful as a model for amateur writers in part because she shows what craftsmanship is all about, in part because it becomes clear that good writing is definitely not ornamental. That everyday language is good enough for literature is made even clearer when Davis recommends studying the chart of the Beaufort wind force scale which goes from 1 to 12 and is based on close observation (as found online, see 'Beaufort scale', *Merriam Webster*). I will just provide a few examples:

0 means 'Calm': 'Sea like mirror' and 'Smoke rises vertically'
3 is 'Gentle breeze': 'Large wavelets; crests begin to break; foam of glassy appearance; perhaps scattered white horses' and 'leaves and small twigs in constant motion; light flags extended'.

9 is 'Strong/severe gale': 'High waves; dense streaks of foam along the direction of the wind; sea begins to roll; spray affects visibility' and 'Slight structural damage (chimney pots and slates removed)'.

('Beaufort scale', *Merriam Webster*)

The point here is the careful observation, the attention to detail.

A basic lesson to learn is the distinction between telling and showing and the value of showing over telling. There are at least two problems with sentences like 'She was nice to me' or 'I loved my grandfather because he was such a kind person', or 'My grandmother had very traditional values' One is that they are vague – how was she nice to you? 'In what ways was he kind?' we want to ask. The other is that we do not get a chance to judge the characters for ourselves.

What is a good example of showing? Perhaps the Swedish writer Olof Lagercrantz's memoir *Min första krets (My first circle)* (1982), a title referring both to his immediate family and to Dante's Inferno. The most important thing we learn about Lagercrantz's mother is that for years she sat at home crying and that eventually her depression became so severe that she had to be taken to a mental hospital. As for his father, we learn that for a long time he watched his wife in bewilderment and then one day decided to give her twenty Swedish crowns to buy herself some flowers. It is an anecdote that makes it clear that we are dealing with a person who knows nothing about mental illness or indeed what it means to give someone flowers. There is no need for Lagercrantz to tell us that his father was good but unimaginative, we have been shown, we have been able to draw our own conclusions. To be told would have felt like a lack of trust on the part of the writer.

Showing can generally be done quite effectively through anecdotes. A particular kind of anecdote that I have talked a lot about over the years is what I call the life-symbol. Speaking autobiographically, a life-symbol is a story – usually from fairly early childhood, often concluding in a remark – which one retrospectively comes to see as symbolic of who one is and what one has become. A couple of examples from my own life: when I was around a year and a half, I was taken on my very first trip to Denmark to meet my grandparents. At that point I was still an only child, overprotected and no doubt spoiled rotten. At my grandparents' house I suddenly found myself surrounded by much older cousins on whom I was eager to make an impression. I pulled down a thin cushion from the sofa, laid it on the floor, climbed up on it and jumped down. I did this over and over and each time I did it I shook my head and said, 'Dangerous, dangerous'. My understanding of myself is that I've spent my entire life thinking that I am taking a risk when I'm actually not – and that I have always been quite happy to have an audience.

An individual can have several life-symbols. Another one of mine that I am happier about because it seems to show a certain integrity is from the age of four or five. A visiting relative looked at me and said: 'You have your father's eyes, little one.' I answered: 'They may look like my father's but they're actually my own.' Life-symbols are, of course, interesting from an existential point of view – if we don't like what a life-symbol says about us we might take a decision to grow and change – but from a literary point of view they are a means of characterization. Fiction writers can invent life-symbols for their characters. A Finland-Swedish short story writer from a hundred years ago, Runar Schildt, wrote a (semi-autobiographical) novella called 'Häxskogen' – 'The Bewitched Forest' (1920) – about a writer – his name is Jacob Casimir – who is low in self-confidence and despairing about the chapter he is currently working on. His sense of self is closely tied up with an episode from his childhood when he and his cousins were all together in the family summer home – the setting of the novella – and an aunt gave each child a toy egg, explaining that it would contain some little object that will predict the recipient's future. One little girl finds a ring and understands that she will get engaged and marry, a little boy finds an anchor and understands that he will become a sea captain, but when Jacob Casimir opens his egg, he finds that it is empty. When the other children show him their presents and want him to show them his he refuses and simply closes his hand round the egg out of an overwhelming sense of shame. It is, of course, the shame that is interesting here: a more self-confident child would have announced loudly that he had been given an empty egg and would have demanded a new one. Jacob Casimir, however, is a man who can only see the empty egg as a symbol of his own failures and the ultimate emptiness of his life.

Another way of showing is through what a character says. Instead of saying 'My grandmother had old-fashioned values' I could quote her remark when she passes a box of chocolate round: 'Only one piece, please! A little tastes as good as a lot'. Even 70 years ago her son – my uncle – dared to protest against this dictum. One day he finally burst out: 'Yes, but the taste doesn't last as long'.

Standing remarks or phrases – or proverbs – that you heard in childhood are worth reflecting on, they represent the values of the times: when I was little no one ever said, 'Spare the rod and spoil the child' but I did have an old aunt who said: 'Your will is in the pocket of your mother's apron', meaning that a child should have no will of her own. Fortunately, I did not understand it when I heard it, perhaps because my mother never wore aprons. Over the years I have given much thought to how enormously values have changed during my lifetime; along with child raising, gender roles, sexual mores and attitudes to ethnicities other than one's own, are obvious examples. If younger generations are to understand older people – or indeed if we are to understand ourselves – we need to be aware of how much – and in many cases how lastingly – we have been affected by the values of our formative years.

But where do these exercises lead, you might ask. What about the actual memoir, the *book* that the people taking the course want to produce? Well, most people who join a course in life writing tend to be terrified at the very thought of *the book*. They worry about where it ought to begin. Ought it to begin with their birth? Or should they begin with their parents, how their parents met or even with how their parents were born? At this rate they are likely never to begin at all. It is much better not to be concerned about chronology but to begin wherever you want to begin, perhaps to begin with whatever made you want to write in the first place, and to rely on the fact that with a laptop text can easily be moved around. It is perfectly possible to carry on writing individual memories, individual scenes and portraits – pieces just one or two pages long – letting one memory lead to another, without any particular worry about where the whole thing is going. Writing, the American novelist E. L. Doctorow – best known for his novel *Ragtime* (1975) – once said, is like driving a car in the dark: at any given moment you can only see a small part of the road, but you can trust that the road goes on. Some discipline is required, though: when a memory, an image, an idea or whatever comes to you, you should write it down immediately, regardless of where you are or what you are doing. However, convinced you are that you will remember it later you very likely won't. It is also a good idea to make writing – or looking over what you have written – a part of your daily routine, if only for half an hour or so. You need to keep the project alive in your mind.

You don't have to aim at covering all of your life, but it is hard to imagine life writing that leaves out childhood. The Swedish writer Olof Lagercrantz who wrote a biography of one of the real giants of Scandinavian literature, August Strindberg, once told me that he kept having to add to the chapters on Strindberg's childhood as it became clearer and clearer to him how much of the great man's later life could only be understood in the light of his childhood experiences. The same goes for pretty much every other life. To settle for a childhood memoir is fine, of course, and many people do – childhood and youth seem to have a special glow – but surely there is also a lot to be said for taking the time to recall and reflect on the experiences and insights of all those later years? They could indeed be said to be worthwhile precisely because they seem so much less distinct. There is no need to describe every mile of your life journey but there are bound to be stations that are worth stopping at. Being in a group can once again be a great help: each person's memories trigger the memories of the others (see also Lehmann & Brinkmann, this volume).

Eventually, when the pages start piling up, when there are 40 or 50 or so of them, it's time to read them through in one go and see what patterns can be discerned, what themes recur and might be possible to develop further, and if they can be arranged in chronological – or some other – order. At this point it might be worthwhile to look for – and think about – climaxes or turning points, points, that is, where one's life took a new direction. What caused the turning point? Was it caused by chance, circumstance or by a deliberate decision? But there is no absolute necessity to stitch the pieces together, it's perfectly possible that they will work best as a mosaic or a patchwork quilt. Most lives, after all, are more like mosaics or patchwork quilts than neatly structured stories.

* * *

What, then, have the results of my writing courses been?
They would seem to have been more existential than literary.
Some examples:
A recently retired man wrote about his mother's death in a car crash 30 years earlier. He had been in shock at the time, he had never learned the details of the accident, he had not seen the body, and, because the whole event was so unclear to him, it had continued to haunt him.

After writing about it, he contacted both the police and the hospital where his mother had died, both were extremely helpful in retrieving the information he asked for and he achieved a sense of closure.

Another man who had never talked to his children about his very difficult divorce managed to write about it in such a way that they ended up feeling that they understood both their parents better. A 70-year-old woman wrote about a childhood throughout which she had felt unloved. She had had an older brother who had died at the age of two and she herself had been born 11 months after his death because the family doctor had encouraged the parents to 'replace' the dead as quickly as possible. This turned out to be a huge mistake, the parents were still stunned with grief, the mother attended to her little daughter's physical needs but was unable to form an emotional bond. What happened during the course was that this woman wrote more and more fully about her mother and *her* feelings and as her sympathy for her mother's situation grew her resentment became less acute.

Another older woman, deeply religious, who lived on a farm and grew organic vegetables was so obsessed by a difficult neighbour that she could not talk or write about anything but him. The fact that he did not farm organically was the least of her frustrations, he was also loud and rude and had endless visits from people who were just like him. She had tried to be nice to him, she had tried to complain but nothing helped. Gradually I came to see that her problem was that as a good Christian she was frustrated by the fact that she had been faced by someone who was – literally – her neighbour and whom she could not love. She was still frustrated when she left, but after a week or so I received a postcard that said: 'Thank you for the course. I have finally realised that though the good Lord tells us to love our neighbours as ourselves there is the occasional neighbour whom God will have to love all by himself.'

In all honesty I have to admit that the outcome has not always been happy. In one case an older man spent a whole weekend course writing about his loathing for his entire family – parents, siblings, children – and on the last day, just as we were getting ready to have a final cup of coffee before leaving, he said: 'When I get home, I will have the family tomb erased.' The class was struck speechless and all I could do was to ask him if he wanted to talk to me privately. He said yes, so the class went off to coffee, the two of us stayed on. I asked him how he was feeling, he said he was angry but still glad that he had taken the course. That writing courses can release all sorts of powerful emotions was something I had known for a long time, but this particular incident was still a learning experience: some emotions may be too much to handle for someone who is not a therapist. I tread more carefully these days; I look out for warning signs. (see also Lehmann and Brinkmann, this volume)

When I began writing about my workshops, I became a trifle embarrassed because it seemed to me that the examples I was giving had nothing to do with what this book is supposed to be about. But I have changed my mind. The important lesson here is that writing involves so much more than recording what we know and feel. Writing is a journey, a process of exploration during which we come to feel and know more than before. And one reason we come to feel and know more is that the tools of writing – the search for the exact word, for nuance, for the most revealing point of view requires us to look more closely at ourselves and the world.

References

'Beaufort scale', *Merriam-Webster.com Dictionary*, Merriam-Webster, https://www.merriam-webster.com/dictionary/Beaufort%20scale (accessed 30 January 2022.

Davis, L. (2019), *Essays*, London, UK: Hamish Hamilton.
Lagercrantz, O. (1982), *Min första krets (My First Circle)*, Stockholm, Sweden: Wahlström & Widstrand.
Mattsson, G. (1994), *I dag (Today)*, Nya klassikerserien, Helsingfors, Finland: Söderströms.
Mazzarella, M. (1992), *Hem från festen (Home from the Party)*, Helsingfors, Finland: Söderströms.
McCarthy, M. (2013), *Memories of a Catholic Girlhood*, New York: Vintage Books.
Schildt, R. (1920), *'Häxskogen' och andra noveller ('The Witch Forest' and Other Short Stories)*, Helsingfors, Finland: Schildts.

Selected autobiographical writings of Merete Mazzarella

- *Först sålde de pianot (First They Sold the Piano)*, 1979, about my childhood.
- *Att spela sitt liv (To Play One's Life)*, 1981, about my early adult life.
- *Att spela Afrikas stjärna (To Play 'The Star of Africa')*, 2008, about grandmotherhood.
- *Resa med rabatt (Traveling at a Discount)*, 2010, about retirement.
- *Det enda som egentligen händer oss (The Only Thing That Really Happens to Us)*, 2012, and *Solkattens år (The Year of the Sun Cat)*, 2013, both about remarrying late in life.
- *Från höst till höst (From Autumn to Autumn)*, 2021, a diary from the first year of the pandemic.
- *Den violetta timmen (The Violet Hour)*, 2022, a book about my brother.

I have also written a handbook in autobiographical writing, *Att berätta sig själv (Telling One's Story)*, 2013.

All books by Merete Mazzarella have been published by Schildts & Söderströms, Helsingfors, Finland.

11

Other Voices: George Oppen, Dementia, and the Echo of Lyric

Alastair Morrison

Dementia and the lyric

When we think of poetry about old age, or indeed poetry about ageing generally, the vast portion of what we think of is lyric poetry. To some extent this is only representative, an effect of the lyric's dominance in modern Western poetries. But there are also reasons of topical affinity. In exemplary cases, the lyric catches a still point of reflection, an introspective or recollective experience set against and bounded by time. In English, many of the initiating poems of modern lyricism deal with childhood, but retrospectively rather than in the voice of a child. An awareness of loss and mortality comes with melancholic consolation, offering exactly the kind of ageing selfhood that a liberal individualist society would want. If not exactly *in control* of its passage through time, the poetic speaker nevertheless retains a clear outline against that passage, through the capacities for self-knowledge and deliberate speech that furnish the basic coherence of a lyric poem.

Exactly those affinities, however, which make ageing a natural condition for the lyric speaker make dementia an intolerable one, even an unspeakable one. Philip Larkin begins his 1973 poem 'The Old Fools' with an inquest into the experience of the residents of a care home: 'What do they think has happened, the old fools, / To make them like this?' (2003: 131). That question is never answered. Instead, the poem pursues a series of first-hand reflections on mortality, reflections which conspicuously separate the speaker from the people he is considering.

> ... and them crouching below
> Extinction's alp, the old fools, never perceiving
> How near it is. This must be what keeps them quiet:
> The peak that stays in view wherever we go
> For them is rising ground.
>
> (Larkin 2003: 132)

In the absence of what, by lyric logic, is the most basic element of subjecthood – the concentrating, delimiting knowledge that one is going to die – the experiences of these people are unimaginable. The figure of alpine sublimity in this passage points to Wordsworth, as may Larkin's powerfully affixing description of old age as 'hideous, inverted childhood'. In Book 6 of *The Prelude*, Wordsworth is by turns captivated and disquieted by the unfathomable plenitude of the waterfall at Gondo Gorge and must turn away to reconstitute himself in private thought (2014: 254–5). In 'The Old Fools', the speaker similarly responds to a confrontation with the unmanageable or the meaningless by turning back to the solidity of the self. What started as an inquest into the consciousness of others – what do *they* think has happened? – ends with an idea of knowledge attainable only through private, first-person, lyric experience: 'we will find out' (2003: 132). In a proposal meant to be all the more salutary for its bleakness, the only way to know anything about dementia is to have it.

In the cultural history of dementias, 1973 can feel a remote date. The panic then beginning over the new epidemiological prevalence of these conditions in developed countries seems now at least tempered. The second childhood motif is rightly out of fashion, and the assumption that meaningful personhood ends where dementia begins has been exposed and challenged from a variety of disciplinary perspectives. Tom Kitwood (1997) and others have put dementia at the heart of person-centred models of healthcare, and books like Anne Basting's *Forget Memory* (2009) have influentially argued a much-expanded sense of what is possible in a life with these illnesses. A great deal of important work could be named here, including pieces by Steven Post (1995), Schwinnen and Schweds (2015), and Kontos, Grigorovich, and Colobong (2020). And yet the problem of dementia for lyric poetry remains. Christian Wiman's poem 'Spirits', from the 2020 collection *Survival is a Style*, works from a perspective similar to that of Larkin's poem. 'My friend's father is forgetting the world / but he remembers sex' (2020: 16). The father's outrageous behaviour prompts the speaker to questions about 'the relation between chemistry and consciousness', the liminal pores of lyric personhood. As in Larkin, the questions are never answered.

> … was there a short as in a storm the fuse box flashes sharply
> And all the windows but one go dark?
> Is my friend's father's mind divided like a cocktail,
> One part grace and two parts loss, with a splash of wrath?
>
> (Wiman 2020: 16)

There is none of Larkin's abrasive jocundity here. The father remains a person, someone whose distinctions are worth seeing and whose derogation would do harm. But the turn away and within is the same. The poem ends as the speaker and his friend

> … clink our drinks – whiskey, neat – and feel,
> Each in his own way, the tiny, divine starburst in the brain
>
> (Wiman 2020: 16)

The conclusion is a bracing reminder that consciousness without dementia is chemical and contingent too. Yet a contrast remains in place. Expanding on the poem's title, the whiskey plays against the cocktail of the earlier line: the 'spirit' of the lyric voice is singular, individuated, *neat*, while subjecthood with dementia, to the extent it can be described at all, is dashed, mixed, composite. The Christian trope of transubstantiation that runs through the poem, whereby the permeable materiality of the body becomes the private miracle of the soul, finds its limit case in dementia.

A poem like 'Spirits' illustrates the limits of a merely 'anti-stigma' position with regard to dementia. Some recent histories of poetic reception suggest that, for the modern Western reader, a poem is unrecognizable as such except insofar as it can be read in lyric terms (Jackson 2005: 70). Something similar seems to be true of subjecthood with dementia; where we do not hear that same integrated self-possession that we also expect in a lyric voice, we may not feel that we are hearing a subject at all. This may be dismissive, as per Larkin, but it could also be understood as respectful, a refusal to presume or bespeak. Having learned to be polite and even positive about life with dementia, then, we may easily remain stranded in an old sense of the gulf between minds with dementia and minds without it.

Alternatives to the lyric

What kind of poetry would take us further into this gulf? As far as dementia is concerned, is the lyric norm of continence a simple anathema, something best discarded as quickly and completely as possible? In fact, I suggest, a premise of personhood at least *something* like that of the lyric is going to be essential in respecting the privacy, dignity, and self-direction of those with dementia, and in treating problems of communication and consent with due gravity. There is also the pragmatic point that lyric poetry's dominance is not going away, and that accommodations to be made within the lyric are likely to be immanently advantageous. Several contemporary poets have taken dementia as an occasion to probe the boundaries of the lyric from the position of caregiver. In her 2006 collection *Tarkovskijs heste* (*Tarkovsky's Horses*, trans. 2010), Danish poet Pia Tafdrup follows her father's institutionalization and death with dementia in poems which take his interiority as their focus, but which always register a tendentious point of origin in someone outside him. Projects like Tafdrup's might contribute the larger investigations of literary caregiving modelled by scholars like Amelia DeFalco (2016), and could supply an account of what the lyric in particular means in these contexts – how it highlights important limits to our insight into others, even as our responsibilities do not end with the acknowledgement that our insight is fallible. It would be unfortunate, however, to take up the question of how poetry *ventriloquizes* dementia without first having attended to how a poet with dementia might imagine this enterprise. This is true in the same way that, when a loved one bespeaks the wishes of a person with dementia in an instance of necessity, they benefit from a sense of this person's values, desires, and proclivities, and ideally, instructions about when and how far to assert decisional power in the interpretation of these things, though these are not always available in time.

What I want to look at here, then, is how selfhood with dementia might be expressed in revised lyric form, retaining that form's emphasis on a tenacious subjecthood while accommodating conditions of interdependence which are not only practical but have also to do with thought, feeling, and expression. I answer that question by way of example. In 1978, the same year that he received his late diagnosis of Alzheimer's disease, the American experimental poet George Oppen published his final collection of poetry, *Primitive*. Commentators have occasionally pointed out the salience of dementia to *Primitive*, but only in negative terms, as a factor in the alienation, and especially the alienation from its own language, which is taken to be the book's theme. So far, we might say, so lyric: the worry that the language one uses is not one's own is quite consistent with the genre's antisocial aspect. Taking this worry to its conclusion, one might argue that the ultimate expression of lyric interiority is silence, and Oppen himself once commented, years before *Primitive*, that 'because I am not silent, the poems are bad' (Izenberg, 2011: 105). What criticism of *Primitive* has missed is the way that this collection, and the challenges of life with dementia that it registers, changes Oppen's earlier stance. Rather than simply failing to be silent, it explores the compromise of not being so, calling attention to the fact that it does, in the face of numerous boundaries to understanding, exist as language at all. In the stages leading up to *Primitive*'s publication, Oppen became increasingly reliant on assistance from his wife, Mary Oppen, who played roles described as both secretarial and editorial. The presence of others' voices within one's own is one of the collection's central themes, and its openness to a partial giving over of expressive autonomy in the name of expressing *something* has to be squared with the discontinuities and non-identities the poems also register. Speech across the boundaries of subjecthood is configured as risky but indispensable, necessary if not necessarily welcome in all instances. The lyric value of personhood is retained, even as lyric sovereignty is cautiously, pragmatically waived.

To some tastes, this reading of Oppen will seem an insufficient break from the lyric, in terms both of what dementia calls for or what Oppen has to offer. Despite good cases for its pre-eminence, the lyric is not the only game in town. Gillian White even suggests that, in later twentieth-century American poetry, a hegemonic and prescriptive avant-gardism positions lyric expression as an object of shame, something both solipsistic and ideologically submissive (2014: 12). Assertions of dominance on this scale are bound to be debatable in their turn; Mary Oliver has more Pulitzers for poetry than Charles Bernstein. But however powerful we take the lyric to be, it is easy to anticipate the question of why we would want to imagine subjectivity as necessarily parcelled into finite little interiors, or to make reflective coherence a validity test for poetic language. By way of alternatives, we might consider a reflection on mortality by A. R. Ammons.

> When the tree of my bones
> rises from the skin I said
> come and whirlwinding
> stroll my dust
> around the plain
>
> so I can see
> how the ocotillo does

(Ammons 1986: 18)

Rather than as frightening, the distribution of subjecthood beyond the bounds of the person is here imagined as convivial. Of course, part of the charm (or alternately the false consolation) of Ammons's poem is the retention of familiar intentional language to describe a state of affairs in which, presumably, intentions linguistic or otherwise do not obtain. For this kind of truly subjectless language (or alternately the paradoxical *intention* of subjectless language), we could look to figures from Gertrude Stein to Craig Dworkin, or, in some lights, to George Oppen. What licenses the expressive coherence that keeps Ammons from this group is the poem's status as proleptic: the speaker is imagining a condition he does not presently occupy and doing so according to the limits of his position now. In this respect, though completely different in tone, the poem occupies a position of deferral or not-yet-thereness like that of 'The Old Fools'. To write the subjectless poetry Ammons does not write, conversely, would be to claim in the present the more distributed kind of being that Ammons pushes into the future. In *The Prelude*, Wordsworth is awed by the dissolutory power of Gondo Gorge, but also recoils from it: avant-garde poetries often seek or claim to inhabit borderlessly what the lyric puts just beyond its borders.

The kinds of poetry that eschew a single speaking voice are too rich and various for easy generalization, and certainly for easy disparagement. Problems arise, however, when an illness, and particularly an illness in which questions of personal dignity and autonomy are so crucial, is taken as a kind of passport to alternative states of being, aesthetic, political, or otherwise. It is not hard to imagine a dementia-inspired poetics asserting the rapturous disassembly of that bourgeois artifact, the self. At best, this would mean making real people with dementia into metaphorical placeholders in a philosophical turf war, which has little intrinsic interest in them; Deleuze and Guattari on schizophrenia should echo loudly here (1972). At worst, it could lead us back to the presumption – perhaps not so remote after all – that people with dementia don't really have personhood, this time perhaps as a hopeful first step toward persuading the rest of us that we needn't see ourselves as persons either. Either way, any scruple about how such representations might interact with the wishes or interests of those who have dementia becomes baseless. When there are no separate subjects, there is no problem of bespeaking. There is only life, engaging in language. Rather than treating care as undesirable because it compromises personhood, as in extreme versions of the lyric, this second position treats personhood as undesirable because it rules out care. But in life with dementia, it seems clear, the efforts of others are a crucial part of *how one remains oneself*, even while these efforts are always in danger of misapprehension.

A history of compromise

The seamless permissiveness of 'life engaging in language' is a long way from George Oppen, whose experimentalism, while often focused on the interpenetrations of subjectivity, materiality, and language, is also consistently sceptical, mindful of the boundaries of insight and expressive access. It is a very different kind of impersonalism than the one mentioned above that helped launch Oppen's career, one which worked by abnegation rather than dissolution and which has its origins in interwar modernism.

Ezra Pound's call for 'direct treatment of the "thing", whether subjective or objective' is perhaps this sensibility's pithiest articulation (2005: 94). Pound wrote a forward to Oppen's first collection, *Discrete Series* (1934), and if Oppen the Jewish communist is always ambivalent about the antisemitic and fascist-aligned Pound, this ambivalence is nonetheless articulated in the terms of Oppen's own commitment to modernist impersonalism. In Oppen's early work, this commitment appears as a strict practice of phenomenological reduction, which rules out all but the most basic inference with regard to other subjectivity. Poems in *Discrete Series* often record action in the world without the inference of a grammatical subject:

> Tug against the river
> Motor turning, lights
> In the fast water off the bow-wave:
> Passes slowly.

(Oppen 2008: 19)

From this undelineated canvas, it is not surprising that Oppen should move to nonstatic, materially interwoven ideas of the human being. His second collection, *The Materials*, is separated from *Discrete Series* by 28 years, during which time Oppen fought in the Second World War and, as a communist during the McCarthy years, lived in political exile with Mary Oppen in Mexico. For all that distance, the collection's new interest in life-stages remains grounded in the dynamism of the physical. From 'Sara in Her Father's Arms':

> Cell by cell the baby made herself, the cells
> Made cells. That is to say
> The baby is made largely of milk

(Oppen 2008: 51)

The poem ends by addressing an interlocutor.

> .. What will she make of a world
> Do you suppose, Max, of which she is made.

(Oppen 2008: 51)

Thought, the action whereby one 'makes something' of the world, is here a physical process, a reorganization of matter comparable to the growth of bodies and cells.

If we can assume that what applies to thought applies also to poetic language – the title *The Materials* would in that sense be a straightforward self-reference – then poems like 'Sara' confirm Michael Davidson's reading of Oppen, as a poet 'dissatisfied with all claims to closure' (Davidson 1997: 71). For Oren Izenberg, the porous and inclusive category of what we are compelled to recognize as alive and minded is Oppen's response to the genocides of the twentieth century, and the stark boundaries around identity that licensed genocide. Izenberg's reading captures the powerful effect of the Holocaust on Oppen's thinking, as well as his deep sense of wonder at the very possibility of consciousness in what he often described as a 'mineral' universe. But Oppen's insistence on life's material presence is rooted in disclaimer rather than in dilation. Even as the poems compel the reader to register *that* the creatures around us feel, they sharply eschew claims about *what* those creatures feel. This is why Oppen's critical writing so often stresses 'opacity' and 'impoverishment' of expression. Another poem in *The Materials*, 'Birthplace: New Rochelle', illustrates how this impoverishment continues the boundedness of the lyric.

> An aging man,
> The knuckles of my hand
> So jointed? I am this?
>
> (Oppen 2008: 55)

To be 'jointed' is to be both connected and segmented, and the relations between knuckle and hand, ageing male body and self, are metonymic but also incomplete. An affirmative answer to the poem's question is inevitable, but the very fact of its asking – the postulation of an 'I' that could puzzle over being 'this' – invokes an archetypally lyric alienation. Without being in any way separate from material process, consciousness is also private, occult within that process, such that to look at one's ageing body is to look at oneself from outside. The same doubleness also marks 'Sara in Her Father's Arms'. The concluding question of 'what will she make of the world . . . of which she is made' gives us the child mind as part of the continuous flux of the concrete universe, but then also as occupying a position of distinctness there. This is the basis of the child's predicted contemplation, and while this contemplation itself can be predicted, its content cannot. The figure of cells works the same way. On the one hand, the baby's cells appear as a temporary arrangement of the material world. But a cell is also a fixed enclosure, one not infrequently invoked to describe the solitude of the mind: 'Nuns fret not at their convent's narrow room; / And hermits are contented with their cells' (Wordsworth 2014: 401).

If Oppen on the one hand refuses the subject/object distinction that undergirds the lyric stance, while on the other refusing the flat openness of undelimited material interaction, this seems like an impasse. Oppen on several occasions described his work in terms of *failure*: as Stephanie Burt points out, given what Oppen seems to have taken as success, failure can be seen as the poems' condition of possibility (Burt 2008: 561). This is not only a question of expressive and denotative boundaries transgressed in the acts of putting words to paper and publishing them as poetry. During his military service and political exile, Oppen abstained from writing poetry because he felt that the need to speak about these situations would lead him to violate the expressive strictures he championed. To some extent, his return to poetry in the 1960s comes from the remission of these politically charged personal circumstances, in the form of his and Mary Oppen's return to the United States. Yet moments of commentary and intervention recur in the later poetry, alongside the scruples and anxieties about them, in ways that suggest a shifting answer to the constant question of what can validly be spoken of. A particularly charged instance of this question appears in Oppen's second-to-last collection, *Myth of the Blaze* (1975), in a long poem called 'The Book of Job and a Draft of a Poem to Praise the Paths of the Living'. From fragmentary references to damaged bodies, murderous mobs, dye-makers' tools, and the sea, all rendered uncertainly as 'image', the poem suddenly breaks into declaratory mode:

> ... and the ant
> hath her anger and the emmet
> his choler the exposed
> belly of the land
> under the sky
> at night and the windy pines unleash
> the morning's force what is the form
> to say it there is something
> to name Goodman   Schwerner   Chaney
> who were beaten not we
>
> (Oppen 2008: 240)

Andrew Goodman, Mickey Schwerner, and James Chaney were the three civil rights activists murdered by the Ku Klux Klan in Mississippi in 1964 (the poem is also dedicated to Schwerner, to whom Oppen had an indirect family connection). Coming into coherence here, the poem suddenly offers a clear scene of action, an insistence on the real and particular subjecthood of bodies in the material world, even those of ants and emmets, and a sense that articulating this reality is an ethical obligation. But this is a hazardous act: what exactly it *is* we name in naming Goodman, Schwerner, or Chaney is not clear, the experience of violence for which we might seek to commemorate them is inaccessible to us ('not we'), and the question of how to speak is cause for irresoluble anxiety ('what is the form / to say it'). Insofar as these lines answer that question in their own form – on the logic that the only way to talk about it is to ask how to talk about it – we might note their eschewal of clear demarcation. Sentences are uncapitalized, unpunctuated, and enjambed, such that assembling them is an active and uncertain process for the reader, and sometimes not satisfactorily possible. But looking for sentences is the only way to read the poem. Oppen is enlisting his reader in an effort, flagged explicitly as hazardous but also as hermeneutically and ethically necessary, of bespeaking.

In Oppen's 'Job', the purpose of this anxious bespeaking is commemoration, and the central question seems to be whether it is acceptable to make these young men into symbols for something larger than themselves. The connection to the biblical Job links this question to that of theodicy, the aspect of theological justification dealing with why the divine plan should include suffering and atrocity. Oppen, as Peter Nicholls points out, specifically rejected theodicean interpretations of the biblical Job, identifying the God who appears in this book not with the omnipotent benevolence described in Judeo-Christian tradition but instead with the demiurge of Plato's *Timaeus*, a distant and amoral figure who lays out the blueprint of the universe but takes no interest in individual destiny (Nicholls 2007: 167). Some of this refusal of moral interpretation finds its way into Oppen's own poem. The hushed clearing among the pines feels like a scene of sacrifice, like Abraham's of Isaac, but the poem pointedly declines to play out this script: the three men are not scapegoats, or otherwise figures in a divinely appointed drama. But the refusal is also not absolute. What can be said is that these men were *there*, that something real happened to them, and that some response is necessary, though it is not clear what this should be. Having denied itself providential certainty the poem falls not into silence but into the more provisional world of politics: if the woodland clearing suggests an Abrahamic typology of sacrifice, it also suggests the iconic scene of a lynching.

In other words, it is necessity rather than security that licenses bespeaking. To say the names is to falsify the 'poverty' of our access to other experience in the material world, to belie the separateness of others as we enfold them into our senses of things. And yet to not do this is to suborn injustice, both in these three murders and the larger pattern of racial abuse the three men were challenging.[1] For the Larkin and Wiman poems, with their clear-eyed refusals to transgress the frame of the lyric, there is no problem of action. Nothing is owed to the friend's father or the care home residents other than some recognition of a similar vulnerability in oneself, if this is really an obligation to other people at all. Both speakers enjoy a privilege that falls disproportionately to men, especially men of the professional class: neither is asked to provide the person with dementia any actual, practical assistance, much less to help them decide or express anything. Oppen would have qualified for this privilege as well, and it is not only as benefactor but also as beneficiary that he imagines the line-crossings that Wiman and Larkin do not. In 'Job', where he imagines himself bespeaking others, the scenario is relatively unvexed. As participants in the struggle for civil rights, Goodman, Schwerner, and Chaney had to a considerable degree already made their perspectives clear, and no particularly ambitious claim about the nature of their experience was necessary to argue that their murders were iniquitous. The prospect of Oppen's own dementia, however, which arose soon after *The Myth of the Blaze* was published, makes bespeaking both more difficult and more inescapable.

Oppen on dementia

Critical writing has mostly treated *Primitive*, Oppen's next and last book, in terms of the poet's vexed relationship with his Jewishness, and with the Hebrew language he did not speak, following a visit to Israel (Taggart, 1979: 148). When dementia is mentioned, it is usually only to underscore a dynamic of confusion whose principal subjects are ethnicity, community, and language. Nicholls goes a step further, suggesting that in its banishment of the familiar, the new immediacy of lost associations, dementia

---

[1] In this sense of bespeaking as both sometimes mandatory and always dangerous, Oppen is close to what Linda Martin Alcoff would later argue more explicitly in 'The Problem of Speaking for Others' (1991). The difference is that, where Alcoff emphasizes the importance of receiving criticism from those for whom one speaks, Oppen is concerned with a scenario where the chance of an action's inappropriateness is never resolved because those spoken for cannot speak back. In 'Job', this is because they have been murdered, but more complicated versions of the worry also attach to some experiences of dementia.

gives Oppen the 'impoverished', 'primitive' linguistic response he had always sought (2007: 183). These readings tend to present dementia as very tacit in its presence as subject matter, or even as a kind of silent backdrop to the collection. The most cited poems, 'A Political Poem' and 'Disasters', which are also first and second in the collection, in themselves largely justify this secondary placement of the dementia theme. But a later poem, 'Neighbors', stages a version of what, in the decades since, has become one of dementia's emblematic scenes:

Thru our kitchen window I see the house

next door a frame house under the asphalt shingles

the wooden framing and I don't know what I am doing

here the neighbor the actual neighbor we are even

    friendly

in a way and I don't know what I am doing

(Oppen 2008: 284)

This encounter may prompt abstract meditation on interpersonal or intercultural otherness, and the poem seems amenable to such reflections:

Here there is more

to wake to

than these old boards these many

boards and the voice of the poem a wandering

foreigner more strange

(Oppen 2008: 284)

The meeting between speaker and neighbour is a moment of apparently unbridgeable 'foreignness' that evokes the alienating trip to Israel. The poet's presentation as 'wandering / foreigner' may even call up the figure of the 'Wandering Jew', lending this encounter a kind of allegorical expansiveness. But this is no reason to forget the more prosaic scenario of the poem, or the more literal referent of the word 'wander': a man with accelerating dementia has wandered into his neighbour's yard and realizes upon seeing her there that he does not know what he is doing. This situation makes it impossible to end the poem with a recognition of radical otherness – he needs her help! – though that otherness is the ground upon which further interaction must take place. As he recognizes his own position, the speaker recognizes a dependence on this woman, which pulls him from isolated reflection: 'not poets only / waking all / are in her hands' (284). The last section of the poem uses Oppen's familiar syntactic incompletion to create an effect of stammer, while also poignantly registering consciousness of its own inarticulacy:

> shall we
>
> say more
>
> than this I can
>
> say more there it
>
> is I can
>
> say more we have hardly begun
>
> -
>
> in time we see
>
> the words fail this
>
> (Oppen 2008: 284–5)

If we understand these words as coming from a man confronted in his neighbour's yard, trying to explain himself or asking her help, the fear of misunderstanding and the shame of inarticulacy must be very powerful. But he must brave this imperfection. The poem ends:

> we know we
>
> will speak
>
> to each
>
> other we
>
> will speak
>
> (Oppen 2008: 285)

When we read the poems of *Primitive* in the full light of its encounter with dementia, what we find is not an intensification of the negative poetics Oppen had heretofore sometimes sought (though never claimed to achieve), but instead a sense of pragmatic legitimacy in those kinds of bespeaking the earlier Oppen sometimes regarded as failures – and which he was already reconsidering in *The Myth of the Blaze*. If these are poems about being surrounded by strange language, they are also poems about how this language is tolerable and can in fact help one constitute oneself: they are poems about the need to be spoken for, and to make use of others' voices, as the basis of individual expression and of survival.

In the collection's earlier poems, which seem most directly related to the trip to Israel, dementia is a somewhat oblique presence, but they help set the stage for dementia by setting up those antimonies that dementia, emerging as a theme alongside examinations of caregiving, bespeaking, and the pragmatic use of compromised language, will eventually overcome. 'A Political Poem', the first in the book, opens to a strange landscape, posing the question of belonging in quite absolute terms:

> For sometimes over the fields astride
> of love?   begin with
>
> nothing or
>
> everything   the nerve
>
> the thread
> reverberates
>
> in the unfinished
>
> voyage loneliness
>
> (Oppen 2008: 265)

As in earlier poems we have the characteristic, variously linkable sentence fragments, nerves that seem to reverberate in several directions but link finally into no exclusively definite pattern. Yet the voyager's choice seems stark: love or loneliness, nothing or everything. Both options – basically, incorporation into the project of Zionism or exile from one's own Jewishness – seem unacceptable, and dementia is hinted at in the second of them: 'this sad and hungry / wolf walks in my footprints fear fear' (2008: 265). This is selfhood reduced to bare animal foundations, a figure for the poet without the group identity he is questioning. It is also a proleptic figure for the poet in dementia, losing history, language, and connection. The second poem, 'Disasters', attaches this troubled crux more explicitly to questions of speech. First, there is an apparent abdication of the poet's right to speak of socially important matters:

> Of politics I am sick with a poet's
> Vanity   legislators
> of the unacknowledged
>
> world *it is*   *dreary*
> *to descend*
>
> (Oppen 2008: 267)

'Legislators of the unacknowledged world' is Oppen's version of Percy Shelley's famous description of poets as 'the unacknowledged legislators of the world' in his *Defence of Poetry* (Shelley 2006: 1199). In registering this role as distasteful, the poem recapitulates Oppen's earlier sense that political motivations would take poetry beyond the rigorous epistemological limits appropriate to it. Nicholls mentions analogously how, on his trip to Israel, Oppen felt both moved and underqualified to challenge Israel's treatment of Palestinians (2007: 185). But the poem also registers the loss implied in this refusal to speak:

> Of a poet's vanity if our story shall end
> Untold to whom and
>
> to what are we ancestral
>
> (Oppen 2008: 267)

Vanity, it turns out, points to a poet's refusal of externals just as much as to any presumption to dictate, and this is a repudiation of Oppen's own previous asceticism, at least when taken to extreme conclusions. In 'Political Poem', the poet's withdrawal meant hunger and loneliness; here it means an abandonment of both ancestors and descendants. Engagement with Jewish issues is 'legislative' in an uncomfortable way, but disengagement from Jewishness brings connotations of loss and isolation, which are elliptically suggestive of worries about dementia.[2]

It is in 'Disasters' that *Primitive* begins to articulate a revised position on the limits of poetic speech. The poem ends in a troubled panorama of collective and perhaps specifically Jewish destiny:

> voice among the people the salt
>
> and terrible hills whose armies
>
> have marched and the caves
> of the hidden
> people.
>
> (Oppen 2008: 269)

If the poem's opening was a statement of reluctance to be exactly this kind of 'voice among the people', it seems to have been carried here by a figure who appears in its penultimate section.

---

[2] Part of the backdrop to this worry, no doubt, is the loss of so many Jewish lives, and the memories and continuities these lives might have provided, in the Holocaust. Linking this loss to the prospect of his own dementia – its threat to his own ability to share and pass on group memories – Oppen would invoke an analogy to the preoccupation observed by Sue Vice, where fiction dealing with Holocaust survivors disproportionately has them experience dementia as a way of troubling the goal of commemoration (2020: 107–14).

> *O I see my love I see her go*
>
> *over the ice alone* I see
>
> myself   Sarah   Sarah   I see the tent
> in the desert of my life
>
> (Oppen 2008: 269)

A helper to the poet's old age, a Sarah to his Abraham, offering him a tent in the wilderness and fortifying him to the act of speech that becomes the poem itself: it is difficult to imagine who this could be but Mary Oppen. But while Mary's presence here is always desirable, the poem continues to register an awkwardness, a fundamentally lyric discomfort, with its dependence on her. Her presence never feels entirely natural. The image of Sarah walking on ice – confusingly discordant with the Israeli landscape with which the poems of *Primitive* have so far dealt – may point to the fact that Mary was not Jewish and felt, as per her own recollections, entirely out of place in Israel (Nicholls 2007: 185). As a surface for walking on, ice is also dangerously temporary, a provisional way forward just as a tent is a provisional shelter. It is through a contingent and sometimes awkward act of filling-in, then, rather than by smooth activation of typological identity, that help is given, voice found, and the extremes of solitude and dissolution navigated. The figure of the wife is much like that of the neighbour later in the book: someone badly needed, but who cannot know automatically *what* is needed.

Primitive's third entry, 'The Poem', steps into the gap that the Sarah of 'Disasters' opens. Again, there are worries about speaking for or of that which is outside oneself. The impulse to make the poem arises from 'a direction' . . .

> of things in us burning burning for we are not
> still nor is this place a wind
> utterly outside ourselves and yet it is
> unknown and all the sails full to the last
>
> (Oppen 2008: 270)

Like the two previous entries, 'The Poem' hesitates between a privacy that threatens to isolate and an engagement that threatens to dissolve. In the above passage, this hesitation hangs on an ambiguity of syntax: poetic speech may, on the most obvious reading of the lines quoted above, arise internally, and never fully connect with the things spoken about. Alternately, if we read the lines as saying that 'place' is not something 'utterly outside ourselves', they amount to an attack on the very idea individual coherence. But the decision between these alternatives is not as absolute as in 'Political Poem'. 'The Poem' mitigates the opposition of solipsism and dissolution with a dialectical suggestion of how language, which is not quite one's own, is also how one constructs oneself. Crucial to this shift in 'The Poem' is its rather loaded incorporation of earlier poetic sources:

To save the commonplace save myself Tyger
Tyger still burning in me

(Oppen 2008: 270)

The prompting to poetry, though it comes also from external sources like William Blake's 'The Tyger' (1794), is also 'in' the poetic speaker and part of how he saves himself, just as parts of Blake's text make up 'The Poem's' own body. 'The Tyger' is in this way a revision of the wolf in 'Political Poem', an unwilled aspect of the speaker, which may compromise his sufficiency as a lyric self, but which now also links him to a community of speech and a prospect of continuity. Communities of speech are not seamless or conflict-free, of course. As well as 'Tyger Tyger, burning bright', the 'burning burning' of the previous quotation echoes the 'Fire Sermon' section of T. S. Eliot's *The Waste Land*, where the repetition of that word points to a longed-for unmaking of the self (1969: 70). 'The Poem', with its stated imperative to 'save myself', works to an opposite end; its 'burning' seems to refer to an expressive impulse, or to life itself, rather than to self-immolation. Eliot and Oppen represent almost antithetical idioms in modern poetry, but this rather contrarian re-use continues one of *The Waste Land*'s key dynamics: just as Blake's 'The Tyger' is itself about the constructedness of the embodied creature – 'What the hammer? What the chain, / In what Furnace was thy brain?' (2006: 197) – *The Waste Land* owes its own macaronic body to a mass of quotations incorporated from previous sources; much of 'The Fire Sermon' comes from the Pali Buddhist discourse of the same name (Ādittapariyāya Sutta).

At points, *Primitive* does stage the unmaking of the coherent self, the comingling into undelineated perpetuity. 'If it all went up in smoke', begins a poem of that name, 'there would still be the smoke' (2008: 274). But this assurance has the proleptic quality of Ammons's 'Mansion', offering consolation for eventual mortality rather than actually *recommending* a way of being, or not being. In the present tense, meanwhile, moments of heterogeneous contact are always marked with tension and the chance of inappropriateness: Sarah on the ice, the discordant voice of Eliot in 'The Poem', the poet in his neighbour's yard. This risk of inappropriateness is inextricably linked to the precarious and insufficient condition of life under which these presences are necessary. In 'The Poem', for instance, the 'unknown' wind filling the ship's sails is menacing, even as it revises an image of deadly isolation that appeared two poems earlier in 'A Political Poem', the 'loneliness / of becalmed ships and violent men' (Oppen 2008: 265).[3] Rather

---

[3] This image of isolation, in turn, points back to references to sailing in Oppen's first book, *Discrete Series*. The consistent nautical imagery of *Primitive* is also more explicitly tied back to *Discrete Series* in the final poem, 'Till Other Voices Wake Us', which briefly presents a recollection of Oppen as a young writer. This is not new to *Primitive*. As Izenberg points out, a passage from Oppen's first collection which quoted Henry James was itself invoked and rewritten in Oppen's second book, and the pattern continues from there (2011: 82). In its recurrence, the association between mishap at sea and existential loneliness could begin to seem typological for Oppen, but I suggest that, in the way he persistently differentiates a present poem from its past references, Oppen is in fact staging a much more imperfect relation to the past, one in which the past self is properly another voice. In earlier poems, these (not-quite) self-references are often self-rebukes. In *Primitive*, the question is more about what in these other voices is salvageable, what use they might be to the goals of present life.

than dissolving it, these contact moments secure the speaker's singular presence: lyric selfhood is qualified because it is *emerging from*, rather than collapsing into, more decentred or interpenetrative models of subjectivity. In a set of figures that appear throughout the collection, the speaker is awoken out of oceanic unconsciousness, by the speech of another. In 'A Political Poem', as we have seen, the sea has already come to represent an unsurvivable isolation. Then we have the conclusion of 'The Poem'.

> in the appalling
> seas language
>
> lives and wakes us together
> out of sleep the poem
> opens its dazzling whispering hands
>
> (Oppen 2008: 270)

Other poems, like 'Waking Who Knows' and 'Gold on Oak Leaves' deepen this pattern with further contrastive images of sea and waking daylight. In 'Neighbours', which is *Primitive*'s second-to-last poem, the wandering poet 'wakes to' the woman in her yard. The final poem, 'Till Other Voices Wake Us', draws all of these instances together in a concluding reprise of literary allusion:

> lights have entered
> us it is a music more powerful
> than music
>
> till other voices wake
> us or we drown
>
> (Oppen 2008: 286)

This is Oppen's reworking of the famous last lines of Eliot's 'The Love Song of J. Alfred Prufrock'.

> We have lingered in the chambers of the sea
> By sea-girls wreathed with seaweed red and brown
> Till human voices wake us, and we drown.
>
> (Eliot 1969: 17)

Eliot is drawing a contrast between divine or cosmic access, represented in the mermaid's song the speaker is denied, and the ordinary human social life, which seems to be destroying him. Oppen's poem subverts this contrast: the music *is* the voices, and it is interpersonal contact that keeps the self out of the sea. The fact that Eliot is himself one of the 'lights (that) have entered' here is, as in the allusive passages of 'The Poem', a reminder that this interdependence is not a smooth comingling, but a process marked by missteps, impositions, and redresses. The lyric self is compromised in its associations, and this is a problem, but it is also the only way for the self to persist at all. The presence of others is what allows us to be ourselves.

In the opening page of his most famous poem, *Of Being Numerous* (1968), Oppen had written that:

There are things
We live among 'and to see them
Is to know ourselves'.

(Oppen 2008: 163)

The quotation marks indicate this idea's source in the French philosopher Jacques Maritain.[4] Maritain's psychological model, drawn from Thomas Aquinas and before that from Aristotle, understood the living being as identical with its actions. In this conception, thought and experience arise not only *with regard* to material objects but as part of materiality, such that the thing we call a person is in fact a fundamentally interactive dynamic of things in the world. Maritain ventured this idea in opposition to liberal individualism, or, in more philosophical terms, to the Platonic tradition's idea that the mind merely *shows itself* in material action, while always remaining apart, occult, constituted elsewhere (it would be anachronistic to Plato, but not to Maritain or Oppen, to tie this privatist psychology to the lyric). The sequence of awakenings that plays out across *Primitive* is in many ways consonant with Oppen's earlier interest in Maritain: the mind is not a hermetic structure, self-consciousness comes about in a condition of interaction and connection, and extreme forms of lyric individualism are off the table. But *Primitive* has also departed somewhat from the earlier formulation, giving qualified legitimacy back to ideas of lyric personhood. In the opening passage from *Of Being Numerous* quoted above, all the action is that of the mind, though it does not take place 'within' an enclosed mental space. The result is an axiom without explicit temporal dimensions: to possess consciousness is to be in a state of interaction. If *Of Being Numerous* is about interconnectedness as a bare indisputable fact, *Primitive* is more specifically concerned with asymmetrical dependence, a condition which makes separateness feel more important even as it feels less tenable. Compared with *Of Being Numerous*, *Primitive*'s repeated motif of *being woken* is both more contingent and more dialectical: other agents continually give rise to what *then* becomes an individual consciousness. In this dialectic, *Primitive* has moved back toward a more lyric stance, since it is an awakened, singular person who must be saved from drowning in order to speak the poems. This is a dialectic without synthesis; the other voices remain other within the poems they make possible, just as the fingerprints of an empowered editor, or any caregiver who helps make decisions, may always trouble the person being helped. This circumstance is both unfortunate and worth working with. As opposed to the unidirectional assertion in *Numerous*, we now see both a foregrounding of values

---

[4] It seems likely that Oppen is thinking in particular of Maritain's *Creative Intuition in Art and Poetry* (1953). As Stephen Cope observes (2008: 258) the phrase does not occur exactly in this volume, but the paraphrase is broadly identifiable, and Oppen was immersed in this work at the same time he was working on *Of Being Numerous*.

of individual personhood and a qualifying injunction that these values must sometimes be transgressed in order to be best pursued. Both biographically and in the sequence of the collection, this echo of the lyric originates in the experience of an intellectual life with dementia, where memory, expression, and mental direction benefit from the care of others.

The concept of personhood seems indispensable if we are to treat people with dementia ethically. The status of inner life, and the imperatives of privacy, autonomy, and self-expression have been and must be at the forefront of the revolutions in our thinking about these illnesses. And yet too absolute an insistence on these imperatives can rule out forms of aid – especially with artistic endeavours and the expression of feelings and ideas – that contribute to life with dementia in indispensable ways. In their very existence, the poems of *Primitive* illustrate the potential of such assistance.[5] They also offer a nuanced and considered perspective for thinking about this assistance, whether as recipient or as provider. The other voices these poems include and depend on are cause for caution. Like all acts of bespeaking, they are at risk of being inappropriate. At the same time, they help make possible the very thing their inappropriateness could harm, the very subject that lyric prohibition seeks to protect: a person's own voice.

References

Alcoff, L. (1991), 'The Problem of Speaking for Others', in *Cultural Critique* 20: 5–32.
Ammons, A. (1986), *The Selected Poems*, New York: Norton.
Basting, A. (2009), *Forget Memory: Creating Better Lives for People with Dementia*, Baltimore: Johns Hopkins University Press.
Blake, W. (2006), 'The Tyger', in D. Wu (ed), *Romanticism: An Anthology*, Malden, MA: Blackwell.
Burt, S. (2008), 'George Oppen and the Limits of Words', in *Modernism/Modernity* 15 (3): 557–565.
Cope, S. (2008), *George Oppen: Selected Prose, Daybooks, and Papers*, Oakland, CA: University of California Press.
Davidson, M. (1997), *Ghostlier Demarcations: Modern Poetry and the Material Word*, Oakland, CA: University of California Press.
DeFalco, M. (2016), *Imagining Care: Responsibility, Dependency, and Canadian Literature*, Toronto: University of Toronto Press.
Deleuze, G. and F. Guattari (1972), *L'Anti-Oedipe*, Paris: Les Editions de Minuit.
Eliot, T. S. (1969), *The Complete Poems and Plays*, London: Faber.
Izenberg, O. (2011), *Being Numerous: Poetry and the Ground of Social Life*, Princeton, NJ: Princeton University Press.
Jackson, V. (2005), *Dickinson's Misery: A Theory of Lyric Reading*, Princeton, NJ: Princeton University Press.

---

[5] We can think of Oppen as theorizing, from the other side, the facilitation of creativity in those with dementia taken up, in diverse and wonderful ways, by Killick (2018), Kontos et al. (2020), Synnes et al. (2021), and many others.

Killick, J. (2018), *Poetry and Dementia: A Practical Guide*, London: Jessica Kingsley.
Kitwood, T. (1997), *Dementia Reconsidered: The Person Comes First*, Maidenhead, UK: Open University Press.
Kontos, P., A. Grigorovich and R. Colobong (2020), 'Towards a Critical Understanding of Creativity and Dementia: New Directions for Practice Change', *International Practice Development Journal* 10 (3).
Larkin, P. (2003), *Collected Poems*, ed. A. Thwaite, New York: Farrar, Strauss and Giroux.
Maritain, J. (1953), *Creative Intuition in Art and Poetry*, New York: Pantheon Books.
Nicholls, P. (2007), *George Oppen and the Fate of Modernism*, Oxford: Oxford University Press.
Oppen, G. (2008), *New Collected Poems*, ed. M. Davidson, New York: New Directions.
Post, S. (1995), *The Moral Challenge of Alzheimer's Disease*, Baltimore: Johns Hopkins University Press.
Pound, E. (2005), 'Imagisme', in L. Rainey (ed), *Modernism: An Anthology*, Malden, MA: Blackwell.
Shelley, P. (2006), 'A Defence of Poetry' in D. Wu (ed), *Romanticism: An Anthology*, Malden, MA: Blackwell.
Swinnen, A. and M. Schweda, eds (2015), *Popularizing Dementia: Public Expressions and Representations of Forgetfulness*, Bielefeld: Transcript.
Synnes, O., M. Råheim, E. Lykkeslet and E. Gjengedal (2021), 'A Complex Reminding: The Ethics of Poetry Writing in Dementia Care', *Dementia* 20 (3), 1025-1043.
Tafdrup, P. (2006), *Tarkovskijs heste,* Copenhagen: Gyldendal.
Tafdrup, P. (2010), *Tarkovsky's Horses and Other Poems* (trans. David MacDuff), Tarset: UK, Bloodaxe.
Taggart, K. (1979), 'The New Primitive', in *Chicago Review* 30 (3): 148–151.
Vice, S. (2020), '"Never forget": Fictionalising the Holocaust Survivor with Dementia', in *Medical Humanities* 46 (2): 107–114.
White, G. (2014), *Lyric Shame: The "Lyric" Subject of Contemporary American Poetry*, Cambridge, MA: Harvard University Press.
Wiman, C. (2020), *Survival Is a Style: Poems*, New York: Farrar, Strauss and Giroux.
Wordsworth, W. (2014), *Wordsworth's Poetry and Prose*, ed. N. Haumi, New York: Norton.

Index

A Life in Poems (Sousa) 87
'A Political Poem' (Oppen) 196, 201–202, 201n.3
Age-ing to Sage-ing (Schacter-Shalom) 144
'Ageing Together' (Major) 160
Alex (course participant) 121
Alves de Sousa, José Newton 4, 84–85, 88–94, 96
Alves de Sousa, Maria Ruth 84–85, 91
Alzheimer's Poetry Project (APP) 28–29, 34–38, 40
American Psychological Association 127
Ammons, A. R. 190–191, 201
Andersen, Cecilie Wold 118
Aristotle 1, 128
Arnold, Matthew 155, 158, 161–162, 165
'Art-of-living' 63, 63n.3
As You Like It (Shakespeare) 114
'Autobiographical learning' (Randall) 144
autobiographical writing 4, 14, 16, 44–45, 47, 118, 122, 142–144, 175

Bachelard, Gaston 48, 54, 56
Bakhtin, Mikhail 73, 77
Baldwin, Clive 57
Barthes, Roland 61
Basting, Anne 40, 188
Bayley, John 31
Beaufort wind force scale 180–181
Beloved (Morrison) 36
Berger, Peter 150
Berman, Harry 145
Bernstein, Charles 190
'Beyond Autonomy and Language' (project) 28
'bilateral involvement' 142
Birren, James 145
'Birthplace: New Rochelle' (Oppen) 193
Bjørnsonfestivalen (2018) 43, 56
Blake, William 37, 201

Bohr, Niels 156
Bond zonder Naam 34
Bonnefoy, Yves 24
'The Book of Job' (Oppen) 193–194
Brinkman, Maike 34–35, 96, 134
Brinkmann, Svend 163, 170
Bronowski, Jacob 155
Brooklyn Memory Center 34
Bruinja, Tsaed 39
Bruner, Jerome 142
Burt, Stephanie 193

call-and-response 37
case study
    ethical considerations 96–97
    interview 93–96
    introduction 81–82
    my father 86–93
    poet and professor 84–86
    poetic experience 82–84
Cash, Johnny 166
Chaney, James 194–195
Chimes at Midnight (Welles) 110
Chronic Obstructive Pulmonary Disease 20
Claus, Hugo 4, 28–33, 40
'Claus-effect' 30
'Cogito ergo sum' (Descartes) 31
cognitive functioning 27, 31, 36, 125–126, 128
Cohen, Gene 142
Cohen, Leah Hager 9–10
Coleridge, Samuel Taylor 162, 166
Cording, Robert 10–11
COVID-19 pandemic 5, 34, 39, 63, 68, 88–89, 127
Cowley, Malcolm 138
'Creative reminiscence' (Bohlmeijer et al.) 145
creative writing 49, 117
Crisp, Jane 150

Culler, Jonathan 54
cultural play theory (Huizinga) 169
Cummings, E. E. 155

Danneels, cardinal Godfried 30
Danto, Arthur 22–23
Davidson, Michael 192
Davis, Lydia 180
De Culturele Apotheek 34–35
de la Cruz, Juan 85
de Lange, Frits 150
de Medeiros, Kate 169–170
De vrouw met de sleutel (van der Meer) 37
de Wit, Veerle 32
De wolken: Uit de geheime laden van Hugo Claus (Claus) 32–33
DeFalco, Amelia 189
Defence of Poetry (Shelley) 199
Deleuze, Gilles 191
dementia
    Alzheimer's Poetry Project 33–40
    conclusions 40
    as a disability 28–29
    Hugo Claus case 29–33
    introduction 2–4
    and the lyric 187–204
    and lyrics 187–189
    more just futures 27–28
    and Oppen 195–204
    poetry of 9, 11–13, 15–17, 19–20, 23–24
    prevention/treatment 128
dementia care
    background 43–44
    close reading 50–57
    conclusions 57
    crafting of poems 48–50
    poetry writing in 43
    theoretical perspectives 44–48
'dementia's tragic promise' (Freeman) 19–20
Descartes, René 31
'Disasters' (Oppen) 196
Discrete Series (Oppen) 192
disengagement theory 143
Do I Look at You with Love: Reimagining the Story of Dementia (Freeman) 9
'Dockery and Son' (Larkin) 162
Doctorow, E. L. 182

Donne, John 155
Doty, Mark 47, 56
'Down by the Salley Gardens' (Yeats) 168–169
dualistic thinking 142
Duchamp, Marcel 22
'duration-block' (Husserl) 45
Dworkin, Craig 191
dying/death 9, 24, 29–33, 40, 44, 103–104, 106
Dylan, Bob 122

Eakin, Paul John 139
Eddington, Arthur 155
Edwards, James 23
ego 108–109
'ego integrity' 138, 144
Einstein, Albert 156, 163, 163n.4
Elegy for Iris (Bayley) 31
Eliot, T. S. 3, 157, 201–202
emotional experiences 46, 120
'emotional intelligence' 141
entelecheia (Aristotle) 1
episodic sense of the self 45–46
Epstein, Robert 62
Essays (Davis) 180
euthanasia 31–32, 40
existential pathways 117–118
experiential wholeness concept 83–84, 94
expressive writing 117

'faction' (creative non-fiction) 137
Feminist Queer Crip (Kafer) 28
'Fire Sermon' (Eliot) 201
Fish, Stanley 49
Fleming, Patricia 164
Fonseca, Aleilton 83
'forget memory, try imagination' (Basting) 40, 188
'found poetry' 10
Frank, Arthur 139
Freeman, Mark 22, 83, 137–138, 144, 148
Freud, Sigmund 9, 108
Frost, Robert 52, 162
Fuchs, Thomas 46

'gerotranscendence' (Tornstam) 143
Gestalt theory 165
ginko 64, 67–70, 67n.10, 73–74, 77

Giroux, Joan 68
Glazner, Gary 34
God 96, 103, 140
'Gold on Oak Leaves' (Oppen) 202
Goodman, Andrew 194–195
'Growing Old' (Arnold) 158, 165
Guattari, Félix 191
Gullette, Margaret 32
Guthrie, Woody 122

haiku
    on ageing 74–76
    conclusions 77
    introduction 4, 61
    and older adults 63–66, 65n.8
    polyphony in 73–74
    in practice 66–73
    and writing course 120
'the haiku moment' (Giroux) 68–69
'haiku walk' 67
'Haiku-kai' 64
Hamington, Maurice 38
Hamlet (Shakespeare) 100, 114–115
Hampl, Patricia 148
Hardy, Thomas 161–162
Hauser, Mike 164–165
Heidegger, Martin 24
Hemingway, Ernest 31
Henry IV, Part 1 (Shakespeare) 101, 111, 114
Henry IV, Part 2 (Shakespeare) 4, 99–115
Henry V (Shakespeare) 106
Herberghs, Ciska 27
Herberghs, Leo 27–28, 40
Herrick, Robert 166
Hinduism 83
Hirshfield, Jane 49
Holocaust 192–193
Home from the Party 176
How To Be an Even Better Listener (Mundle) 146–147
'How to recognize a poem when you see one' (Fish) 49
Hugo Claus: Een groepsportret (Claus) 31–32
Huizinga, Johan 169–170
Huke, Marte 118–120, 127
'Huntington Road' 131
Huntington's disease 122, 131

'Hurt' (Reznor) 166
Husserl, Edmund 45–46
Huxley, Aldous 155
Hydén, Lars-Christer 46

'I Still Matter' (Fleming) 164
In Search of Lost Time, Swann's Way (Proust) 178
'The Incredible Ageing Man' (Hauser) 164
indexical referencing 46
Ingold, Tim 68
Intensive Journal Process (Progoff) 144
Izenberg, Oren 192–193

Japanese poetry 120
José Newton *see* Alves de Sousa, José Newton
'Joy of knowing' 70–72
'Joy of thinking' 72–73
Jung, C. G. 144

Kafer, Alison 28–29, 40
Kaufman, Sharon 3
Kaufman, Shirley 3
Keats, John 170
Kempton, B. 78
kidzuki 67
Kierkegaard, Søren 175
Killick, John 49
killjoy 108, 108n.6
King Lear (Shakespeare) 114
Kingsley, Charles 163–164, 167
Kitwood, Tom 188
Koch, Kenneth 2
Koffka, Kurt 165
Kontos, Pia 46
Kropf, Nancy 145
Ku Klux Klan 194
kukai 64–66
Kunitz, Stanley 1

Labouvie-Vief, Gisela 142
Laceulle, Hanne 128, 131
Lagercrantz, Olof 181, 183
'Landscape of action' (Bruner) 142–143
'Landscape of consciousness' (Bruner) 142–143
Larkin, Philip 162, 165, 187–188, 192

'Law of Mind' (Peirce) 159, 162, 165
Lawrence, D. H. 157
Leavis, F. R. 155
'Legislators of the unacknowledged world' (Oppen) 199
Lehmann, Olga V 163, 170
Leo Herberghs Poetry Prize 28
'Let Me Die a Youngman's Death' (McGough) 166–167
Lewis, Rhodri 100, 100n.2
'Life review' (Erikson) 144
'Life review therapy' (Bohlmeijer/Westerhof) 147
life-as-story 137, 139
'lifeworld' concept 69, 77
light bulb image 177
Lima, Assis 85, 88
'Lines on Retirement, After Reading Lear' (Wright) 166–167
Literature House 118
'The Little Boy and the Old Man' (Silverstein) 168
'lived experience' concept 31, 40, 48, 54, 77
Living to Tell the Tale (Marquez) 122
Lord of Misrule 108, 108n.6
Lotherington, Anne Therese 29, 32
'The Love Song of J. Alfred Prufrock' (Eliot) 202
Loving Later Life (de Lange) 150
Lukić, Dragana 29, 32
lyric
    alternatives to 189–191
    compromise 191–195, 195n.1
    and dementia 187–204
    language 100
    Oppen on dementia 195–204, 199n.2, 201n.3
    stories 47–48, 51–52

Macbeth (Shakespeare) 114
McCarthy, Mary 176, 179
McGough, Roger 166–167
Major, Clarence 160, 166
Maritain, Jacques 203
Marquez, García 122
Marshall, I. 67
The Materials (Oppen) 192–193
Mattsson, Gustaf 177, 177–178n.1

medical/individual model 28
Melick, Bert van 27
Memories of a Catholic Girlhood (McCarthy) 179
mental health 62, 127–128, 128
'metaphor therapy' 140–141
metaphoric competence
    conclusions 149–150
    introduction 137–139, 137n.1
    meaning of 140–143
    mystery 139–140
    philosophic homework 143–144
    play 144–148
Milosz, Czeslaw 24
Minagawa, N. 65–66
mindfulness 62, 82
'mineral' universe 193
Mittler, Peter 29
Morrison, Toni 36
Mortier, Erwin 30
Mundle, Robert 146–147
Murdoch, Iris 10, 31
My first circle (Lagercrantz) 181
Myth of the Blaze (Oppen) 193–195, 197

narrative
    development of 148
    introduction 1, 1–5
    and its discontents 12–14
    poems 53
    resilience 145–146
    speaking in de-narrativized way 19
    turn 142
'Narrative coherence' (Hyvärinen) 139
'Narrative debris' (McKendy) 139
narrative gerontology 137
Narrative Gerontology (course) 137, 137n.1, 140
'Narrative habitus' (Frank) 139
'Narrative imagination' (Andrews) 137–138
Narrative Knowing and the Human Sciences (Polkinghorne) 139
Nemerov, Howard 50
Nicholls, Peter 194–196, 199
'Nine Inch Nails' (rock band) 166
Noche Escura del Alma (de la Cruz) 85
Norões, Everardo 88
Nu en straks (Bruinja) 39–40

O Canto das Gerações Novas (Alves de Sousa) 84
'Ode on a Grecian Urn' (Keats) 157
Odense House 38
'Of Being Numerous' (Oppen) 203
old age
    case study 82, 86–88, 92–93
    and Haiku 63, 72
    introduction 2–4
    lyrical 113
    nostalgic 109–111
    rebellious 111–112
    and Shakespeare 99–101, 105–109
    usurping 114–115
    virtuous 117–133
'The Old Fools' (Larkin) 187–188, 191
Oliver, Mary 190
'On Transience' (Freud) 9
Oppen, George 5, 190–204, 199n.2, 203n.4, 204n.5
Oppen, Mary 5, 190, 192, 200
Oppenheimer, Robert 155
oral poetry method 34
Orr, Gregory 47–48, 51, 129–130
orthogonality 163
Os Cadernos de Malte Laurids Brigge (Rilke) 82
Othering 28, 32

Paz, Octavio 23, 83, 129
Peirce, Charles 159, 162, 165
personhood 204
'philosophic homework' 138, 144
Piaget, Jean 142
'Piano' (Lawrence) 157
Pillemer, Karl 124
Plath, Sylvia 156
Plato 194, 203
Poe, Edgar Allan 157
'The Poem' (Oppen) 200–202
'the poetic experience' (Paz) 23
poetic instants (Bachelard) 48, 54
'poetic instants' concept 82–83
poetic repurposing 22–24
poetic windows 54
'a poetics of being' (Ricoeur) 138
'Poetics of selfhood' (Freeman) 137–138
Poetry Facilitator 34–36, 38

Poetry and the Fate of the Senses (Stewart) 47
Poetry as Survival (Orr) 47
'Poetry travels alone' (Alves de Sousa) 90–91
poiesis
    and Aristotle/praxis 128
    and creativity 126
    empowering possibilities of 120–122
    finding a writing style 129
    Greek origins of 82
    introduction 1, 4
    and Susan Stewart 47
'Political Poem' (Oppen) 199–201
political/relational model 28–29
Polkinghorne, Donald 139–141, 146
'Polonaise' (van Ostaijen) 35–36
polyphony 74, 74n.12, 77
Popova, Maria 155
'post-critique' 33–34
'post-formal operational thought' 142
Pound, Ezra 3, 192
praxis 128, 132
The Prelude (Wordsworth) 188, 191
Primitive (Oppen) 5, 190, 195, 197, 199–201, 203–204
Progoff, Ira 144, 147
Proust, Marcel 178
'Provide, Provide' (Frost) 162

Q methodology 156–159, 161–163, 165, 168–170
'Q Methodology' (Stephenson) 4
Q sorting 156

R methodology 156–157
Ragtime (Doctorow) 182
Randall, William 129
Ray, Ruth 149
re-genre-ation 145
Reader Leader 36–37, 39
'Recht op waardig sterven' 29–30
reflective self-consciousness 45–46
relativistic thinking 142
Reminiscence and the Self in Old Age (Sherman) 143
Retelling a Life: Narrative and Dialogue in Psychoanalysis (Schafer) 140
retirement 63–65, 118–119, 126–128

Reznor, Trent 166
Ricardo, Cassiano 94, 94n.4
Rich, Adrienne 54
Richard II (Shakespeare) 103
Richard III (Shakespeare) 114
Ricoeur, Paul 1, 54, 138, 141
Rilke, Rainer Maria 48, 82
Rimmon-Kenan, Shlomith 138
Romeo and Juliet (Shakespeare) 100, 114
Rorschach blots 146
Rosenow, Ce 38
The Rule of Metaphor (Ricoeur) 141
Ruset, Arne 49

Sai'jiki 66, 66n.9, 70
'Sara in Her Father's Arms' (Oppen) 192–193
Sarton, May 139
Sartre, Jean-Paul 156
Schacter-Shalomi, Rabbi Zalman 144
Schaevers, Mark 32
Schafer, Roy 140
Scharwyerveld dementia ward 34
Schildt, Runar 182
Schwerner, Mickey 194–195
science
    ascending downward 169–171
    introduction 155–156
    poetry responses 157–169, 160nn.1–2, 163n.4, 164n.5, 168n.6
    Q methodology 156–159, 161–163, 165, 168–170
self-negation 24
Shakespeare, Tom 29
Shakespeare, William 4, 33
Shakespeare's old age
    introduction 99–101, 100n.2
    irresponsible paternity 101–102
    last grasp 103–107, 103nn.3–4
    lyrical 113
    nostalgic 109–111
    rebellious 111–112
    responsibility as law 107–109
    usurping 114–115
Shared Reading (SR) 28, 34–40
Shelley, Percy 199
Sherman, Edmund 143, 149
Silverstein, Sheldon 168
Simonsen, Henrik 3
Snow, C. P. 155

somewhat 113, 115
'Song to Woody' (Dylan) 122
'Song' (Wharton) 159
'Sonnet 107' (Shakespeare) 33
'Sonnet XV' (Claus) 33
Speaking in Parables: A Study in Metaphor and Theology (TeSelle) 147
Spearman Sir Charles 156–157
'Spirits' (Wiman) 188–189
Stein, Gertrude 191
Stephenson, William 156–158, 161, 165, 175
Stevens, Wallace 3, 9
Stewart, Susan 47, 54–56
storytelling 46, 117, 148
    see also writing
Strawson, Galen 2, 48
Strindberg, August 183
Summa, Michela 45–46
'Sunday Morning' (Stevens) 9
super-ego (Freud) 108
Survival is a Style (Wiman) 188
Swinnen, Aagje 169–170
'Symbolic tool concept' (Vygotsky) 66
systematic thinking 142

Tafdrup, Pia 189
tanabata 70
Tandy, Cindy 145
Tarkovsky's Horses (Tafdrup) 189
Teixeira, Faustino 85
The Tempest (Shakespeare) 109, 114
TeSelle, Sallie 147
texistence 138
theodicy 194
therapeutic writing 122–123
thinking
    dualistic 142
    relativistic 142
    systematic 142
Thoreau, Henry David 68
'Those who pass slowly but calmly' 94–95
'Three joys of the everyday' 66–67
'Three joys of haiku' (Minagawa) 65–66
'Till Other Voices Wake Us' (Oppen) 202
Timaeus (Plato) 194

'To Virgins, to Make Much of Time'
 (Herrick) 166
Tornstam, Lars 143
The Transfiguration of the Commonplace
 (Danto) 22
transubstantiation 189
Trilling, Lionel 155
Trondheim Public Library 118
The Sacred in Contemporary Haiku
 (Epstein) 62
'The Tyger'(Blake) 37, 201

unselfing 15–17, 22

van der Meer, Vonne 37
van Hulle, D. 33
van Leeuwen, Joke 38
van Ostaijen, Paul 35
Vergeet dementie onthou mens
 (campaign) 30
Verploegen, Helen 34
vertical time (Bachelard) 48
'Vier manieren om op iemand te wachten'
 (van Leeuwen) 38
virtuous ageing 117
virtuous ageing (Laceulle) 128
vulnerability 13–14, 126, 128
vulnerable reading 99, 99n.1
Vygotsky, Lev 66

wabi-sabi 71–72, 71n.11, 74, 77
'Waking Who Knows'(Oppen) 202
Warhol, Andy 22
The Waste Land (Eliot) 201
Weil, Simone 21–23
well-being 127–128, 131
Wells, Orson 110
Wharton, Edith 159–161

Wheelock, John Hall 137
'When You Are Old' (Yeats) 157–158
White, Gillian 190
Whitman, Walt 129–130
Williams, William Carlos 3
Wilson, C. B. 155
Wiman, Christian 188, 195
The Winter's Tale (Shakespeare) 109, 114
'Wisdom as Integrated Thought'
 (Labouvie-Vief) 142
Wolf, Werner 37
Wolfe, Thomas 139
Woods, Angela 2
Woodward, Kathleen M. 2–3
Wordsworth, William 188, 191
Wright, David 166–167
writing
 conclusion 131–133
 courses 118–119, 131
 dialogical function of 122–123
 discussion 127–131
 expressive 117
 and haiku 120
 introduction 117–118
 as a legacy 123–125
 lives 175–184
 motivation 125–127
 perspectives on 120
 therapeutic 121–123
 workshops 125
 see also storytelling

Yeats, William Butler 158, 168–169
'Young and Old' (Kingsley) 163, 167
'Youth and Age' (Coleridge) 162

Zahavi, Dan 44–45
Zeilig, Hannah 2, 29

www.ingramcontent.com/pod-product-compliance
Lightning Source LLC
Chambersburg PA
CBHW052108300426
44116CB00010B/1575